Cadillac V-16s
Lost and Found

If you have a home computer with Internet access you may:
- request an item to be placed on hold.
- renew an item that is not overdue or on hold.
- view titles and due dates checked out on your card.
- view and/or pay your outstanding fines online ($1 & over).

To view your patron record from your home computer click on
Patchogue-Medford Library's homepage: www.pmlib.org

Cadillac V-16s
Lost and Found

*Tracing the Histories
of the 1930s Classics*

CHRISTOPHER W. CUMMINGS

McFarland & Company, Inc., Publishers
Jefferson, North Carolina

LIBRARY OF CONGRESS CATALOGUING-IN-PUBLICATION DATA

Cummings, Christopher W., 1952–
Cadillac V-16s lost and found : tracing the histories of
the 1930s classics / Christopher W. Cummings.
p.   cm.
Includes bibliographical references and index.

ISBN 978-0-7864-7570-4 (softcover : acid free paper) ∞
ISBN 978-1-4766-1239-3 (ebook)

1. Cadillac automobile—History—20th century.
2. Antique and classic cars—United States.   I. Title.
TL215.C27 C86 2014   2013050521

BRITISH LIBRARY CATALOGUING DATA ARE AVAILABLE

Manufactured in the United States of America

*McFarland & Company, Inc., Publishers
Box 611, Jefferson, North Carolina 28640
www.mcfarlandpub.com*

To the V-16 people.

To the executives, engineers, designers, marketers, advertisers, salespeople, and technicians, known and anonymous, who conceived, designed, built, sold and serviced these magnificent vehicles.

To the businessmen, professionals, performers, social figures, old money, newly flush and others who ordered and purchased the cars over the course of a tempestuous decade through rough economic weather.

To the bold, idiosyncratic and fascinating folks who saw, during the years when many others didn't, the enduring, intrinsic value of the sixteen-cylinder Cadillacs, and who preserved the cars, saved the spare parts, and passed along the knowledge.

To the authors, historians and hobbyists who have gathered the lore, the legends and the factual information that gives context to the surviving cars, informs us about the lost examples, and permits modern owners to keep their cars alive and running.

To the heirs, collectors, museums, entrepreneurs, and individual enthusiasts (and those who support, enable and love them) who keep, maintain, show, drive, and admire the cars, ensuring that the stories of these great classics will live on.

To the future owners and aficionados, in the hope they will appreciate and conserve these magnificent reminders of an age and way of life long past.

Table of Contents

Introduction

There are some natural phenomena, inanimate objects and mechanical devices that somehow seem to be endowed with personalities, and that seem to behave as if they had minds and wills of their own, however rudimentary. People have named storms, ships and combat aircraft as though they were living beings. I suppose there may be some literal truth to the expression "he puts something of himself into his work," and perhaps a complex and carefully made machine does somehow retain some fraction of the spirit of its maker. I submit that the high classic automobiles built from the late 1920s up to the Second World War demonstrate this.

My favorites among classic cars are the V-16 Cadillacs of the 1930s. Each of these cars was essentially hand built. The customer was encouraged to personalize the car he ordered with a wide selection of body styles, color choices and interior appointments, as well as a range of optional equipment and furnishings that anticipated all but the most eccentric whims. Cadillac spared no expense and cut no corners in crafting the nearest thing to a fully custom-built luxury automobile produced by a corporation in the business of mass-produced transportation. The only restraint was concern for the way a particular variant would reflect on the public perception of the V-16 product generally.

Even if each V-16 Cadillac doesn't really have a living soul or something like it, each one has a story to tell. The original owner was a man or woman of means (or perhaps a company or institution). And the choice to order such a sumptuous conveyance was not made lightly (for the price of a 1930 Cadillac V-16 sedan, ten fully-optioned Chevrolets could be had). Then almost coincident with the advent of these cars, the American economy was overwhelmed by the Great Depression. Many V-16 owners could no longer afford to own them. Other owners hid their cars away to avoid ostentation in front of the less fortunate. Still others traded in their cars in the ordinary course. Large, elegant cars that required careful attention and lots of fuel quickly lost most of their market, and many languished at dealerships or in garages or barns. Two major wars with earnest scrap drives severely culled the ranks of what were then just old, used cars. And the moth, mouse and tinworm took their toll as well.

Each Cadillac V-16 that survives today somehow withstood the ravages of time, neglect and the elements, whether in a garage, in the open or otherwise. Some came through as nearly unscathed originals, while others had to be rescued and painstakingly restored. Still others still show substantial wear and tear, while retaining that ineradicable air of class and breeding with which Cadillac and Fleetwood designers, engineers and craftsmen infused them.

The words that follow in these pages came together as I began to meet other Cadillac V-16 owners and to learn about their cars. At first there was just a handful of tales, but more and more of these automobiles presented themselves with colorful histories that begged to be told, in interviews with the owners. So the project kept growing.

Initially I meant to look only at the first Cadillac V-16s, those made and shipped in the 1930 and 1931 model years. That was because in my judgment those cars are the most beautiful, the high point of the classic ideal before it gave way to the streamline imperative that rules so powerfully today. But along the way I became acquainted with a number of the later V-16s, including the mid-'30s cars and some of the flathead 16s of 1938 through '40. Their stories had an added piquancy because far fewer of them were made, because they show how a spectacular concept was developed and adapted to changing tastes, and because it took a certain courage and optimism to place an order for such an extravagant conveyance in the face of a persistent economic undertow.

And I consciously tried to find and tell the stories of the big sedans. These were the cars that were ordered most often, the cars that did the most work transporting owners and passengers in regal style and in all manner of weather, and the cars that are the most overlooked in today's exaltation of convertibles.

All of these stories deserve to be told and remembered, and I believe that they can tell us something about ourselves and our nation's history.

1. Sic Transit Gloria Mundi

When the conquering hero in ancient Rome enjoyed his triumphal parade through the streets of the Imperial City, a slave rode in the chariot with him, whispering in his ear "All glory is fleeting." In February 2006, there was auctioned on eBay a body tag from a Cadillac V-16. The style number was 4330-S, the straight-sill five-passenger sedan without a divider window. The write-up for the auction stated that it was from a parts car, but gave no further elaboration. EBay permits viewers to submit questions to sellers during their auctions, so I asked the seller of this item if he could tell me anything about the car that the plate had come from—such as the engine number—and I asked if he had any pictures of the car. He responded as follows:

> Hi, I just had some of the remains from the car. I had Quite a few Cadillac parts that were lying around So I made a Conv. Coupe From The doors Cowl and other parts that I had. Thanks for asking...Andrew

The car might have been wrecked too severely to repair. Or it might simply have deteriorated to such a degree that bringing it back would have been economically unreasonable. Or a previous owner may have taken the original chassis and running gear for another project, and this fellow was left with an amputated body.

One day in 1930, this tag adorned a magnificent chariot being delivered to its first owner, a spectacular rolling work of art, hand crafted and exquisitely fitted. Gleaming and imposing, it boasted silk window shades, fine wool carpets and trim, and lines that spoke in the language of formal elegance without being ponderous. And, of course, there was that incredible engine. The hefty price paid for the car didn't come close to covering Cadillac's cost in building it. Now, all that could be said with certainty is that although some of its parts may reside in one or more other vehicles, the car that originally bore body number 76 of the Series 4330-S five-passenger sedans will never again roll down the street.

---

2. Kiwi Cadillac

A 1930 Series 4330 imperial sedan, body number 12 (of fifty built), was sold new in San Francisco. Its history is told by eminent Cadillac historian Maurice Hendry, assisted by Yann Saunders, creator of *The (New) Cadillac Database*, and former owner Barrie Grant. The identity of the original purchaser is not known. But in 1933, the car was acquired used from Don Lee Cadillac's San Francisco office by the second owner, Sir Jack Newman, owner of Newmans Coach Lines in New Zealand. Sir Jack had the controls converted to right-hand drive and he took the car home to New Zealand. He used it personally and for V.I.P. transport in his business.

Mr. Hendry provided me with the following interesting details concerning the purchase and shipment overseas. Newmans Coach Lines was established by the Newman brothers in 1879 as a horse-drawn carriage service. The company changed over to automobiles in about 1911, and Cadillacs became their favorite service cars. Standard Cadillac automobiles were lengthened and modified to take bus bodies. Jack Newman was a second-generation board member of Newmans and he was in the United States to visit the Cadillac factory in Detroit. While in San Francisco, he had seen a 1930 V-16 sedan at Don Lee Cadillac, and he told the dealership that he would buy the car if they could modify it to right-hand drive while he was in Detroit. Clarence Dixon, who would later establish his own Cadillac dealership in San Francisco, performed the modifications to the car.

The agent in San Francisco for Newmans Coach Lines was George Roberts, a New Zealander who had shipped many Cadillacs to New Zealand over a period of years. The arrangements were for Mr. Roberts to deliver the car to Jack Newman's hotel on the Sunday morning of his departure for Vancouver, where Mr. Newman and the car would board the liner *Niagara*, leaving for New Zealand on Tuesday morning. Mr. Roberts arrived at the hotel with the V-16 before 8:00 a.m. on Sunday morning, but there was no sign of Mr. Newman and his bed had not been slept in. Mr. Dixon and friends had taken Mr. Newman to a football game the day before, and there had been a convivial night at the Dixons' afterwards. The friends were still asleep on the carpet of Mr. Dixon's lounge.

Mr. Newman set out about two hours behind schedule, but he still wanted to see the redwood forest on the way to Vancouver. The Golden Gate Bridge would not open for another four years, so the alternatives were to drive around the harbor or to take the ferry. Mr. Newman took the ferry, saw the redwoods, and covered the 1,200 miles to Vancouver on what were then country roads, passing through customs twice and catching the ship by Tuesday morning. He had "no trouble," he told Mr. Hendry, "but I did hustle the V-16 along, was cruising at 80 m.p.h. much of the way."

By 1940, the original engine had been replaced (with number 701096) as an easier and quicker alternative to a full valve job. In 1939, Bill Gould had purchased the by-then no longer fashionable limousine. He removed the Fleetwood body and mounted a "caravan" body in its place. Mr. Ray Chapman fitted a locally-built station wagon body in place of the caravan for the next owner, Straits Air Freight Express. The reconfigured conveyance was used to haul people back and forth on the hilly coastal route between Nelson and Takaka on the South Island of New Zealand.

Meanwhile, the original body found its way to Wadsworth Motors of Tapawera, and was installed onto a Nash chassis for use as a school bus. In 1946, a newspaper ad appeared "Cadillac V16 station wagon for sale—£375." Mr. Grant, then 13 years old, read the advertisement, which was his first knowledge of a Cadillac V-16 in New Zealand. He decided he had to have one. He clipped the ad and put it away, but kept the idea in his head. Subsequently, while cleaning his room, young Mr. Grant inadvertently destroyed the ad ("big cry," he says).

There were five or six subsequent owners of the V-16 until 1958, when Mr. Grant made up his mind to find that Cadillac. Because his brother-in-law worked in the car registration office at the post office, he was finally able to track the car down. Once he'd located it, he set off to have a look at it. But he was told that he'd have to buy the car sight unseen. The owner said he'd had it with buyers making low-ball offers once they had seen the car. He was determined to get £100.

Disguised as a station wagon. This 1959 photograph shows the car as Barrie Grant purchased it. This may be the only 1930 Cadillac V-16 "woodie" station wagon ever made. Note the Cadillac script on the tailgate and "CADILLAC V16" lettering in the windows. The original Fleetwood body had found its way onto a Nash chassis to serve as a school bus (courtesy Barrie Grant).

Mr. Grant drove away "most upset," and promptly became lost. Then he saw the back end of an ugly wooden car body protruding from a shed. Stopping to have a look, he chided himself for wasting time. But when he lifted the "bonnet" he was beside himself—a V-16 Cadillac engine rested between the frame rails. Of course, he had to have it. He went straight back to the owner's house, but the man had left until evening ("gone bush for the day" as Mr. Grant put it). Mr. Grant drove 80 miles back to where he was staying, and that night he phoned the owner and said he'd buy the Cadillac. Not having the £100 purchase price at hand, he had to phone his employer (another 80 miles away) and implore him to wire the money to a post office near the car.

The next day he headed back to the owner's house, picked up the money at the post office, made the purchase and drove home in the Cadillac. It was quite an experience, according to Mr. Grant. The electric fuel pump that had been installed on the car wasn't really up to feeding a thirsty sixteen-cylinder engine. Top speed on level ground was 30 m.p.h. and progress up hills was very slow. Going downhill was no better. The brakes were marginal at best. And the transmission kept slipping out of second gear, so he had to stay in first.

Car and new owner arrived home safely, and the next day, Mr. Grant proudly drove his new ride to work. "When the boss saw it, he laughed," says Mr. Grant, "as he knew I would be working for him for the next 2 years until I paid him back." The long restoration journey began soon afterward, with the removal of the improvised coachwork. The station wagon body served as a playhouse for Mr. Grant's daughter, and the rest of the car became Mr. Grant's playhouse for the next 40 years.

Mr. Hendry located the original body in 1959, and Mr. Grant purchased it. To say that a full restoration was required is something of an understatement. Needless to say, certain parts had gone missing over the years, and there were few or no resources available for obtaining or manufacturing replacements. For example, the windshield was missing and the wood framework for its opening was exposed, bereft of the metal coverings that defined the shape of the glass and held it in place. Mr. Grant was left to his own devices in fashioning a new windshield and frame, and under the circumstances the results are excellent.

Mechanically, the car is restored to original with the exception of the fuel delivery components. Mr. Grant and Mr. Hendry were unable to locate a reliable source for the stock Cadillac Johnson carburetors, and instead Mr. Grant installed Solex carburetors (model BX4U3 with adjustable main jets and 38 mm venturis) and two six-volt electric fuel pumps. The car gets about 11 miles per gallon cruising at 55 m.p.h.

The restored limousine was sold after the turn of the last century to the Museum of Wearable Art in Nelson for NZ$140,000. Mr. Richard Grimes of the museum was kind enough to provide photographs of the car as it sits today.

As has been noted, the windshield on this car is unique. Closed-model V-16s that did not have the Pennsylvania Fleetwood split and V'd windshield were built with what was known as a "V-V windshield." V-V stood for "Vision-Ventilation," and referred to the fact that the windshield could be partially rolled up into the header to open a ventilation gap between the windshield's lower edge and the cowl. Opening the windshield up to about an inch allowed in-rushing air to be scooped by the curled lip of the instrument panel and directed downward to the feet of the driver and front passenger. Raised beyond

Body and chassis reunited. After nearly two decades of going their separate ways, the body is finally back on its chassis. Clearly, Messrs. Hendry and Grant had no small project in front of them at this point. The "after" pictures show the extent of their accomplishment (courtesy Barrie Grant).

that, the windshield allowed the air to waft into the occupants' faces. This car now has a fixed windshield glass crafted by Mr. Grant without benefit of parts or patterns for the "V-V" feature.

The outside door handles on this car are a style that was used for phaetons, coupes, convertible coupes and Madame X sedans (although a purchaser who asked Cadillac to substitute alternate trim items would almost never be refused). Sedans in the 4200 and 4300 style series ordinarily used outside door handles shaped like a letter "J" laid horizontally. The chrome-plated vent doors on the hood were an available option, and sometimes owners of V-8 Cadillacs installed chrome-plated hood doors to make their cars look more like V-16s.

Mr. Hendry was also able to locate the original parts crate that came to New Zealand with the car. Among other goodies, it contained original factory radiator hoses with the Cadillac logo, and a spare pair of headlamp lenses in their original factory packing.

Whatever technical criticisms one may be tempted to make, this is a beautiful and handsomely restored classic, saved from the fate that befell so many others, by devoted people

Restored and resplendent. The observant viewer will notice a number of respects in which this imperial sedan departs from stock 1930 Cadillac construction or practice. The re-created windshield, as described above, is one difference, distinguished by the bright-metal frame and the squared lower corners. The pivoting windshield wipers are another variance (stock windshield wipers shuttled horizontally right and left across the glass) (courtesy World of WearableArt and Classic Cars Museum).

Blackwall tires make these cars appear longer. It's hard to tell from the one side view exactly what's going on with the valence panels ("dust shields" in factory parlance) between the running board and the bottom edges of the doors. The chrome-stripped panels that should flank the courtesy light (a door for the battery box to the front and a decorative dummy to the rear) are not in evidence. Mr. Grant told me that the battery resides in the normal location (below the right front door), and that a 12-volt battery "for starting only" has been fitted under the left front mudguard (courtesy World of WearableArt and Classic Cars Museum).

who appreciated a treasure of automotive history. Mr. Grant and Mr. Hendry performed a minor miracle in reconstructing this Cadillac at a time and in a part of the world in which the level of information, access to replacement parts and existence of reproduced parts were not nearly what they are today.

---

3. A Ghost Appears Briefly

In August 2005, Kruse International sold at auction the estate of the late Karl Kleve, an eccentric and eclectic collector in the Cincinnati area who was known for storing a huge assortment of cars and parts in open fields, barns and junkyards. Among the marques represented were Duesenberg, Rolls-Royce, Packard and Bugatti. Mr. Kleve is said to have believed that a car was less likely to be stolen if he disassembled it before storing it. Accordingly, many of the cars in the estate sale were in pieces, with little assurance that all the parts were there.

Relevant to this discussion is a partially-dismantled 1930 Cadillac V-16 Series 4375-S seven-passenger sedan. As big as a limousine, but not equipped with a glass division between the front and rear compartments, this style was a roomy and elegant family car, or an impressive business vehicle. There were 501 Series 4375-S cars built in the 1930–31 extended model year, which is more than any other model in the entire eleven-year run of V-16 production.

There were quite a few photos of this particular car on the Kruse website, parked in a

The 1930 Series 4375-S sedan parked in Mr. Wallace's garage. The elderly tires have come apart in the course of transporting the car from the late Karl Kleve's residence. The fabric roof insert is almost gone, and the missing body parts give the car the look of an old-school hot rod. The size of the radiator needed to cool the big V-16 engine is readily apparent, as is the strength of the frame. Original two-tone brown paint is offset by orange primer liberally applied by a previous owner (courtesy Thomas Wallace).

barn or warehouse without its fenders, running boards, hood, lights or radiator shell. The body and frame looked straight and structurally sound, and the old tires had been inflated for the photos (though they were clearly not holding the air very well). A lot of the original two-tone brown paint was visible, highlighted liberally in various places with red primer.

The engine was in place, but missing its carburetors, and showing extensive make-do modifications to its fuel and electrical systems, intended to keep an exotic car running in spite of dried-up parts sources. What was left of the upholstery and the fabric roof insert was ragged, and the window glass was almost opaque from discoloration of the plastic safety layer. The visible structural wood seemed to be sound, even if some of the ornate inlay on the decorative panels seemed to have deteriorated. This was a car that had seen extensive use and long storage, and now it was in need of a great deal of restorative care.

I visited the website often to examine the exposed mechanisms and structures visible in the photographs. Then, not long before the date of the auction, the photos of the Cadillac V-16 suddenly disappeared from the Kruse website, and the woman at the other end of the company's information line couldn't say what had happened. One could only assume that this lot had been sold separately. A ghost from the Classic Era had shown itself and then

View of the forward part of the engine. Distributor cap with plug wires coming out of the top is a design introduced in 1932, as is the generator with an air scoop on top (lower part of photo, aimed toward radiator). Fluted radiator hose is the original design. Reproductions are available today. Cylindrical holes in radiator top tank are for ignition coils, intended to keep them at a steady temperature (courtesy Thomas Wallace).

vanished back into the mists. Poring over the pictures had been a delightful entertainment, but it looked as though the rest of the story would remain a mystery.

Some time after the auction, there appeared on the Antique Automobile Club of America message forum an inquiry about buying parts for a recently-acquired V-16 sedan. Through that posting I was able to get in touch with Mr. Thomas Wallace of Dayton, Ohio, the new owner of Karl Kleve's V-16 sedan. Mr. Wallace shared with me his own photos and some of the background information. He'd bought the car with the intention of restoring it, fully realizing the magnitude of the task he'd taken on. On the plus side, many of the parts not seen in the photos were present and were included with the car.

One of the things Mr. Wallace shared was a copy of the car's "build sheet," the factory form that identifies the car, its paint and trim specifications, any optional equipment, where the factory shipped it, and its order and shipping dates. Somehow, these records have survived for most years of Cadillac production, and they provide a number of clues to a car's origins and early history, even if they rarely indicate the original owner's name.

In those years, Cadillac used the car's engine number the way a VIN number is used today. That's how the owner registered and licensed the car, and it was the way the car was identified in any correspondence with the factory. This car was engine number 700783, meaning that it was the 783rd V-16 Cadillac of regular production, and indicating that it was shipped from the factory in March of 1930. The destination was Cadillac's Philadelphia branch on Shackamaxon Street, with the instruction to tag the car with the name "Sallade," a not uncommon family name in Pennsylvania. Without more, it's not possible to know of the original owner was a person named Sallade, or if that was the name of the employee picking the car up for the purchaser or for the selling dealership.

The body and fenders were painted in Alhambra Tan, with a lighter shade of the same color for the window offsets, lower body panels and wheels. A double hairline in gold bronze was to be the body pinstriping, and the rear axle ratio was the slower 4.75:1 gearing reserved for hilly locales. Another tantalizing but inconclusive clue about the original owner—perhaps a coal mining company? A company executive?

The only factory-installed options indicated on the build sheet were wire wheels and fender-mounted spare tires (standard equipment, though rarely seen, was wood wheels and a rear-mounted spare). From the photographs, though, it's possible to identify some dealer-installed items. There is a little electric blower in the lower right rear corner of the engine compartment, right next to the exhaust manifold that would have been for a "Kelch" heater. It would have blown air through a jacket surrounding the exhaust pipe to provide warm air

Rear part of engine and firewall. Vacuum tanks for fuel delivery system are the two orange cylindrical items on the firewall flanking the engine. Extra plumbing work has required removal of the chrome-plated dome covers for these tanks. Stack of pipe fittings and valves atop right-hand intake manifold are a prior owner's addition. Rod wrapped in electrical tape that runs along the valley between the cylinder banks changes the distributor position to retard the ignition. Tape is probably to stop spark plugs (visible next to the rod) from arcing and misfiring. Rectangular oil level indicator and its wire are visible next to rear corner of right-hand valve cover (courtesy Thomas Wallace).

View where lower right-hand edge of firewall meets frame. Object in middle of picture, next to vertical portion of exhaust manifold, is the blower for a Kelch heater system. Outside air heated by the exhaust pipe would be blown through tubing into the passenger compartment via floor registers. This technology was abandoned for automotive heaters shortly after this car was built (courtesy Thomas Wallace).

to be piped into the passenger compartment. That particular technology provided heat sooner after starting the engine than hot water heaters, but the obvious safety concerns seem to be why Kelch heaters fell by the wayside. Also visible in one or two of the photographs, on the driver's-side windshield pillar there are holes where an accessory spotlight was once mounted. All of these are additional partial but inconclusive clues.

There is one rather intriguing instruction on the build sheet, though. It says simply: "STRAIGHT WINDSHIELD." The Series 4375-S model had an almost vertical windshield by design. It did have a 7-degree rearward lean, however, to spare the driver most glare and extraneous reflections at night, but unless you look carefully, these cars appear to have just what that enigmatic instruction specified. Why would it be necessary to call for a "Straight Windshield" on a car that, practically speaking, already had one? From the photographs, it does not appear to this observer that engine number 700783 has a straighter windshield than any of its sister cars.

Thomas Wallace told me that he was working with people at the noted restoration facilities Platinum Classic Motorcars and Dick Shappy Classic Cars to acquire not just the necessary parts but also the knowledge about how the car was built and how it should be put back together. An accomplished woodworker, Mr. Wallace remanufactured the missing vanity unit for the left-hand side of the passenger compartment, having asked me for photos

Driver's compartment. Extent of deterioration of windshield glass is clearly apparent. Original carpet remains on portion of toeboard above steering column and pedals. Correct greenish tint of instrument numbers was more readily apparent on the Kruse website photos (courtesy Thomas Wallace).

of mine to work from. I made sure he was aware of the resources I rely on—the Cadillac-LaSalle Club, *The (New) Cadillac Database*, the people who remanufacture and provide essential parts, and so on. A restoration such as this is a worthy but difficult enterprise, and with all the help in the world, a substantial financial outlay is unavoidable.

The future for this Cadillac had brightened a good deal since the time of Mr. Kleve's passing. But then, in 2009, Mr. Wallace disclosed that he had sold the car to a private individual who preferred not to be identified. Fortunately, that fellow also intends that the car receive a full and correct restoration. And late word is that he is making significant progress. With any luck, this grand motor car will be seen on the street again before many more months have passed.

4. Ferdinand, the Gentle Bull

In 1930 Edward C. Baganz, a Great Lakes steamship captain, purchased a new V-16 Cadillac Series 4330-S sedan and brought it home. When his wife saw the massive vehicle, she exclaimed, "You don't expect me to drive that big bull, do you?" According to their son

Captain Edward C. Baganz, ship's master and V-16 Cadillac purchaser. Shown here standing aboard a Great Lakes ore carrier, he was away at sea for nine months out of the year. The *Philip R. Clarke* was his last ship and this photograph was taken in 1962 (courtesy Theron Baganz).

Theron, however, she changed her impression after actually driving the "big bull." He said that with the synchronized transmission and vacuum-assisted brakes, she found the car to be an easy drive, compared to the 1928 6-cylinder Buick coupe she had been driving. So she named the car after the gentle bull immortalized by Munro Leaf in his book *The Story of Ferdinand* (and the subject of a popular song in the '30s). To this day the car is known by the name Ferdinand.

Captain Baganz allowed (and perhaps fostered) a certain vagueness as to exactly how he had acquired Ferdinand. Relatives and neighbors understood that he had bought the car used. Theron suspects that for all practical purposes it was a new car. He recalls that the Sweeney Coal and Brick Company in Michigan had ordered three Cadillacs—a convertible, a seven-passenger closed car and Ferdinand—but if they took delivery of Ferdinand, they didn't keep the car for long. Bill Andrews, a Cadillac salesman who knew Captain Baganz, began to drop by and said, "Try this one." Eventually he tried the car, liked it and made the purchase. According to Theron, when Ferdinand joined the family, the odometer showed 80 miles. The interior of the car was redolent of mothballs, for whatever light that sheds on the question. In the end, because of the national economic climate in 1930, it was probably much more socially acceptable to have purchased a fancy luxury car used than to have bought it new.

Ferdinand has engine number 702545, and he is a five-passenger sedan, without a divider window between the driver's and passengers' compartments. Generally, such a car would have been an "owner-driven" car (as opposed to chauffeur-driven). And with Ferdinand, this was certainly the case, as he was definitely a family car. Sometimes cars were used both ways—my

Ferdinand in his prime. Note the parking aids attached to the front fenders to help the driver calculate where the corner of the car is in relation to cars or other obstacles. Theron's mother was a petite woman. The fabric spare tire cover is a Cadillac accessory (courtesy Theron Baganz).

1930 imperial sedan was built to be chauffeur-driven, but it was ordered with cloth upholstery in the driver's compartment, instead of the usual leather. That sort of departure from the usual configuration often meant that the owner wanted to drive the car at least part of the time.

Because his father was operating a ship on the open water for nine months of the year, Theron acceded quickly to the job of keeping the Cadillac clean. And because he was the "man of the house" in his father's absence, and because the scrupulous observance of driver's licensing requirements was not what it is today, he began to drive the big V-16 sedan at an early age. Whether in the driver's seat or riding as a passenger, Theron has collected a fascinating array of experiences with Ferdinand over the years.

When he was 12 and driving Ferdinand on Michigan's Harsens Island, a fellow in a 1938 Ford approached, straddling the center line through a 90 degree turn in the road. As the two cars passed, the Ford was "gored" in the left rear quarter, sustaining considerable damage, but Ferdinand was unharmed. However, because Theron shouldn't have been driving in the first place, his parents paid to have the Ford repaired, and in the process, showed a frightened Theron how much they loved him. Five years later a drunk driver and ice on the road combined to produce another "goring" of a Ford. After the collision, Theron's girlfriend asked "Did we hit him?"—such was the difference in weight between the Cadillac and the Ford. A policeman saw what happened and sent Theron and the uninjured Ferdinand on their way. The third accident, in 1950, involved a Chevy drifting over the center line and being struck in the left rear quarter. This time, Ferdinand suffered a slightly bent front fender that some work with a hydraulic jack quickly repaired.

On a bitterly cold day in the winter of 1943, when he was 14, Theron, his family and

Theron and Ferdinand visiting family in Ohio. Theron is on the back seat of the bike operated by his cousin, in this 1939 or 1940 shot taken in Columbus (courtesy Theron Baganz).

a buddy of his headed off for an afternoon of ice skating on Harsens Island, where the family had a summer cottage. As the day wore on, Theron became concerned about Ferdinand sitting for five or six hours in the sub-zero weather. Theron asked his dad if he could start the car and take it for a short drive up to the small town on the island to keep the engine warm. His father didn't think that was a very good idea, as Ferdinand was their transportation home. Later, when it was time to get ready to leave, his father asked Theron to get the car started. But the effects of the cold weather on the viscosity of the engine oil, on the volatility of the gasoline, and on the efficiency of the starting and ignition systems thwarted Theron's efforts to persuade the engine to run. A tow truck had to be summoned and Ferdinand was towed out to the main road. Then with the transmission in gear, and the tow truck pulling the car, it was started by letting the clutch out. But unfortunately all the earlier cranking had put a considerable amount of cold, but still combustible, fuel/air mixture into the car's exhaust system. When the engine started, it lit off that mixture and *both* mufflers blew out spectacularly. Needless to say, the trip back was very noisy, and Father was very unhappy.

Theron remembers very vividly an apparent paranormal incident with the car when he was ten (give or take a year). He and his mother and father were at his aunt's house in Columbus, Ohio, for Christmas. His parents had gone to pick up his grandparents a few miles away. In their absence, Theron had a clear picture in his mind, and knew before they returned that the goddess that adorned Ferdinand's radiator cap had been broken, and had lost her shawl. Theron was devastated when he saw the car come up the driveway, and the radiator ornament was just as he had seen in his mind's eye—broken. On the way back to his aunt's house, his parents had stopped for gas, and the attendant had dropped the cap and its attached figurine on the concrete.

In the not-so-long-ago days when attendants would automatically check every customer's oil, coolant and battery electrolyte, the decoration of radiator caps with sculpture thrust upon the serviceman the puzzle of where to put the item and how to handle it when inspecting and topping off the fluid. And there was a Cadillac anti-theft accessory that attached the radiator cap by a short chain to a bar inside the radiator top tank that let the cap be removed, but not taken more than a few inches from the filler neck. Theron's father had vacillated between using the chain tether (and watching the cap and mascot be laid on the radiator shell or the painted surface or the hood) or leaving the cap free (and letting the attendant hang it on the headlight cross bar or do something else with it). Theron figures that his parents' ongoing worry about the goddess may have given rise to his expectation of the worst that evening.

In any event, the billowing shawl that had flowed smoothly from the mascot's hands, clasped behind her head, was now in need of some well-thought-out repair work. When they returned to Grosse Pointe, Michigan, Theron's father drilled both pieces and inserted a spline to fasten the flowing garment back where it belonged. Years later, Theron repeated that repair job when he was doing some other work on the car.

On the Fourth of July in 1947 or '48, Ferdinand had an adventure that was a throwback to an earlier time, but it was very real when it happened. Theron and his friend Jack were taking their girlfriends to the Grosse Pointe Yacht Club for a swim and dinner. About a mile away, along the lakeshore, they encountered a car full of fellows throwing firecrackers so that they exploded underneath the car, or under other cars on the road. Theron called out to them to cut it out or get pushed off the road into the lake. The road had three lanes, and just as Theron and his party reached the yacht club drive, two cars closed in front of him from either side and stopped. A thug jumped out of one of the cars, came over to Theron's

Deputized and capable. This is a 1947 photograph, about the time of the run-in with the hoodlums near the Grosse Pointe Yacht Club (courtesy Theron Baganz).

window and put a knife to his throat. It just happened that the Grosse Pointe Shores police station was located right across the street from the yacht club, and some officers saw the commotion and came running out to respond. In the moments before they arrived, Theron and Jack had been engaged in serious diplomacy to convince the hoodlums to consider another course of action. Meanwhile, 4th of July traffic was backing up behind the impromptu roadblock, and horns were sounding. When the delinquents saw the police officers running toward them, they jumped back into their cars and fled. One of the officers hollered, "Think you can catch those guys?" Theron answered, "Heck, yes!" Two officers piled into the back seat with Jack and his girl, and two more climbed onto the running boards, one on either side, and the V-16 took off after the two carloads of thugs, catching up with them about a mile up the road. Several squad cars joined the chase, and the bad guys were caught and taken back to the station. It turned out they were known felons and had a list of prior offenses. Returning to the yacht club, Theron and his friends had a fun afternoon after all.

Ferdinand earned his keep in the Baganz household. In later years, Theron's father used the no longer new and fashionable car to haul building materials and for other mundane tasks. The powerful drivetrain and substantial weight of the car were put to use moving a garage far enough to make room for an addition to that structure (so it could be used to garage Ferdinand). A roll of roofing paper tossed into the passenger compartment unfortunately broke one of the footrest support brackets. After ten or fifteen years the big classics of the early thirties were seen as very old fashioned and out of date—just used cars.

Theron had fun drag racing from stoplights. The big V-16 would pull ahead of practically any other car, so long as he didn't have to shift out of first gear (in other words, up to

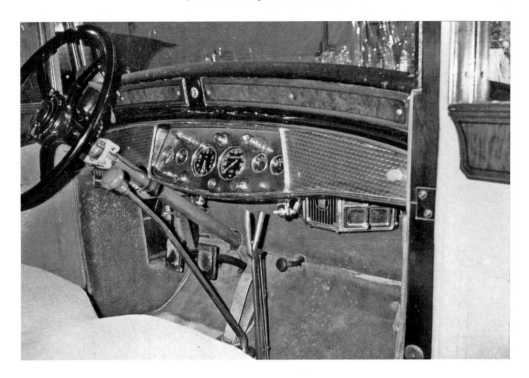

Ferdinand's dashboard. Slight green tint to the numbers on the instruments is authentic and it was unique to the V-16 cars (V-8s and V-12s used white lettering). Mounted to the dash is a Cadillac accessory heater. In this recent photograph, the ornate wood inlay trim retains its original finish (courtesy Theron Baganz).

about 40 m.p.h.). In 1949, the father of a friend of Theron's had gotten a new Oldsmobile Rocket 88 with the overhead valve V-8 engine, considered to be very fast at that time. Ferdinand would beat him off the wire. Theron often wonders whether Ferdinand was really that fast, or if it was just that his size and sound scared them into submission. Like Paul Schinnerer in California, Theron drove the car around for some period of time with the hood removed, to show off the impressive powerplant. That was after a year of disassembling, refurbishing and detailing the engine. He considered installing downdraft carburetors, and even re-bodying the car as a convertible coupe, but ultimately left the car in stock configuration.

In 1950, a time-saving technique almost brought the car to a spectacular end. Theron had taken to filling Ferdinand's commodious gas tank by inserting the hoses from two pumps into the Cadillac's filler pipe at the same time, squeezing the handles and setting the locks. He relied on the automatic shut-off switches in the hose nozzles to stop the flow of fuel when the tank was full, and while the pumps worked, he had time to talk with the station attendants. This particular time, one of the hoses did not shut off, and while he chatted, a pool of gasoline began accumulating underneath the car. By the time Theron saw what was happening, the puddle was about 6 feet in diameter, and as the flammable liquid flowed over the tail of the car and fell onto the hot exhaust pipes, it made ominous hissing sounds, but fortunately failed to ignite. Theron switched off the pump, opened the driver's door and released the hand brake. He and the station attendant gingerly pushed the car away from the spreading pool and the gas pumps, then wiped off the gasoline with shop towels.

In the 1950s, Theron began courting the lovely young lady he would later marry. He had a good friend at the time who also loved the car and who took it upon himself to keep it polished. Before every date Bill was there, shining the finish to where he could see his face in the door panel to comb his hair, and Theron set off on his date knowing his car looked sharp.

Theron's fiancé poses demurely next to the big Cadillac. Note the aftermarket turn signal lamps peeking over the top of the front bumper. Electric turn signals did not become common on cars in the United States until the end of the 1930s (courtesy Theron Baganz).

Young Theron Baganz in the 1950s. This photograph was taken when Theron was courting the young lady who would become his wife (courtesy Theron Baganz).

Inevitably, the young couple began to tire of the unavoidable attention the car attracted. Policemen would pull them over just to take a closer look at the car. And courting "in a fishbowl" can be difficult. Theron considered selling Ferdinand, or even transplanting his V-16 engine into a 28-foot Hacker speedboat. Doc Rund, a local car dealer, repeatedly came by and offered to trade a nearly new Cadillac convertible, but in the end Ferdinand stayed in the family.

Theron says that he has taken apart just about every part of the car, with the exceptions of the rear axle, the shock absorbers and the brake booster. He says that on at least one occasion, his father had the car up to 95 m.p.h. Theron himself only took it up as high as 90. These cars were powerful, but heavy, and the lighter roadsters and cabriolets were more likely to reach 100 or more.

Dangerously worn tires (and difficulty in finding replacements that fit) caused Ferdinand to be placed in storage, though he did participate in a parade in 1960. Since then, he's been hibernating, patiently waiting for Theron to finish replacing the valve seals and fire up the big engine once more. The car has 86,000 miles on the odometer, and the interior, though not perfect, has held up extremely well. The exterior is in very respectable original condition, as well. I've been coaxing Theron to get Ferdinand back on the road, and when he does, that will be a fine day. It's not every classic automobile that has stayed in the same family from delivery to the present day.

5. A Veteran Driver

This car, like the car from the Kleve estate featured elsewhere in these pages ("A Ghost Appears Briefly"), is a Series 4375-S sedan that was regularly used. This one just fared a whole lot better. It belonged to J.C. Stevens, Jr., former owner of the Cortland, New York, Oldsmobile and Studebaker dealership, who was by most accounts a lovable, if occasionally difficult, eccentric. When he died in 2002 at the age of 79, his estate included this and over 80 other automobiles from antique and brass-era cars through the 1960s. According to his family, this Cadillac was his favorite, and the last car that he did a lot of work on. He got it from an old barn in a farmer's backyard, possibly in Missouri. The engine had been damaged, and Mr. Stevens had to find a replacement. Again according to a family member, the car was set up so that Mr. Stevens could switch off the ignition on one side of the engine or the other for making carburetor adjustments. Mr. Stevens is reported to have driven the car as recently as 1983, and to have participated with it in several Antique Automobile Club of America Glidden Tours.

The cars in the Stevens estate were auctioned in 2006. At that time, this Cadillac V-16 wore what appeared to be an original maroon and black lacquer finish that had held up pretty well. The bumpers appeared to have been replated, together with the radiator shell and the wheels. Some of the other brightwork looked as though the standard chrome plate finish had been stripped, leaving the underlying brass exposed. At first glance it looked like a fine coating of surface rust, but examination of the close-up photographs revealed a burnished, uniform finish inconsistent with pitting and rust. In addition, the background plate that surrounds the dash gauges (originally brass with a black finish overlaid with white cross-

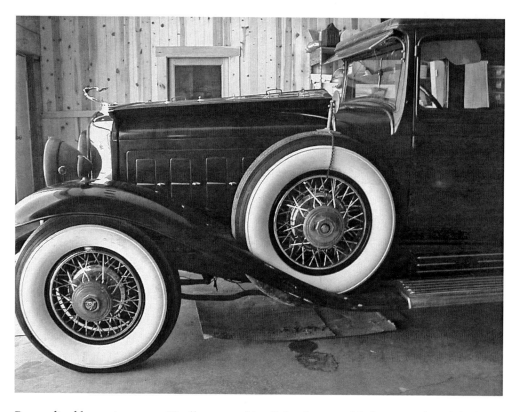

Personalized by a prior owner. Headlamps, parking lights, horns and hubcaps are denuded of their chrome plating. Chrome-plated wheels are a contrast. Support brackets for the smoked-glass sun visor in front of the windshield have either been replaced or bent to hold the visor at a sharper angle than the factory set (courtesy Karl Kahlberg).

hatching) has clearly been either rubbed down to its native brass or otherwise decorated with a gold-colored finish, implying that the same treatment could have been given to the hubcaps, horn trumpets, lights and radiator stoneguard.

The support brackets for the smoked glass sunshade above the windshield appear to have been bent downward to a sharper than normal degree, but it's hard to imagine how that could have been done without breaking the glass.

The engine displays some examples of unorthodox plumbing, both on the intake manifold vacuum ports and in connection with the vacuum tanks and carburetors. The vacuum tanks on the firewall appear to be larger than the stock units. Instead of the original flexible fuel line to the carburetor (flexible metal hose covered with bright metal braid) there's a solid line constructed from copper pipe and brass fittings. It's not clear from the pictures whether the vacuum tanks have been bypassed altogether in favor of an electric pump. At any rate, some modification was undertaken to keep the car running in the face of substantial challenges, including hard-to-find replacement parts and a scarcity of knowledgeable repairmen.

Opposite: Engine compartment. Vacuum tank on right is larger than the stock unit. Copper fuel and vacuum lines with brass joints, valves and fittings are home-fabricated replacements for the originals. Hose clamps can just be seen around the exhaust manifold expansion joints (underneath the intake manifold). Distributor cap had been replaced when this photo was taken (courtesy Karl Kahlberg).

Dash and instruments. Clock and speedometer have switched places. Panel that surrounds instruments has been rubbed down to the underlying brass from the original black with white cross-hatch design. Engine-turned trim panels that flank V-16 instrument cluster have been removed, leaving exposed the black base panel (courtesy Karl Kahlberg).

The three pieces of each exhaust manifold on a V-16 connect with slip joints to allow for expansion and contraction without leaking. Over time those joints can develop looseness and can permit exhaust gases to escape. Short of removing the manifolds and re-doing the slip joints (cutting lengths of tubing to fit and replacing the old connectors) a variety of stopgap remedies have been used. Some owners have packed the joint with asbestos and placed a hose clamp over the packing to hold it in place. Since asbestos became a vilified bad guy in the war against cancer, that solution has not been readily available. Here, however, the manifold joints sport a 1¼ inch black band covering each joint, with a wide hose clamp holding it in place. Exactly what the black band is composed of is not apparent. Nor is it clear if there is any packing in the joint underneath the band.

Inside the car, as noted, the dash panel surrounding the gauge faces has been given a gold-colored finish that may be attractive but is not original. Cadillac shipped the car with a black panel, cross-hatched in white. The finish has been rubbed off here, leaving the exposed brass. The panel also had white lettering to designate the choke handle and the companion handle for the spark advance. That I have not previously seen these knobs engraved with the first letter of its assigned function (as we see here) does not necessarily mean that Cadillac didn't do that. It would not be the first time that I learned something about these cars that surprised me.

The cigar lighter is missing, as are the hoods for the instrument panel illumination lamps. One of those lamp covers has been replaced with one from a V-8 or a V-12. Also from a V-8 or a V-12 is the speedometer. The scale on a V-16 speedometer goes up to 120 m.p.h., where the highest speed shown on the V-8 or V-12 speedometer is 100 m.p.h. A V-16 roadster, stripped of all unnecessary weight, could have exceeded 100 m.p.h. and test runs at the General Motors proving grounds are said to have exceeded 110 m.p.h.

The instruments have been moved around. The speedometer and clock have switched places, as have the oil pressure and temperature gauges. The appliance to the lower left of the instrument cluster is the windshield wiper switch, minus its handle. On the lower right of the cluster, the instrument panel light switch has been replaced with a generic on/off switch of the sort used for a table lamp—wonderfully resourceful, but not technically correct.

Overall, the car stood as a proud and valiant survivor that appeared determined to keep running in spite of some age and wear. This is a car you might not even want to begin restoring. There's a massive amount of distinctive character to this vehicle, and its sometimes quirky variations from strict authenticity contribute agreeably to that personality. Although the owner of such a car might choose to undertake a full restoration (or even a significant cosmetic restoration), even left just as it is, a car this original and still presentable and usable can stop the show at any gathering. And the owner could drive it without fretting about marring a "trailer queen's" perfection.

In the fall of 2008, my friend and fellow V-16 owner Theron Baganz became acquainted with Karl Kahlberg of Snowflake, Arizona. Mr. Kahlberg, as it turned out, had purchased the late J.C. Stevens's maroon and black Series 4375-S V-16 sedan at the auction, and was trying to locate the engine originally installed in the car (engine number 703106). As noted above, the original engine was replaced some time ago (it currently has engine number 701324).

When I called Mr. Kahlberg and introduced myself, he told me a sad tale of purchasing a car he had always wanted to own, and then finding that what he purchased was not at all what he imagined he was buying. He had learned about the car by way of an advertisement

Sad remains of distributor cap. The intricate three-piece 1930–31 V-16 distributor cap as it was when Mr. Kahlberg received the car. The auction company provided an intact replacement (courtesy Karl Kahlberg).

in *Hemmings Motor News* in July 2006. From the text of the ad and from discussing the car by telephone with people at the auction company he came to understand that the car was in "Number 3" condition, running, authentic and complete.[1] He had inquired about placing bids by phone at the upcoming auction of the Stevens estate cars, but says that he didn't hear from the auction company on the day of the sale, and when he called to find out what was going on, he was informed that he had won the car. Surprised, he waited for delivery, and when the big Cadillac was unloaded from the transport vehicle, he was dismayed to find that it could not be started. For one thing, the distributor cap was badly broken. Subsequent discussions between Mr. Kahlberg and the auction company resulted in replacement of the distributor cap and some engine work being done to get the car running. Mr. Kahlberg was in the middle of constructing a kit-build log cabin home at the time, and could not devote time and resources to completing the car's recommissioning, so it had to wait. In late 2008, Mr. Kahlberg was asked by a potential purchaser if he would be interested in selling the V-16 sedan.

I'm not in a position to sort through the events and analyze how the misunderstanding arose between the auction company and Mr. Kahlberg. And I am certainly not accusing anyone of wrongdoing. The photographs that the auction company provided to me in the time leading up to the sale showed a car that had been well, if devotedly, used, and that certainly wore a patina. The same information was not in Mr. Kahlberg's hands, for whatever reason. From this vantage point, it's enough to repeat the timeworn advice to prospective purchasers to make sure that they truly know what they are pursuing when they set out to buy a car. This applies whether the seller is a private individual, a dealer or an auction house. If relying on photographs, ask for a lot of them, and make sure that they show enough of the car in sufficient detail to give a sense of any flaws or problem areas. If possible, examine the car in person, or have someone you trust and who knows what they're looking at do so for you.

And ultimately, one must remember that no classic car, no matter how well preserved or restored, is a new product with a warranty against defects. Everything original on the car is decades old, and has aged, whether visibly or not. And some of the materials used during the Classic Era, even when new, lacked the durability and dependability of modern-day equivalents. I know people who have spent hundreds of thousands of dollars for a stunning car from a reputable seller and have still had to spend significant amounts of money to straighten out various issues that showed up after the purchase. As they say, it goes with the territory.

6. Frozen in Time

One of the most evocative pictures I've ever seen of a Cadillac V-16 is one that was listed for auction on eBay a few years ago. The condition of the car and the context speak volubly about life, history and the way people deal with both.

It's a picture of a 1930 Cadillac V-16 sedan and its driver. There is no date or ready indication of when the picture was taken. The weather is warm, judging from the short sleeves and the fact that the Cadillac's V-V windshield has been cranked up to allow ventilating air to flow under the glass, over the top of the dashboard and into the driver's compartment.

The car is either a Series 4375 seven-passenger sedan, or a Series 4330 sedan for five passengers, and whether there is a divider window or not is not readily discernible (the angle from which the picture was taken makes it difficult to state with certainty which of the two series designations applies). But for our purposes, it is enough to say that the automobile is one of the large sedans that were the most frequently ordered of the 1930–31 V-16 models. The big sedans are huge, powerful, formal cars, but graceful in their own way and quite refined. Whether owner-driven or chauffeured, they made an impressive arrival statement. They were ordered only by people with substantial means—a new fully-optioned Chevrolet could be had for less than a tenth the price of the V-16.

The Cadillac shown here is said to have belonged to Mr. W.A. Ranke, who owned a painting and decorating business in Chicago, Illinois. He also owned three Pierce-Arrow automobiles, likely including the car in the background of the photograph.

The man at the driver's door, dressed in well-worn work clothes, wears a billed cap not unlike one a chauffeur would wear. With his right foot on the running board, his left hand on his hip and his other hand grasping the steering wheel though the open driver's window, his pose is one of confidence and competence. In the background, another man strikes a similar pose with a Pierce-Arrow touring car from the 1920s.

The big Cadillac is clearly not new—the tread of the road wheels is worn smooth, the great headlights have been replaced with smaller units from another make, and the little parking lights have disappeared from the crests of the front fenders. The twin trumpet-

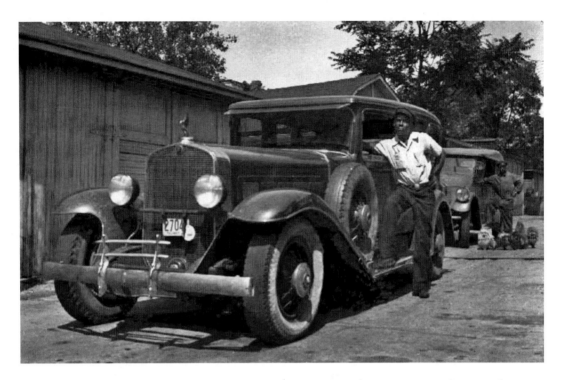

1930 Cadillac Sedan and earlier Pierce Arrow touring car. Even with tires worn smooth, tiny replacement headlights, and the patina of daily use, this V-16 is still a majestic motor car. Many of the big sedans were used hard, but they proved to be tough and reliable (courtesy Cheryl Whitfield).

belled horns that once flanked the radiator are also missing. A nonstandard bumper guard has been clamped to the Cadillac's wide, single-bar bumper, and the ornament from a late-thirties Packard V-12 graces the radiator cap. But the owner has kept his car running and it clearly means a great deal to him.

Almost as soon as the Cadillac V-16s came to market, economic, technological and cultural forces conspired to make them obsolete. A severe and tumultuous depression knocked the wind out of the sales prospects for fine, custom-built luxury cars. Improvements in metallurgy, engine design and fuel chemistry soon meant that a V-8 engine could be made to run every bit as smoothly and powerfully as a sixteen. And the classic styling of the late twenties and early thirties was shouldered roughly aside by the onrushing "streamlining" craze. By 1940, the car in the picture would have been considered every bit as old-fashioned as a Model T (and it would have been significantly harder and more expensive to maintain).

But throughout the long years from the time that the "new" wore off until the great classics were "rediscovered" in the 1960s and '70s, there were people from all walks of life who appreciated the unique and ultimately timeless appeal of these vehicles. Certainly many of the cars were neglected, junked or donated to wartime scrap drives. But many were conserved from the ravages of time, weather and collision damage. Some of the cars were parked in garages and stored for years or decades. Some were driven and carefully maintained by people who refused to give them up. And others were bought and appreciated by people who could never have afforded them new, but who, because of the depreciation caused by changing fashions, technology and economics, became able to acquire them.

Keeping the cars running was a challenge throughout much of their lives. After a few years automobile manufacturers lose interest in supporting older models, geared as they are to selling new product. And certainly the V-16 engines were thirsty, a significant factor even in the days of gas prices well under 50 cents. And the cars were complex, having incorporated what was cutting-edge technology for the time—hydraulic valve silencers, vacuum brake assist, dual carburetion and dual ignition. Replacing parts and obtaining competent service required ingenuity and persistence. Tires for the nineteen-inch wheels became rare and expensive. The availability of Model A Ford parts never really dried up, but owners of more exclusive cars did not enjoy the same convenience. It's clear from the picture that the owner of this Cadillac had to stretch a bit to keep it running.

For some time I wondered what might have become of the cars, the two men and the lively little dogs featured in the photo. The eBay listing didn't say, and there was no accompanying caption or tag. In April 2008 I figured out how to contact the woman who listed the picture on eBay, and she informed me that the 1930 Cadillac had been sold out of the estate of one of Mr. Ranke's descendants in 2005. She thought that the men in the picture had been employees of Mr. Ranke at the time the photograph was taken, and she believed that the car was still around. If the veteran V-16 could be located and its survival confirmed, that would make a gratifying postscript to the story told by the photograph.

7. Bound for Spain

The original owner of the five-passenger sedan that bears engine number 700476 is unknown. What is known is that for several years in the 1970s, the Series 4330-S sedan was owned by Ronald Renaldi of South Lake Tahoe, California. When I spoke with Mr. Renaldi (still living in California, as he had been when he owned the car) he had no recollection of the car's history or to whom he had sold it. In 1972 he found out that the car was for sale in Utah. He flew to Salt Lake City in his Piper Comanche, accompanied by his wife and son, to see the car. He bought it on sight for $7,500 and returned home. The next week, he had a friend fly him back to Salt Lake City to retrieve his car. This time he brought along his wife and his friend Joe Mikula, an accomplished mechanic with a broad knowledge of Cadillac V-16 and V-12 cars. The trio drove the car back to Lake Tahoe without any serious problems until they reached Spooner Summit, just shy of their destination. The car simply quit, and after investigating they concluded that one of the two condensers in the distributor had failed. Mr. Mikula looked through the selection of V-16 parts he had prudently brought along (including a complete distributor) and they were able to install another condenser and complete their journey. A few years later, Mr. Renaldi sold the Series 4330-S and turned his attention to other projects.

Mr. Renaldi has owned about 400 collector cars in his lifetime, but he has loved Cadillac V-16s from his early teen years. He said that he prefers the 1934–1937 V-16s and their more sophisticated driving characteristics. The later cars benefited from the continued rapid pace of technological advancement in the automotive industry. Independent front suspension (introduced on Cadillac cars in 1934) has been the rule for so long that it is difficult today to appreciate what a stunning difference it made in terms of comfort, handling and even safety. And of course, the engines themselves were upgraded with mechanical fuel

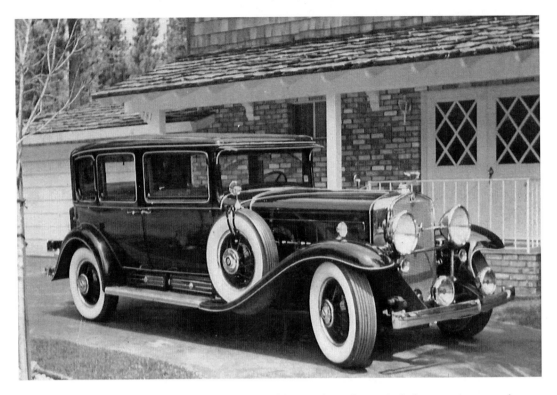

The 1930 Series 4330-S sedan when Ronald Renaldi owned it. The smoked glass sun visor over the windshield is still in place, but the enormous V-16 headlights have already been replaced with the somewhat smaller 1929 or 1930 units (courtesy Ronald Renaldi).

pumps, quieter air induction systems and other improvements. My point of view differs because of my partiality to the stately lines of the 1930–31 V-16s, the final development of the carriage before the streamlined car began to appear, and the first of the illustrious V-16 model run.

I first saw pictures of this car when it was listed on eBay in the spring of 2007. The listing included shots of two documents relative to the ownership history. In 1969, a registration card was issued to James E. Newton of Salt Lake City. Unfortunately, there was no more information about Mr. Newton than appeared on the card. But it was a clear "snapshot" of where the car was at the end of the 1960s, shortly before it came into Mr. Renaldi's hands.

A Florida certificate of title, issued in 2003, showed joint ownership by Robert L. and Bennett H. Vaughn of West Palm Beach, Florida. The date of the previous title was shown as May 12, 1983 (or is it 1993?). The eBay listing had been placed by a friend of the car's owner, who was selling on account of health problems. Thus, some of the information I received was necessarily "as told to." For instance, I was told that the then-current owner had held the car for seventeen years.

The various photographs show a well-preserved example of the Series 4330-S five-passenger sedan. The upholstery is intact and clean with no evidence of moth or water damage. One thing that caused one of my eyebrows to rise was the upholstered board above the windshield to which the rearview mirror is attached. These closed cars were equipped with what was known as a "V-V" windshield. "V-V" stood for "vision and ventilation," and it referred to the fact that the windshield glass could be raised to allow a stream of ventilating air to enter the car's passenger compartment through the gap between the lower edge of the windshield glass and the instrument panel. The driver raised the glass by turning a small crank located on that upholstered header board and about a third of the way across the top of the windshield from the driver's doorpost. On this car there was neither a crank nor a hole where the crank would have been. That meant that it was likely that the board had been re-covered with carefully matched upholstery material. Or it could also mean that the car had been completely reupholstered at some time.

The silk window shades look like new—white and spotless—and could be original, but without being able to visit and examine in person, the jury will have to remain out on that question.

The body is straight and without rust, insofar as the pictures tell the whole story. The paint is shiny and uniform, and consistent with a well-cared-for original car. The pinstriping illustrates a facet of classic car design often overlooked today. It was a very widespread practice to outline windows and trace body contours with one or more fine lines of contrasting color. In the case of the early Cadillac V-16 cars, there was a separate box on the "build sheet" where the color and specifics of the car's "body stripe" were designated. These stripes were applied by hand by talented and patient artists, and they became an integral part of the look of a finished car. A friend who was very interested in cars of various sorts during the 1930s recalls that one could easily spot a repainted car, because the absence of pinstriping made it stand out from the rest.

Three photographs of the engine were included. The engine shown was a correct early V-16, but there were some interesting quirks. There was additional plumbing indicating that a heater for the passenger compartment had been installed. Unlike today, in 1930 a heater was not automatically included, even for new luxury cars. A V-16 buyer could select a heater that used the hot water in the engine cooling system, or one that used the exhaust pipe to heat air entering the passenger compartment.

The carburetor shown on this car is a correct V-16 carburetor, but from the way its "S"-shaped air horn is attached, it could be identified as a later version of that carburetor than would originally have been mounted on an engine with a number as low as 476. The first V-16s came with exposed carburetors and no intake tubes. During 1930, however, Cadillac directed service men to retrofit the intake tubes to the early cars as they came in for maintenance or repair.

The distributor cap on a 1930 or 1931 V-16 should have a flat top, with the spark plug wires appearing to pour out of the side of the maroon Bakelite cap. This engine sported a distributor cap with the more conventional vertical "towers" familiar to most backyard (and professional) mechanics. That type of cap was used on 1932 and later V-16s. The write-up in the eBay listing indicated that the engine would turn over, but that it had not started and run recently. The seller speculated that the car needed a new distributor cap, and subsequently theorized that the problem might more likely be one of carburetor cleanliness and adjustment.

The bumper-mounted "Trippe" driving lights are a sought-after accessory for Classic Era cars. They were a popular add-on accessory at that time, and they continue to add flash to the cars even in the present. The only thing fancier would be one or a pair of "Pilot Ray" lamps, driving lights that swivel to shine in the direction the front wheels are turned.

Not entirely unexpectedly, there were some other missing or not strictly correct items. The headlights on the 1930 and 1931 V-16s were the largest-diameter headlights ever installed on Cadillac automobiles. The chrome-plated bell behind the enormous lens had a compound

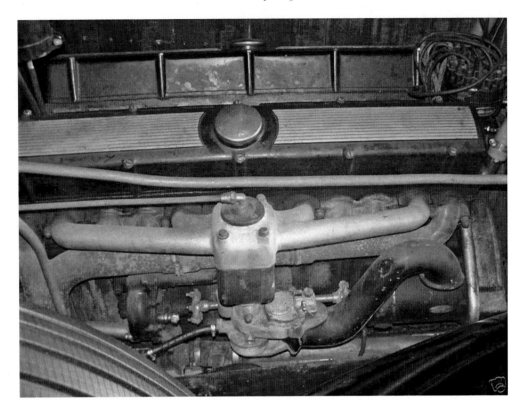

Right side of the engine. The thick copper pipe running along the side of the valve cover and above the intake manifold returns coolant to the right-hand radiator hose from a heater mounted on the passenger-compartment side of the firewall. The almost-vertical copper pipe at the left edge of the photograph brought liquid from the water pump to the heater. The distributor cap is a 1932 or later type (courtesy Dave Bowersock).

flare, and the screw at the top of the lens door was a simple slotted knurled design. The pattern scribed into the back of the lens on the V-16 headlight was entirely made up of vertical and horizontal lines. (Prior years' headlamps and those on the 1931 V-12 and V-8 cars have curved lines molded into the lenses.) The headlights on this car have a simple flare to the "bucket," curved lens lines, and a top screw bearing an enameled Cadillac crest, such as the 1929 and 1930 V-8 Cadillac models wore. Evidently, someone had occasion to replace the original headlights with lights from a prior year.

A final unique point about this car is the electric windshield wiper. With the exception of the closed models in the 1929 model year, Cadillacs in the 1920s and 1930s exclusively used vacuum-actuated windshield wipers. A Series 4330-S sedan, such as this one, would have had a "Visionall" wiper motor that would have moved two vertical wiper blades from one side of the windshield to the other. Instead, this car has a single electric wiper mounted to the windshield header in front of the driver. The car is also missing a smoked-glass sun shade that would have extended from the windshield header just underneath the leading edge of the roof. In the ordinary configuration, that sunshade would conceal the Visionall wiper motor. The Visionall system disappeared, largely due to the disappearance of windshield sunshades (Cadillac abandoned them for 1932) and the appearance of split and V-shaped windshields.

Single electric windshield wiper. Cadillacs from 1930 and 1931 were equipped with vacuum-operated wipers. A sedan such as this would have had a long tube-shaped unit set horizontally across the windshield header that moved two wipers from one side of the windshield to the other (courtesy Dave Bowersock).

The car was listed twice on eBay, and the first auction ended with the bidding falling short of the seller's reserve. In the second auction, the winning bid was $78,200. When I spoke with the seller afterwards, he indicated that the purchaser was a fellow from Spain who had put down a substantial deposit on the car and was traveling to the U.S. to see it.

In December 2007, the new owner drove the car (in Spain) while a friend or relative followed with a video camera. The resulting clip was posted on YouTube at the following URL: http://www.youtube.com/watch?v=_UcrMkMFg-Y and may still be accessible. The caption accompanying the video read: "Estos son el primer paseo con el cadillac despues de 30 años sin utilizarse" which I translate to mean that this is the first time the Cadillac had been driven after thirty years without being used. In the video, the car is without its hood or fender-mounted spare tires (most likely for easier engine access) and the covers for the battery box and tool box were removed. Other videos were posted the same day (December 8, 2007), including a brief clip of the car driving past the camera with the missing parts remounted (http://www.youtube.com/watch?v=bV-hNKSB3J8) and a session where the crew is trying to get the engine to start and run (http://www.youtube.com/watch?v= BLu00haJEvM). They succeed, but not without a lot of noisy backfiring and some smoke in the engine compartment. They are amused by the black soot sprayed on the bumper of a modern Nissan that was parked behind the V-16.

A half-minute clip from February 2008 (http://www.youtube.com/watch?v=f-jV_

PVb2Qo) just shows the engine running calmly and quietly. The caption reads, "El motor del Cadillac bien afinado." It's been refined and tuned up. Apparently this wonderful old motor car has found an appreciative home.

---

8. Message in a Bottle

In the September 1972 issue of the Cadillac-LaSalle Club's newsletter *The Self-Starter,* a letter was reproduced asking for information about a 1930 Cadillac V-16 sedan that the writer's father had purchased and that the family had lost track of around the end of the Second World War. If anyone responded to the request, they did so directly to the writer, and there was no further mention of the car in the pages of *The Self-Starter.* As far as I can tell, the engine number and body number cited in the letter are not among the known surviving 1930 and '31 V-16s. I can only suppose that the letter went unanswered and the car is lost to the ages, but the story is worth considering.

T.L. Tallentire
R.F.D. # 1
Aurora, Ind. 47001

Dear Fellow Member of the Cadillac-LaSalle Club:

I should like very much to find out what happened to my father's 1930 (?) Cadillac V-16 sedan, Type 452-A, Engine #702415 Job # 4330S, Body # 285. (I put the question mark after the year because my father purchased the car used, Aug. 1, 1932, and there is no mention of the year on the receipt that we have.) I am going to send this letter to everyone listed in the club directory as owning a V-16 or V-12, with the hope that somehow I may just run across someone who has some knowledge of the car. Of course, I hope that it still exists somewhere, but the odds are that it was cut up for scrap.

My father, a Cincinnati attorney, drove the car regularly until 1941, and after that it was parked out here at our country home for a few years. I can well remember riding in it as a little boy, and later on playing in it. If only my father could have been able to see into the future and recognize its potential value! In about 1945 (perhaps a year earlier or later) the caretaker sold it for my father to some man from Lawrenceburg, Ind. (or possibly from rural Dearborn County,) who claimed that he wanted to use it for a taxicab. I feel sure this idea was never carried out! What high rates he would have had to charge in order to make any money, with that 16 cylinder gas-guzzler!

We never heard anything more about the car, and I suppose it ended up in some obscure junk yard. However, I wonder if someone might have been poking around in junk yards, looking for old Cadillac parts, and might possibly have kept some notes on serial numbers of cars he found in them? Could there just possibly be someone in the country who knows something about the fate of old # 702415 (yes, it had a name, "Charlie!") "Charlie" was painted a dark green (Brewster?) and had some black trim. This was the original Cadillac paint job. It had no glass division between front and rear seats, and the front seat was upholstered in the same kind of cloth as the rear seat. The 4330S, of course, was a "Standard" Fisher body (or Fleetwood.) If any member should happen to know anything about the car, or know of any non-member who might, I hope that he will get in touch with me. Any information will be most sincerely appreciated.

From the engine number, Charlie was a 1930 car, and he carried a Fleetwood five-passenger sedan body of the same style as my car (give or take the divider window). The black and dark green color scheme would have presented quite well. The original owner had sold or traded the car in, whether because he wanted to buy the latest fine motor car, or because the Great Depression had necessitated a strategic reallocation of assets. Mr. Tallentire's father probably acquired the car at a bargain price. Once America entered the war and rationing of gasoline and rubber began, the big Cadillac's consumption of those commodities would have become an "issue."

It would be fun to try to track down any relatives of Mr. Tallentire and see if he ever found Charlie. One sincerely hopes that he did.

9. Destination Czech Republic

In 1972, a Cadillac collector near Akron, Ohio (let's call him "Bill Wilson") acquired a Series 4330-S five passenger sedan, engine number 701168 and body number 341. He bought it from an elderly, taciturn fellow in Norwalk, Ohio, who really didn't say much about the car's history, except that he'd had the car for quite a few years, and had bought it from the son of the original owner. Cadillac records show the car was shipped new to Cleve-

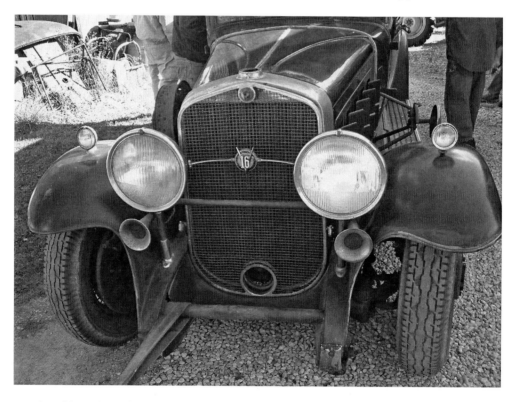

Weathered but solid and handsome. This is the front end of "Bill Wilson's" car before restoration was begun. The paint is rubbed to primer in some spots and some of the chrome has lost its luster, but there's no rust to speak of and it's still a magnificent car (courtesy Thomas Wallace).

land, but the name of the original purchaser is not known. Bill Wilson had found out about the car from a friend who had seen it at a show, and during the 1970s he enjoyed driving it to car shows and on club tours. At this writing, the Cadillac V-16 sedan is being restored at a facility in New York State, for a new owner in the Czech Republic. Before Mr. Wilson and the car parted company, Thomas Wallace took a splendid assortment of photographs, some of which are included here by permission.

Depicted in the photographs is a mostly complete, quite straight, but certainly used car. The condition of the car is pretty much as it was when Bill Wilson bought it nearly forty years ago. The left front fender needs some straightening, but that's the only notable dent problem. In the first picture, the front bumper has been removed for easier towing.

The combination of maroon body and black fenders is a pleasing one on these cars. In this case, the original paint is rubbed down to the primer in places, and in some spots new primer has been applied (e.g., the left rear fender). The man who sold the car to Mr. Wilson was repainting the rear fenders black, but had intended otherwise to leave the car entirely original.

The black rubber strips that formerly served as the tread for the running boards have been replaced by strips of another material, held in place by hand-formed metal straps that

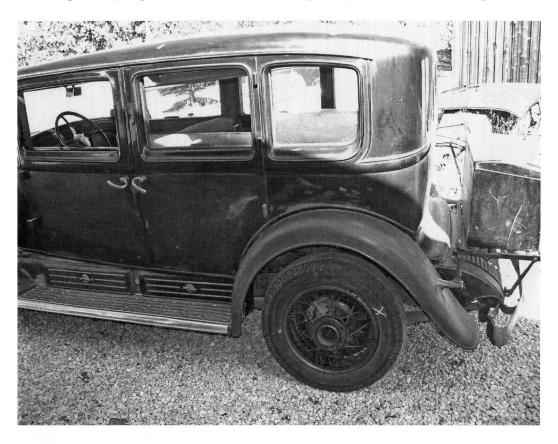

Maroon and black color scheme works well with these cars. The rear fender was stripped and primed by a previous owner who had begun a cosmetic restoration. A partially-lowered silk window shade is visible through rear door window. The rear wheel and tire appear to be a smaller size (18-inch as opposed to correct 19-inch) than the car should have (courtesy Thomas Wallace).

use the same holes as the studs molded into the original rubber strips. An inventive owner during the long years when replacement (and remanufactured) parts were unavailable for these venerable cars devised a way to keep the running boards functional and the bolt holes plugged.

The cloth of the interior is very well preserved and usable, but the window cranks all appear to be missing. Consistent with the Series 4330-S body style, there are no jump seats and there is no partition between the front and rear compartments, except for the back of the front seat. The taillight units can be seen resting on the rear seat cushion. The extra bit of carpet visible in the rear compartment just behind the front seat belongs across the inside of the firewall, with a cutout for the steering column.

The instruments and switches on the dash are all present and correct, and the odometer reads 50,992. The brake and clutch pedal pads are aftermarket replacements (not surprising for such high-wear items).

Overall, what's shown is a pretty nice unrestored car that has given a lot of service in the customary automotive manner. The patina of age is clearly evident, and the originality of the car poses the usual dilemma—to restore or not to restore. In this case, the exterior appearance is probably over the line for most owners—the primer on the rear fenders, for example, clashes with the rest of the finish, and it would be hard to return them to their proper black color without clashing in a different way. Removing the incorrect trunk and adding a new set of 7.50" × 19" tires would have gone a long way towards making a decision

Side view of the engine. Curlicue copper tube is the fuel line to the carburetor, replacing the original that was made of flexible braided metal hose and chrome plated (courtesy Thomas Wallace).

to conserve, rather than restore, more palatable. As it turned out, though, the car was taken through a full restoration, from the bare frame up.

In the photos that Thomas Wallace took, the engine appears to be fairly complete and operable, although the valley cover that was meant to hide the spark plugs and wires, and the chrome-plated covers for the vacuum tank fittings, are absent. And the elegant braided and chromed lines from the vacuum tanks to the carburetors have been replaced with plain copper tubing. (Judging from the deep color in the fuel sediment bowl, the engine hadn't been run in a long time when the pictures were taken.) I am personally fascinated to see what various owners did over the years to solve the routine problems of replacing worn parts and maintaining the function of devices that the factory had long since ceased supporting. For example, on this car a previous owner seems to have applied some orange goop to the points where the vacuum and gasoline lines meet the vacuum tank in an apparent effort to leak-proof the system.

It's a privilege and a treat to be able to see this car as it was before restoration, to see how it stood after surviving an active life of nearly eighty years. Soon it will be returned to a sparkling similitude of newness, showing what a fortunate purchaser would have seen in 1930 when the Cadillac V-16 was the ultimate expression of engineering and esthetic achievement.

10. A Somewhat Shopworn Showgirl

The phrase "Madame X" is redolent of mystery and elegance with an undertone of passion and intrigue. Several explanations have been put forth as to how General Motors styling chief Harley Earl came up with that name for a distinctive subset of the elite Cadillac V-16 offerings in the early 1930s. These were cars with certain advanced styling and construction features that gave them a unique personality and feel, even among the august "catalog custom" cars comprising the V-16 range.

Madame X cars had a number of exclusive attributes in common. They were all closed cars and all were four-door models (although a few coupes were built with some of the Madame X features). All had styling codes or body series numbers beginning with 41 (Series 4130, 4161, 4175, etc.). All of these cars, except for a few built before Fleetwood's Pennsylvania plant was closed, have raked windshields sloped to 18 degrees from vertical, an angle considered quite astonishing for a production car in 1930. The side windows were outlined with slender bright-metal reveal moldings, and through the use of the latest techniques in metallurgy and construction, the windshield pillars and door posts were unusually slender. The result was an air of lightness and grace that belied the actual size and weight of the vehicle.

Inside, the appointments of Madame X cars were somewhat simplified from the other V-16 cars. The inlaid wood decorative panels below the windowsills are not used, in favor of an entirely upholstered door panel. Similarly, below the rear quarter windows, the right and left vanity units were free-standing, instead of being integrated into inlaid wood panels like those found below the door windows on regular V-16 cars. Another simplification was the elimination of roll-down silk window shades, such as are found in the other V-16 sedan and limousine series.

The car that appeared on eBay in late June 2007 was a Series 4130-S five-passenger sedan (no divider window and no auxiliary seating). No more of its history was given than that it had come from California in the mid–1980s (the listing indicated that the car was located in Lyons, New York). Visible in the pictures accompanying the listing were California "black plate" license tags attesting to significant West Coast residence prior to being brought east. Topping the license plate frame was an older (yellow) version of the Cadillac-LaSalle Club medallion, and a single Pilot Ray driving light added interest to the front end ensemble. The seller said that he was listing the car for the owner, who needed to sell for health reasons. The car had been offered on eBay two or three years previous to this listing, and I do not recall what the result of that auction was.

Roy Schneider, author of the definitive account of the history of these cars, *Sixteen Cylinder Motor Cars*, told me that the car had been a familiar sight in the California collector car world. It had been owned by Owen R. Crain, a fellow with a strong interest in cars and mechanical things. Mr. Crain had worked on the car for years and he regularly brought it to club meets. It was not a professional restoration, but it was a very decent car. My source said Mr. Crain's son-in-law was a "pretty damn good mechanic" who had subsequently acquired a V-12 Cadillac, rebuilt the engine and made it into a high performance motor.

In the July 1964 issue of *The Self-Starter*, the monthly newsletter of the Cadillac-LaSalle Club, a two-page spread of photographs appeared illustrating Mr. Crain's progress in restoring

This angle shows off the Madame X styling almost as well as seeing the car from the front. From the beltline down, the Madame X models were the same as their 4300 series counterparts (except for rear-hinged front doors). Deployed trunk rack on this car is from a 1932 Cadillac (courtesy RM Auctions).

the Madame X sedan. The caption referred to the car as a 1931 model, although the engine number (702103) would indicate a production date in June of 1930.[1]

Yann Saunders, who built *The (New) Cadillac Database* on the Internet (where a photo of the partially restored car is posted), disclosed that pictures of this car appear in at least two books: *Great Marques of America* (pp. 40–41), by Jonathan Wood, and *Great Marques—Cadillac* (p. 33).

As presented for sale on eBay, the car was somewhat the worse for wear. The seats had been covered in pleated black leather, in sharp contrast to the wool broadcloth door and trim panels. The trim panels behind the front seat and beneath each of the rear quarter windows were ripped. The tear in the front seat appeared to have been a careless accident, but the lesions under the quarter windows could be explained by the missing right and left vanity units, which would have been located where the cloth was torn. Some moisture damage was evident in the rear upper quarter trim panel and over the corner of the backlight.

The garnish moldings surrounding the windows were painted the same color as the fenders and roof, a scheme I've seen on at least one other Madame X sedan. The theme of the Madame X design was one of clean lines and simple elegance in a contemporary vein; hence the restraint in the use of wood trim in the interior. The seats would have been plain, without pleats, and they would most likely have been covered with cloth coordinated with the doors and trim panels, although an owner who wanted leather seats and cloth on the other interior surfaces would have been accommodated.

The engine appeared to be a healthy, rather complete and functional (based on the description) V-16 engine. The original carburetors and their gooseneck air horns had been replaced, probably with Zenith (or perhaps Solex) carburetors. The oil filter on the center of the firewall is supposed to be contained in a chrome-plated cylindrical case, but here a black painted case has been substituted. The original vacuum tank fuel delivery system appears to be retained, although with rubber hoses. The car came with fuel lines connecting the vacuum tanks to the carburetors consisting of flexible metal hoses encased in braided chrome-plated wire. Until recently, those fancy fuel lines have been very hard to replace, and many owners turned to neoprene hoses or copper tubing at some point or other.

Some interesting photographs of the underside of the car were included in the eBay listing. They disclosed a car that had been driven, as opposed to a restored and stored specimen—no major damage or problems, but some things that a new owner might want to address. The first shot showed that the covers or "gaiters" for the front leaf springs had been removed, as had the louvered splash pans between the engine and the frame rails. The second photo showed slender, modern mufflers, and the third showed that the tailpipes ended just aft of the rear axle, instead of extending rearward nearly as far as the rear bumper.

The car appears to be an excellent "driver" and a definite show-stopper at any venue, just from its rich heritage. When new, Madame X models sold for $1,000 more than corresponding models in the other V-16 lines. That was when a fully-optioned new Chevrolet cost about $675. Bringing this Madame X up to the level of a competitive show car would require some significant expenditures in the area of upholstery, missing parts (for example, engine splash pans, correct carburetors and rear seat vanity units), and general clean-up and detailing. The bidding for this special Cadillac exceeded the seller's reserve price (which was apparently $67,500) with four days left before auction expiration. The winning bid was $69,360.

In October 2007, RM Auctions added this Madame X sedan to the roster of cars it would be auctioning at the annual Fall Meet of the Hershey Region of the Antique

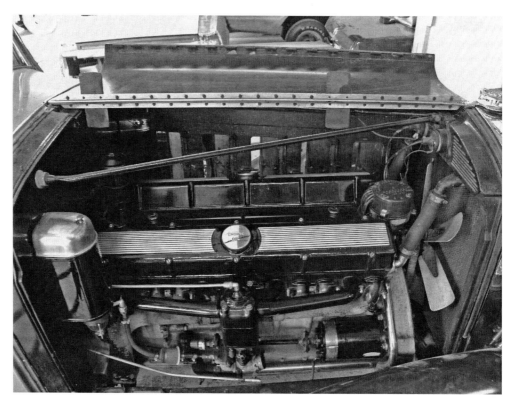

Right-hand side of the engine. Generally correct, except for the non-standard carburetors and oil filter, along with rubber hose for fuel lines (courtesy RM Auctions).

Automobile Club of America in Hershey, Pennsylvania (fondly referred to by old car aficionados worldwide as "Hershey"). The published estimate was $100,000–$125,000, but the car was sold at a price of $93,500. Subsequently, photos of the blue Madame X sedan Owen Crain once owned appeared on a Czech Republic website with a plate on the front bumper announcing the Prague Classic Car Centre, a collector car sales and service establishment.

11. A Surviving Twin

In 1930, if you were a Cadillac customer who wanted a V-16 limousine, there were several ways you could go. You could buy a straightforward imperial sedan, in either a 5-passenger style (with a pair of fold-down opera seats to accommodate occasional extra passengers) or a seven-passenger version (with full-width auxiliary seats). Either of these cars would be spacious, private and comfortable, with the power and performance of the V-16 drivetrain. The passenger compartment could be isolated by rolling up a divider window. Necessary instructions to the driver could be conveyed through a microphone. A gentleman's smoking set on the right and a lady's vanity set and ashtray on the left pampered the occupants. There was even an umbrella in a built-in stand next to the curbside door.

Or you could select one of the even more formal chauffeur-driven styles—a formal town car, perhaps, with a removable fabric roof over the driver and without rear quarter windows. Or maybe a landaulet with a fold-down rear quarter so the rear-seat passengers could enjoy open-air riding.

Or you could be stylistically daring and order a limousine from the 4100 series cars, the so-called Madame X models. For the time, the Madame X design was *avant-garde*. The raked windshield (adopted after about April 1930), the slender window pillars and chrome reveals around the glass lent an air of delicacy to a massive formal car. That was deceptive, because the cars were every bit as strong as their non–Madame X counterparts and their curb weights were nearly identical. New techniques of casting and engineering the structural body parts enabled the innovative styling that gave the cars a dramatically different presence or personality. Inside, the use of stained and varnished wood was greatly restrained compared to the other V-16 series. The garnish moldings surrounding the door and rear quarter windows were painted, and there was no inlaid trim panel beneath the side windows. There was still inlaid wood over the instrument panel, but it was more subdued. The smoking and vanity sets in the rear compartment were free-standing units, instead of being built into window trim.

1930 Series 4175 Madame X limousine. Nick Romanick is behind the wheel of the dark green and black car. The raked windshield, the bright reveal moldings in the windows and the slender windshield and door pillars were unique to the Madame X cars, which cost $1,000 more than corresponding body styles in other style series (courtesy Nick Romanick).

In 1930 and 1931, 86 Madame X Series 4175 seven-passenger limousines left the Cadillac factory. Two of them were ordered by Ingersoll, Ontario, business partners Harold Wilson and Sam McLaughlin, owners of a nut-and-bolt factory. (Sam McLaughlin was the man who sold to William Durant the company that became General Motors of Canada.) The two cars were nearly identical, though the one that Mr. McLaughlin ordered had gold-plated interior door handles and window cranks. Mr. Wilson's car was recently sold out of a private collection in Michigan to Hyman Ltd. Classic Cars. The engine number is 702879, putting the car close to the end of the 1930 model year (the last car shipped in 1930 was engine number 702887). The body number was 74 (out of the total of 86 mentioned previously) and Cadillac records indicate that the new car was shipped to Oshawa on the north shore of Lake Ontario.

The car was owned for over twenty years by Mr. Nick Romanick of Windsor, Ontario, and he was the third or fourth owner. There's an Ontario Motor League decal on the windshield, and Mr. Romanick drove the car regularly (and at highway speeds). He tells of taking the car on club tours, driving annually to Niagara Falls, and participating in the Blossom Tour. He acquired the car from the owner of an automotive parts store by trading a "brass era" 1908 Maxwell runabout for it in an even exchange. The parts store owner had kept the Cadillac in a rented garage that he was no longer going to be able to rent. The Maxwell, though tall, was not as long and was easier to store. At one show, a gentleman asked Mr. Romanick to lift the Cadillac's hood so he could see the engine number. The fellow had been hoping it was the car that Mr. McLaughlin had ordered new.

The 1908 Maxwell that was traded for the Cadillac. Nick Romanick swapped this Maxwell runabout for the 1930 V-16 limousine about a quarter century ago (courtesy Nick Romanick).

Mr. Romanick performed a ring job and a valve job on the engine shortly after taking ownership, because it had several burned valves and wasn't running well. The hinge down the center of the hood was gone, and a replacement had to be found (at Hershey) and Mr. Romanick used small bolts instead of rivets to install it. The fenders and the top of the hood had some dents, and in deference to the Cadillac's wonderful originality, Mr. Romanick did no more than correct the dents and touch up the paint. The body only required a nice polishing.

The car retains many unique details that might have been lost in an extensive restoration. Where the divider behind the front seat meets the right-hand rear door, there is a cloth loop in which an umbrella once rested. Only the worn and torn front seat gives away the car's true age. Everything else is extremely well cared for and preserved. Even the hat net on the ceiling is ready for use. There is an aftermarket radio, and the remote control dial unit is mounted on the steering column in front of the instrument panel.

Part of the intense charm of this very original and carefully cared-for car are the features that eloquently speak of how the prior owners worked to keep this motor car running and presentable. Mr. Romanick told me that the vacuum fuel pumps worked, but that the metal fuel lines would get hot, and the pumps would quit working. So he bypassed the vacuum fuel delivery system and installed two electric fuel pumps in the rear of the car where the fuel lines leave the tank. The switches are positioned below the dash to the left of the steering column, and the pumps are rubber-mounted to minimize vibration and noise. The fuel lines to the carburetors don't start out at the fittings next to the sediment bowls under the vacuum tanks. Instead, they run from holes that have been drilled into the sides of the top covers of the vacuum tanks and they connect to in-line fuel filters attached to the carburetors (required because the fuel no longer passes through the sediment bowls). Moreover, the lines are copper tubing instead of the original flexible hoses with shiny braided wire casings. When the engine was designed, the goal was that any wiring or plumbing that couldn't be hidden would be decorated.

Mr. Romanick bought an add-on turn signal kit at a flea market and installed it himself. The set-up includes a four-way emergency flasher, and it does a great deal to make the car safe to drive in modern traffic. When these cars were new, hand signals were familiar to drivers and were commonly used. Today, a driver employing only the left arm to indicate a turn or a lane change is rare indeed, and many motorists would miss the message. The original horns still look classy, perched below the massive headlights, but Mr. Romanick says that they didn't work very well. So he installed a different set of horns, mounted to the radiator support rods under the hood and operated with a lever on the steering column.

The Pilot Ray driving lights mounted just behind the front bumper were purchased from another old Cadillac aficionado for several hundred dollars (current prices for this impressive accessory are in the thousands). Pilot Ray lights do what many modern headlights do electronically—they point where the front wheels are aimed in a turn, helping the driver to see where he's going. "Pilot Ray lights the winding way," as the advertising slogan said.

The running boards on this car represent something of a design reversal, and were refashioned and installed by Mr. Romanick. The factory originally turned the car out with the steel running board finished in a faux wood grain treatment. Running the length of each board were five black anti-skid rubber strips about an inch wide, set in chrome-plated accent moldings. Bolts molded into the rubber strips went through the moldings and the running boards, and were fastened on the underside with nuts. On this car the running board surface

New owner Tom Sutphen. Now in his personal collection, the 1931 Madame X limousine is seen here when Cadillac-LaSalle Club members were privileged to tour Mr. Sutphen's collection in connection with their 2011 Grand National meet (courtesy David Rubin).

underneath the strips has been painted black and no longer has a wood-grained appearance. Mr. Romanick had wood strips fashioned to fit where the deteriorated rubber had been, and fastened them with metal screws using the existing bolt holes. The job was nicely done and well crafted.

Madame X cars cost an additional $1,000 over the price of the same configuration in another non–Madame X series. A couple of Chevrolets or Fords could be had just for the amount of that difference. The 4100 series represents another example of the pioneering efforts of Harley Earl to advance the frontiers of automotive styling, even in what was a very tradition-bound field, that of ultra-luxury motor cars. They also demonstrate the lengths to which Cadillac was willing to go in order to offer a range of styles that could satisfy all but the most particular or eccentric tastes. This particular example marvelously conveys the majesty and clean elegance of the Madame X design theme, close enough to new condition to give the viewer a real taste of what customers encountered in 1930.

In the autumn of 2008, the car was included in the lot list for RM Auctions' October 10 Vintage Motor Cars of Hershey Auction, with an estimate of $125,000 to $175,000. A lucky bidder took the Madame X survivor for $104,500.

Cadillac-LaSalle Club members attending the club's 2011 Grand National Meet in Columbus, Ohio, were able to tour the private collection of Tom Sutphen. Among the cars to be seen there was a certain green 1930 Cadillac V-16 Madame X limousine, the same one that Nick Romanick had owned. Mr. Sutphen is clearly fond of the car, and it's in good hands.

12. From Parts Car to Show Car

Now living in Bergenfield, New Jersey, is a 1930 Cadillac Series 4361-S five-passenger V-16 town sedan. A relatively early car, the engine number is 700759, body number 52 of 258 built. The build sheet shows an order date of March 25, 1930, and a shipping date three days later, on March 28.

The original color scheme was black with maroon lower door and body panels, and gold-bronze pinstriping. Sometime during the car's life it was resprayed black with red wheels, and there is some evidence of an earlier repaint in green.

A town sedan provided comfortable, elegant transportation for up to five people, and it had an attached trunk. This trunk was a part of the car, although not engulfed by the bodywork the way the trunks of later cars would be. Behind the permanent trunk is a folding rack onto which an accessory trunk could be clamped for even more storage space. The configuration was ideal for a shopping trip or for touring.

At one point, this car was part of the collection of William "Bill" Harrah, the Reno, Nevada, casino owner who amassed during his lifetime a collection of vintage cars and other vehicles that remains a legend thirty years after his death. Harrah's Automobile Collection included hundreds of carefully restored cars, as well as a fully-staffed and equipped restora-

Town sedans came equipped with a built-in trunk, as well as a folding rack to accommodate an additional accessory trunk. Touring accommodations were ample for a family of five. Note cutaway in lower right rear corner of trunk to provide access to the fuel filler cap (author's photograph).

tion facility and a prodigious automotive history library. This V-16 town sedan may have been used by the Harrah collection as a source of parts for flashier V-16 models (apparently having donated parts such as the ignition switch, the speedometer and some trim items).

The current owners, Mr. Tex Sorrell and his family, have had the car for the past twelve years. Mr. Sorrell's first V-16 was a Series 4375-S seven passenger sedan that he bought in the 1970s. That car was pretty far gone, and he quickly became convinced that the magnitude of the restoration it required was more than he could handle (for example, the rockers were severely rusted and the running boards were unusable). Then, in 1995 or 1996, while attending the AACA's Hershey meet, he saw the town sedan we're concerned with in the car corral. RM Restorations had taken the Cadillac and twelve other cars in trade for a Duesenberg, and they were hoping to sell it, rather than take it back to Canada. The engine was not running at that time, and the car had been towed into the car corral with a stout rope. That's unusual, because the normal rules for the car corral require that each sale vehicle be driven in under its own power. Mr. Sorrell thought that the town sedan was much more consistent with his needs, desires and means than the seven-passenger sedan he then owned, and he set about acquiring it. He negotiated the price with the seller for a while, and ultimately agreed to buy. The terms provided that he had a month to decide whether to keep the car or call the deal off.

The previous owner assured Mr. Sorrell that the engine was sound and that the car would run, and after working with the car for a month, the transaction was finalized. The big Cadillac was soon running, and it proved to be a comfortable and reliable vehicle to drive or ride in—so much so that the Sorrells were able to take the car on a Glidden Tour from their home to Altoona, Pennsylvania, and back, a trip of 10 or 11 days, covering about

The Sorrells' V-16 town sedan while on the September 2005 Glidden tour in Altoona, Pennsylvania. The 200-year-old building in the background is a church (courtesy Tex Sorrell).

View of the town sedan's driver's compartment, very much as it would have appeared in 1930. Levers on the steering wheel hub control the hand throttle and headlight switch. The ignition switch, below the clock and speedometer, locks the transmission in reverse or neutral to help prevent theft. Engine-turned or "damascened" decorative panels flank the instrument cluster (author's photograph).

1,200 miles. The V-16 was their sole vehicle on the tour and it performed impeccably. Mr. Sorrell had wanted to experience driving a V-16 on a long journey, where they would be dependent on it, the way an owner would have been in 1930. He was not disappointed.

In caring for their Cadillac, the Sorrells strive to preserve the car's originality at the same time that they enjoy driving it. If something is missing or broken, they are not worried about repairing or replacing it, and the pieces that were cannibalized in the past have been reinstalled. The carpets had deteriorated and have been replaced with authentic materials. But the seat covers that the car came to them with have not been removed. The car does not have the fold-down sun visors that were attached to the ceiling (such as my Series 4330 imperial sedan has). But there is a very interesting accessory visor on the driver's side, with a swivel arm attached to the windshield header board. The holes for the mounting screws on the bracket match exactly the two screws that hold the header board to the windshield pillar. The lower edge of the visor is tinted transparent plastic to help the driver see, even when the sun sits on the horizon.

Some of the pot metal cast parts, such as window cranks and throttle gears, that are notorious for crumbling or freezing in place when they're supposed to move freely, have been replaced with the high-quality reproductions for which the late Charles Selick of Rumson, New Jersey, was known. And one day the Sorrells hope to return the car's finish to the original maroon and black with gold pinstriping.

13. A Hybrid of a Different Sort

Phil King lives on the beach, just north of Brisbane, in Queensland, Australia. Sometime in late 2009 or early the next year, he saw on eBay a Cadillac V-12 being offered for sale by a gentleman in Newcastle. He phoned the seller and arranged to come see the car, which turned out to have a reproduction aluminum sport phaeton body. The engine was incomplete, there was no interior upholstery or trim, and the brightwork and door latches were missing. The asking price was $100,000, and the seller also had a V-12 roadster in similar shape for $70,000. Mr. King decided not to bid on either car when he considered what would be required in money, time and work to complete either project.

Fascinated, nevertheless, by the classic Cadillac multi-cylinder cars, Mr. King phoned a friend who had run a well-known restoration facility in New Zealand, and discussed the matter with him. He suggested that Mr. King call a friend of his who had a Cadillac for sale (he didn't know which year or model). The restorer's friend turned out to be a perfectly delightful fellow, but the car was a V-8. He steered Mr. King to friends of his in Sydney, Keith and Maureen Brailey, who were involved in old Cadillacs. They suggested Mr. King call Brendan Lane-Mullins (also in Sydney).

Mr. Lane-Mullins was the owner of several old classic cars, including a 1930 Cadillac V-16 town sedan and a Cadillac V-8 dual cowl phaeton. He had been a car dealer with a fine home on Sydney Harbor. He had sold that home, leased a factory and made the office into his residence. He acquired a fair number of interesting collector cars and began restoring them, hiring people to help him work on the cars. Unfortunately, he was now in need of cash to pay medical expenses, and that was the reason why some of his cars were on the market. Mr. King flew to Sydney and examined both the V-16 and the V-8, and he fell in love with the sixteen.

The car was parked in a shipping container, surrounded by an enormous amount of what might be called rubbish, but the sort of thing that merits saving for some people. Mr. Lane-Mullins had owned the car since 1993, when he purchased it in St. Louis, Missouri, and since 2004 it had been in storage.

Before placing the car in storage, Mr. Lane-Mullins had enjoyed driving and showing it. Irwin Sinclair, another Australian Cadillac enthusiast, recalls Mr. Lane-Mullins bringing the big Cadillac on a rally in Penrith, New South Wales, sometime in 1995, on which occasion he gave rides to a lot of people. At that time Mr. Sinclair says that it was "an excellent original car." The car ran well, the interior was "great," the paint was "reasonable" and the chrome plating on the radiator was "down."

Before Mr. Lane-Mullins put the town sedan into storage, he had intended to replace the sedan body with a modern replica of the Series 4380 convertible sedan body (also known as an "all-weather phaeton"). He had applied primer to the fenders, the valences below the doors, the dust shield between the front frame rail ends, and the gas tank cover, and he removed the body from the chassis. He'd rebuilt the carburetors and vacuum tanks, cleaned and re-lined the gas tank, and had generally reworked the twin fuel systems which had been blocked from front to rear. He had also begun to remove the interior trim panels (which he saved), although the original upholstery remained quite usable, as Mr. King describes it.

Prior to interring the car in the shipping container, Mr. Lane Mullins had re-installed

The body by itself. Mr. Lane-Mullins had taken the body off the frame when this photograph was taken, and had removed the interior trim panels (courtesy Peter Ratcliff).

the sedan body, with its original paint still intact (but which now contrasted with the primed fenders and dust shields).

After a great deal of digging, moving and re-arranging the stuff in the container, Mr. King was able to get close enough to the V-16 town sedan to have a look at it. After examining it as best he could, he agreed to buy the car on the basis of Mr. Lane-Mullins's assurance that it was complete. He flew home to make shipping arrangements, and flew back to Sydney the next week so he could extricate the Cadillac from its "Tut's tomb" situation, nestled as it was in the shipping container, tightly surrounded by miscellaneous items. It took an entire day to get the car out into the open, since Mr. Lane-Mullins could not help on account of his health problems.

The car appeared to Mr. King to be complete, so he paid Mr. Lane-Mullins the agreed amount and loaded his new prize into a second container he had bought for the purpose. He had the container with its enclosed Cadillac shipped by rail to Brisbane, and flew home to await their arrival.

A week later, when he came to take delivery of the car, he saw that oil was leaking from the container, and he dreaded what he would find inside. It seemed that a muffler that had been left loose on the floor of the container had rolled until it lodged under the oil pan (which is made of cast aluminum alloy). The bounces and rocking of the train journey had produced a hole in the oil pan, and Mr. King was devastated. Fortunately, the damage would prove to be repairable.

Mr. King's car is a 1930 Series 4361-S five passenger town sedan. Two hundred fifty-eight of these town sedans were built in the 1930–31 model years (along with two Series 4361 cars [no "S"] that featured a divider window between driver's and passenger compartments). This body style was also known as a "close-coupled" sedan, and it corresponds to what most modern sedans are like. There are four doors and two rows of seating, with the rear seats as close to the front seats as a reasonable allowance for the rear passengers' legs and feet will permit. Cadillac sedans in 1930 came in three basic sizes, in terms of interior room. The town sedans were the smallest, laid out for two passengers (including the driver) in front and three in back. The next size was also designated "five passenger" but there was significantly more room between the front and rear seats. These cars (which included owner-driven sedans, chauffeur-driven limousines and town cars) typically had movable footrests or hassocks for rear seat passengers, and in some cases had folding "opera seats" that allowed two additional people to be transported in a pinch. The third size included the seven-passenger sedans and limousines (as well as town cars, landaulets and other formal variations). These had even more rear compartment room, and generally sported full-width foldable auxiliary or "jump" seats.

The Series 4361 cars each had a permanent trunk, mounted to the rear of (and separate from) the passenger compartment. If the car was equipped with fender-mounted spare tires, there would be a foldable rack behind the built-in trunk on which an additional accessory trunk could be mounted for even more luggage capacity. (Otherwise, a single rear-mounted spare tire sat behind the trunk.) These cars were fine transport for a family of up to five, without being overly formal.

In the course of following the historical scent trails left by Mr. King's car through time, a very unusual chain of events came to light. The engine in Mr. King's car is number 703002,

Side view of Mr. King's car. The open compartment beneath the front door is for the battery. Aside from some mild surface rust and the delamination of the window glass, the car appears to have weathered the years very well (courtesy Phil King).

and according to Cadillac records still extant, it was originally installed in a Series 4330-S five-passenger sedan (the middle of the three sedan sizes). That car was shipped from the factory on March 8, 1931, to Denver, Colorado. It met an unfortunate end, being "T-boned" by a railroad train. Subsequently, its remains have been used for parts for other cars.

Several photographs of Mr. King's car appear in James Schild's masterly book *Fleetwood: The Company & the Coachcraft.* (Initially printed in a limited run, this book has been out of print, quite rare and expensive whenever it was offered for sale. Mr. Schild has completed and published a revised edition that is even more helpful and informative.) Mr. Schild's book identifies the car as an unrestored town sedan in the Fred Weber collection. Phone calls to Mr. Weber and his associates elicited the following automotive biography.

Sometime in 1930, Cadillac built and shipped a Series 4302 V-16 roadster to a Cadillac dealer on the East Coast of the United States. For some reason, unknown today, shortly after the car was shipped, the roadster body was removed and a Series 4361-S town sedan body was mounted on the chassis in its place. Without factory records and information from the people who were there, it's extremely difficult to say where that town sedan body came from, what car it may once have been part of, and what the engine number and shipping specifics had been for that car. From January 1931 onward, this town sedan that had been built as a roadster was registered with motor vehicle authorities as a four-door sedan.

Why would the bodies have been switched? From this vantage, we can only speculate. Maybe the initial purchaser changed his or her mind, and asked the dealer to provide a car that would be comfortable year-round, as opposed to an open model that would never really be weathertight. And don't forget, in the 1920s and '30s, a closed car was generally considered to be more valuable and more desirable. On the other hand, if the roadster body had been damaged in an accident, the car might have been reborn as a town sedan in the process of being repaired. Moreover, some of the buyers of high-end luxury cars in the Classic Era thought nothing of ordering an additional body in another style, so that their car could provide appropriate comforts for the changing seasons merely by having the dealer exchange the two bodies. (Try that on a modern car!) The original owner of this particular car may have purchased the sedan body for cold weather use, and for some reason the original roadster body was lost (perhaps when the car was sold).

After many years, the car came into the hands of the garage and restoration facility run by Fred Weber in St. Louis, Missouri. It's possible that Dragone Classic Motorcars in Connecticut may have sold it to them. The Webers worked extensively with Cadillac V-16 automobiles, buying up parts, parts cars and whole cars whenever they could. At one time they had twenty-one V-16 Cadillacs in the shop. It was clear to them that this particular V-16 was unusual. The build sheet said that it should be a roadster. All of the serial-numbered engine and chassis components (transmission, rear axle, steering box, chassis, generator, etc.) were correct for the roadster described on the build sheet. There was even a rumble seat step still bolted to the rear bumper bracket. So a decision was made that, as long as this car had the pedigree of a roadster, and in fact started out in life as a roadster, they would convert it back to that body style. In due course a roadster body was substituted for the town sedan body and the car was finished and sold.

The town sedan body was in outstanding condition. Everything was there, the upholstery was like new and the paint was very presentable. It was a relatively easy matter to place the sedan body onto a chassis from among the vehicles situated around the shop in varying states of repair. The engine came from a sedan that Jim Pearson had owned which was only good for parts (the one that had been hit by a railroad train). Once again there was a complete

1930 V-16 town sedan, but it was a hybrid of at least three different cars. When it came time to sell off the assets of Fred Weber's operation, the town sedan made its way to Mr. Lane-Mullins and then to Mr. King.

The dilemma that ordinarily faces the owner of an unrestored but pretty well preserved car (whether to leave the car original, or to embark upon a restoration) was thus complicated somewhat for Mr. King.

Increasingly, old car enthusiasts have come to appreciate the value of keeping a lightly used car in an unrestored state, rather than immaculately restoring it. "It's only original once" is guaranteed to be heard at least once at every car show. Car clubs that hold judged shows often include an HPOF class (historic preservation of original features) in their judging, and cars are eligible for that class if more than a specified percentage of the car's paint, trim, upholstery, etc. has not been re-done. So when someone acquires an old car that presents respectably well without being repainted, reupholstered, replated and so forth, there is a certain amount of pressure or encouragement to "keep it original," rather than embark on a major restoration.

Where the path that a car has taken from the factory to the present day is as complex as the one followed by Mr. King's car, the complexity would seem to open some unusual

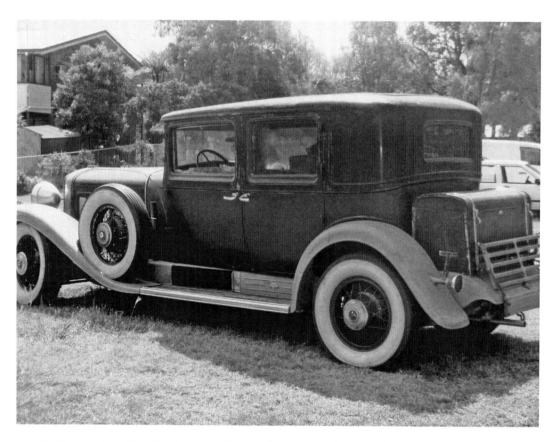

In this view the yellow discoloration of the window glass can be seen. The open compartment on this side of the car was for a tool kit that came with the car, including tire changing equipment, as well as screwdriver, wrenches, a grease gun and a hammer, among other useful implements (courtesy Phil King).

alternatives. Where the car's engine is from a wrecked vehicle, the chassis is from an unknown parts car, and the body was placed on a different chassis (for the first time) when it was brand new, determining what the car was "originally" becomes a philosophical discourse. Is it the town sedan that the body originally graced? Is it the train-wrecked sedan that the engine originally propelled? Is it the car that the chassis first undergirded? Copies of the build sheets for the 1930 and 1931 Cadillac V-16s are all available, but they are sorted only by engine number—if you don't have the engine number, you probably can't find the right build sheet. The build sheets also show the body number and the separate chassis number (distinct from the engine number). But to find a build sheet with only the car's chassis number requires examining all 3,251 sheets until the one with that chassis number turns up. To find the build sheet with only the body number first requires separating the sheets for the specific body style and then finding the specific body number within that subset. When and if someone undertakes the task of cross-referencing the body and chassis numbers and thereby makes it possible to find a particular build sheet without the engine number, the origins of the chassis and body of Mr. King's car can be readily determined.

So, if the question "What's original?" is this difficult to answer for a particular car, it would be hard to gainsay the owner if he chose to place on the car whatever might be his favorite 1930 V-16 body style—roadster, phaeton, town car or whatever. And there would certainly be nothing wrong with polishing up what he's got, a straight, complete and serviceable town sedan requiring not much to make it a beautiful, drivable classic to use and show as he pleases.

At this point, Mr. King has elected to reinstall the detached interior trim bits and to repaint the fenders and valences in a subdued manner to harmonize with the original black finish of the body. Along the way, replacement of occluded window glass would not be out of the question. Meanwhile, he has been addressing some mechanical matters. The engine has been re-commissioned and runs once again. Before long, the car should once again be an impressive and smooth-running representative of the breed.

---

14. Dealer Demo Special?

The Cadillac V-16s that were ordered by purchasers in Canada were shipped through General Motors Canada in Oshawa, Ontario. In late January of 1931, a Series 4361-S V-16 town sedan, engine number 702577, was shipped to Canada. This model was the so-called close-coupled sedan, which came with a built-in (though not enclosed) trunk, and a folding rack to accommodate an additional accessory trunk if the owner so desired. The body was painted Brewster green and the fenders and chassis were black. The wheels were black with stainless steel spokes, and the whole affair was set off by a "gold bronze" pinstripe. Blackwall tires were specified. But the car's build sheet indicates that it was not initially outfitted this way. At the bottom of the document are the instructions: "REDUCO ENTIRE UPPER AND LOWER PANELS AS SPECIFIED. ALSO CHANGE WHEELS." "Reduco" means repaint the body the Brewster green color specified (at the time, "Duco" was used as a synonym for Dupont's recently developed nitrocellulose lacquer paint and the process of applying it to automobile bodies). And the wheel change would have resulted in smart stainless

Built-in trunk with room for another. The town sedan body style included a trunk (note cut-out in lower corner to provide adequate access to fuel filler cap). Five people could travel comfortably, and for longer trips, a second trunk could be mounted (courtesy Brian Keating).

steel spokes. It would not be necessary to call for a repaint of the rest, unless the upper and lower panels had originally been painted black (or another color), and the original setup included different wheels (say, with painted spokes). By the time it was delivered, this town sedan had been tastefully personalized.

According to Cadillac records, this car was originally "shipped to the Factory" on August 12, 1930, and then was returned for credit on January 16, 1931. It was then shipped to Oshawa on January 23, 1931. "Shipped to the Factory" can mean a variety of things, like just going to a Cadillac-owned distributor, or possibly being set aside for the personal use of a GM executive. This scenario was not unusual.

An interesting feature of the January 1931 build sheet is that there appears to be a name for the initial owner of this car. In the line after the words "SHIP VIA" the clerk has typed "DELIVERY TO CUSTOMER AT WALKERVILLE." Until it was amalgamated into the city of Windsor, Ontario, in 1935, Walkerville was a separate town that owed its origins to the Hiram Walker & Sons liquor distillery business. On Walker Road in Walkerville was a General Motors branch plant that built, at various times in the late 1920s and early 1930s, truck and bus chassis and bodies, and complete Chevrolet and Pontiac automobiles.

In open space on the build sheet has been typed "TAG MR COLLACUTT." The instruction to "tag" a car meant that a tag was to be attached indicating that it was for a particular recipient. Thus, a Mr. Collacutt of Walkerville, Ontario, appears to have bought this

"Tag Mr. Collacutt." The build sheet for this car appears to show that it was sold to a gentleman named Collacutt in Walkerville, Ontario, Canada. Apparently, the customer wanted a specific "look" for his car, and Cadillac obliged. Handwritten note "9 qts. Alcohol" denotes prudent addition of antifreeze for late January delivery in Canada (courtesy Brian Keating).

car new. Googling the name Collacutt in Canada yields, among other entries, a travel agency with that name and a coach line. Perhaps a member of the family that started one or both of those enterprises is the original owner of this V-16. Perhaps Mr. Collacutt was a bigwig at the Walker Street GM plant. It's hard to say from this remove.

At some point, Mr. Collacutt sold the Cadillac. In about 1952, Murray Dalglish bought the town sedan in Sudbury. He was told by the seller that when the car was new it had been the personal vehicle of Colonel R.S. "Sam" McLaughlin, the president of General Motors Canada. At the time, Mr. Dalglish was living in Toronto and selling plumbing supplies in the north-central part of Ontario. He used the old Cadillac as a second car and drove it a fair amount for several years. The car's tendency to overheat was the only problem he experienced. Subsequently, he moved to London, Ontario, to work at his brother's Volkswagen dealership. During the first winter in London, Mr. Dalglish stored the V-16 in an unheated shed with a sealed cover to protect it. Unfortunately, the lack of ventilation promoted extensive mold growth inside the car, and Mr. Dalglish was horrified and thoroughly depressed when he found what had happened to the beautiful wool upholstery and trim. He decided to sell the car and for $1,100, one of his salesmen, Max Hartell, became the next owner.

Meanwhile, a classic car enthusiast named Lyall Trenholm eagerly responded to a newspaper ad for the Cadillac, only to be informed that the car had already been sold. No matter how hard he tried, Mr. Trenholm was unable to find out who had bought the car. But he kept trying, and several years later, he determined that it had been sold to Max Hartell. However, by that time, Mr. Hartell had moved to England. Mr. Trenholm tried to contact him there, but without success. Then discovered that the car was still in Canada, stored in a garage at Mr. Hartell's former residence with a canoe resting on its roof. Mr. Trenholm kept an eye on the place, and when Mr. Hartell returned to Canada in 1970 or '71, he met

Murray Dalglish and his Cadillac. Mr. Dalglish was 24 years old when he bought the V-16 town sedan and was selling plumbing supplies in Northern Ontario. What we know as the big classics today were considered old-fashioned curiosities in the early 1950s (courtesy Murray J. Dalglish).

Arriving in style. Facing the camera, from left to right, Marianne Dalglish, her husband Bill Dalglish and Volkswagen Canada Ltd. president Verner Jannsen. Bill Dalglish (Murray's brother) owned and operated Dalmar Motors in London, Ontario. Today he is semi-retired (courtesy Murray Dalglish).

him and asked him if the car was for sale, to which the answer was "no." A month later, though, Mr. Hartell called Mr. Trenholm and said that he was offering the car for sale, but that there were three or four people in line to buy it. Mr. Trenholm replied, "I'm not interested in an auction. I'm coming today to buy the car." He arrived with money and a tow vehicle and began negotiations, but Mrs. Hartell soon joined the conversation. After husband and wife retired to another room for a separate conference, the husband returned and sold the car to Mr. Trenholm for $11,000. It turned out that Mr. Hartell had recently suffered a heart attack. His wife was not interested in figuring out what to do with the big old Cadillac if her husband was no longer around, and she had urged him to sell it.

The Cadillac was a pristine original car when Mr. Trenholm acquired it, without any indication of the mold that had so dispirited Mr. Dalglish. When he drove away from the Hartells' residence, a car followed Mr. Trenholm and his new purchase all the way home. There the driver got out and began begging Mr. Trenholm to let him buy the Cadillac from him. Mr. Trenholm put the man off, but thought that he should find out what the car was worth in case he later decided he did want to sell it. He phoned the McGowan brothers in Branford, Connecticut.

Frank, Bob and Dennis McGowan had a business of buying and selling old cars, and they were well known in the car collecting community. Brother Jack, a banker in New York, would help out at the annual Hershey swap meet. Three of the brothers were members of "The Fabulous Farquahr," a folk band that also sang humorous songs and that was quite popular in the New England region during the late 1960s and even into the '90s. "The Farquahr" recorded two albums (one each on the Elektra and Verve labels). (Frank McGowan, known in the band as "Flamingo Farquahr," passed away in 2004, and brother Dennis, "Condor Farquahr," in 2001.)

Lyall Trenholm asked Bobby McGowan to tell him what a fair price would be for a 1930 Cadillac V-16 town sedan in excellent original condition, and instead of an estimated market value, Bobby offered to buy the car for $45,000. Mr. Trenholm said that he had just phoned for an idea, and left it at that. After Mr. Trenholm hung up and mentioned the offer to one of his salesmen, he said, "Are you nuts? That's more than you make in a year!" So four or five months after finally acquiring the V-16 town sedan, Mr. Trenholm sold it to the McGowan brothers. Bobby McGowan recalls that the car was delivered to a friend's place, and when he went over to see it he was struck by what a beautiful original car it was.

Shortly after buying it, the McGowans sold the car to a collector in Houston, Texas. In 1984, that gentleman advertised the car in the Classic Car Club of America bulletin, and Edward Perkins of Guilford, Connecticut, purchased it from him. Mr. Perkins recalls the car as a "nice original" when he owned it. He would trade it some years later to Charlie Harper of Meredith, New Hampshire. In the summer of 2010, Brian Keating of Plainfield, New Hampshire, became the owner of this V-16 town sedan.

A nice original engine. Everything is correct, with the exception of the black rubber fuel hoses and the porcelain coating missing from portions of the exhaust manifold. This powerplant was designed to be shown off by the owner (courtesy Brian Keating).

Mr. Keating was mostly a motorcycle collector, but when he heard that this exotic old Cadillac was available, he was intrigued. He recalls being told that the car had been inactive for about ten years, and finding that some parts were misplaced or missing (including a carburetor). He negotiated a purchase price that he could swing, acquired the car and began working on getting it running. Even though he knew he was "way out of my league," he "totally enjoyed working on such a vehicle." Patiently taking his time, acquiring parts and learning as he went, he got the car back on the road, give or take some continued work to get the carburetors adjusted and not leaking.

In January 2011 Brian Keating expressed an interest in selling the Cadillac V-16 town sedan and asked me to let people who might be interested know about the car. Among the people to whom I mentioned that the car was available was Lyall Trenholm. Mr. Trenholm immediately asked for Mr. Keating's contact information, raising the prospect that the ownership trail might circle back upon itself.

As it turned out, the Brewster green and black V-16 town sedan was sold to Bill Hill of Temperance, Michigan, in a transaction that left Mr. Keating with cash and a four-cylinder Indian motorcycle. Subsequently on September 4, 2011, the car found a new owner at the Auburn Auction conducted by Auctions America, where it was sold for $101,750.

Later in the fall of 2011 this car was offered for sale on the website of Dick Shappy Classic Cars in Providence, Rhode Island, with an asking price of $159,000. A year later, the car was sold, and a new owner in Russia took up its stewardship.

15. A Tattered Town Car

If the classic car hobby is a religion, its high holy days are four days in early October that comprise the AACA's Eastern Fall Meet in Hershey, Pennsylvania. Hershey draws vendors, cars, parts and customers from all over the world to acres of (often muddy) stalls, show fields and a car corral. You never know what you'll find or whom you'll meet. It's a truly legendary phenomenon.

At Hershey in 2004 was displayed a very unusual 1930 Cadillac V-16. The car was a Series 4391 seven-passenger town brougham, also known as a town car. That's essentially a limousine with removable fabric over the driver's compartment. Bearing engine number 700298 and body number 6 (of 30), it was entirely original and unrestored. The windshield has the split V configuration peculiar to cars built at the original plant of the Fleetwood Body Company in Fleetwood, Pennsylvania. Fleetwood, purchased by General Motors, was in the process of transitioning to its new location in Detroit. The car's original two-tone green paint was mostly there and quite nice in places. The upholstery was almost usable inside the passenger compartment, although the leather gracing the chauffeur's compartment was deteriorated. Still, Hershey-goers of all stripes marveled at this substantially complete and unmolested example of a rare breed.

A town car was a chauffeur-driven car that clearly indicated the owner's social standing and means. A V-16 town car carried an added level of cachet and exclusivity. There were fancier body styles one could purchase from the Fleetwood catalog, but this series was unmistakably in the upper tier. Only the very well off would have ordered such a car new.

Side view of the town brougham. The cover over the chauffeur's compartment completes the roofline for a profile like any of the 1930–31 seven-passenger sedans (courtesy Rick and Nancy Kellman).

Less than a month before its appearance at Hershey, the town car was sold out of the estate of Mr. Jasper G. Wiglesworth. Mr. Wiglesworth was an automobile dealer who began collecting old cars in the 1940s. In 1950 he purchased the V-16 town car from its second owner, a Mr. Paul Berry, who had acquired the car in 1945. No one knows who the original buyer was, but the car is the same body style as the one purchased by opera star Ernestine Schumann-Heink. Mr. Wiglesworth kept the car in storage for the rest of his life. By the time he passed away in 2003, he owned a considerable collection, including 19th-century carriages, fire trucks, farm machinery, motorcycles and motor cars, including a 1913 Mercer Raceabout and an 1895 Benz. Bonhams auctioned the cars from the Wiglesworth estate in Shawnee, Kansas, on September 18, 2004. The green V-16 town car brought $92,000, including buyer's premium and tax. The buyer is described as "an American East Coast private collector." A 1923 Stutz Bearcat went for $65,550 at the same auction.

In spring 2008, the Worldwide Group announced that the veteran V-16 would be offered at its Houston auction on May 3. The price estimate was $170,000–$220,000, and the description credited the car with 35,700 miles. It sold for $154,000.

This automobile presents in a quintessential fashion the dilemma of the "original" car. The saying goes "It's only original once," and the champions of preservation urge an owner to refrain from embarking upon a restoration in direct proportion to the degree to which a surviving car has eluded the consequences of age and the elements. A perfectly cared-for original car showing no signs of wear is the easiest case—if it ain't broke, don't fix it. Leave it the way you found it. The more the natural effects of aging are evident—faded or rubbed-off paint, dull or pitted chrome trim, torn or stained or dry-rotted upholstery—the greater the urge to repaint, replate, re-upholster and so forth. A car such as this one has a tremendous amount of "preservation" appeal, and many shows have preservation-class awards for significant and well-presented unrestored cars. Everything on this vehicle is the way the Fleetwood and Cadillac craftsmen left it (give or take wear and tear). On the other hand, in order to drive the car comfortably, a certain minimum amount of restorative work would be required, and a first-class restoration would produce a spectacular result. The only drawback to that option is the enormous expense the owner would incur. The summary of the Bonhams auction result, quoted below, is entertaining and instructive:

Body by Fleetwood; Engine # 700298; Grey, Black fenders/Black leather, Beige cloth; Estimate $80,000–$100,000; Unrestored original, 4 condition; Hammered Sold at $80,000 plus commission of 15.00 percent; Final Price $92,000—Rollup divider window, vee windshield, dual side-mounts, single Pilot-Ray. Substantial tendelet over chauffeur's compartment, with rollup windows the poor retainer must have sincerely appreciated when it was cold or rainy. Luxuriously appointed rear compartment with window shades, jump seats, footrest and speaking tube. Very original and impressively solid with excellent door fit and operation. Front seat is in tatters; rear compartment seats and trim are so fragile it is unusable. Needs everything but is an outstanding example of a sumptuous Cadillac of the 30's. This is a substantial price for a closed Cadillac but also a very adaptable and useful car in impressively sound condition. The new owner will never recover from the cost of even the most elementary mechanical restoration; the Pebble Beach treatment will end up as an investment that's four or five times the value of the restored car. It's not about money, however.

Engine number 700298. Completely chrome-plated vacuum tank (left edge of picture) is an early design. Later in the 1930 model year, Cadillac began painting the middle section black. Oil level indicator (rectangular item to the left of the black cylindrical oil filter next to the firewall) is also an early design. It was moved to the left-hand side of the engine under the manifolds later in the year. Copper fuel line has replaced the original braided chrome plated flexible hose the car came with. Correct original-style replacements are now available, but for many years could not be had (courtesy Rick and Nancy Kellman).

In May 2008, I made the acquaintance of the couple who bought the town car. Rick Kellman said he'd bought the car for his wife Nancy and that he intends to restore it correctly and completely. Since he brought the car home, he has uncovered some interesting facts. It was shipped from the factory to Chicago on February 25, 1930. But in April 1930 it was diverted to Minneapolis. Nearly a year later, on March 29, 1931, it was sold in Minneapolis, and it was shipped back to Chicago on April 28 for delivery to its new owner. There were a number of instances where a V-16 was shipped first to one place, and then to one or more other locations before a purchaser took delivery for good. That's understandable in light of the upheavals besetting the United States economy at that time.

According to Mr. Kellman, Mr. Wiglesworth believed that the car had belonged to a Dr. Brinkley who resided in Texas, and that perhaps while Dr. Brinkley was at the Mayo Clinic he had seen the car at Northwest Cadillac-LaSalle in Minneapolis. One of the most colorful medical hucksters of the twentieth century was Dr. John R. Brinkley of Del Rio, Texas. He became famous during the Great Depression by using the medium of radio to promote goat glands as a spurious remedy for male reproductive problems. He amassed a sizable fortune and almost became governor of Kansas. But the Kansas State Medical Board revoked his medical license and the Federal Communications Commission refused to renew his broadcasting license. He moved across the Rio Grande to Mexico and began using a high-powered radio station in Ciudad Acuña to further his quackery. Dr. Brinkley owned a number of Cadillacs, and repainted them to match the colors of his mansion.

Dr. Brinkley died in 1942, three years before Mr. Berry titled the V-16 town car in Kansas. Nothing related so far is inconsistent with Mr. Wiglesworth's belief that Dr. Brinkley

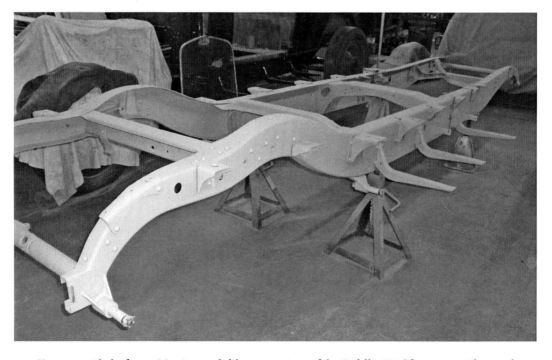

You start with the frame. Massive truck-like proportions of the Cadillac V-16 frame are evident in this view from the right rear. The three brackets pointing to the right support the running board. As the restoration progresses, the car will be rebuilt from the ground up (courtesy Rick and Nancy Kellman).

had owned the car. It may not be as distinguished a provenance as that of Madame Schumann-Heink's car, but it is certainly every bit as colorful.

Mr. Kellman has arranged for a major Midwestern restoration facility to bring the car back to its proper stateliness. Meanwhile, he has been locating some of the few missing trim and accessory pieces and working to find out the rest of this magnificent motor car's history.

16. A Very Clever Car

On April 15, 1930, a professional engineer named Henry W. Struck took delivery from the Boston, Massachusetts, Cadillac distributor of an Almeda gray V-16 roadster. The negotiations had not been simple, and the sales personnel had been put through their paces. Mr. Struck had been unsuccessful in having the rumble seat cushions deleted and the hinges on the cover reversed to make a trunk compartment, such as we are accustomed to today. But he had extracted assurances that the car, with the fast 3.47:1 rear axle ratio and 7.50" × 19" tires, would actually reach 120 m.p.h.

After a reasonable break-in period, Mr. Struck set out to arrange for time trials to test his car's ability to hit the magical 120 mark. Exploiting connections he had with the highway and constabulary authorities, he was able to use a three-mile section of public roadway adjacent to Boston. The course was straight, had no intersections or other side access, and included a two-mile level run in the middle, and gentle rises to each end. The down slope at the beginning would help get up to speed, and the upward slope at the end would help slow down.

With prestige and bragging rights on the line, the local Cadillac agency as well as the factory's zone manager pitched in to help prepare the car for the run. Timing and carburetion adjustments were made after the first five runs, with improvements noted each time. Two more runs were made in each direction, and on three of those passes Mr. Struck's own timing equipment recorded 120 miles per hour. The boast had been proven.

Following that adventure, Mr. Struck carried out a long-term creative project aimed at enhancing the safety and driving convenience of his roadster. By the time he parted with the car almost thirty years later, the added gauges, instruments and controls would nearly obscure the stock instrument panel, and the engine compartment and underside of the vehicle would be fitted with a plethora of additional servos, relays, linkages and plumbing to permit the car to accomplish functions the manufacturer never contemplated. Each additional mechanism or measuring device had been carefully and thoughtfully installed, taking care not to damage or mar the finish of the car itself. Taken together they made the car a rolling laboratory and a demonstration of how various operations could be accomplished in new and different ways.[1]

The driver of Henry Struck's V-16 roadster could advance the car, and stop it as well, using only the accelerator pedal. Depressing the pedal produced the expected result of increasing the speed of the car. Once the operator released the pedal, past a certain point in its travel, it engaged the vacuum system to apply the brakes. Fully releasing the accelerator/brake pedal resulted in full stopping power, a trait that would take some getting used to for the average driver.

Nothing up my sleeve. The standing spotlight, which by 1930 had become passé, is the only outward hint that this roadster might be quite different from others of its breed. The windshield on the roadster body style could be folded flat on the cowl, like a race car. That once-popular feature would die out for good on passenger cars in the early 1930s. Motorists who used it were all but obliged to wear goggles (courtesy William Locke).

Mr. Struck modified the clutch operation on his car as well. The system he devised coordinated a vacuum-operated clutch with the car's speed and the position of the gear shift lever. The effect was to allow the driver to start the car and go up and down through the gears without touching the clutch pedal. What's more, the driver could set the speed with which the clutch engaged, allowing anything from a leisurely progression up to operating speed to a very assertive tackling of hills or severe traffic conditions. A side effect of this feature was that the operator could perform something of an "outdoor parlor trick" with the car.

If Mr. Struck set the automatic clutch operation to its absolute slowest, it could take a full minute to engage. While onlookers watched, he could step out of the idling car, discreetly touch the clutch engagement lever, and walk quite a distance in front of the car, and, if he timed it just right, turn around and call out to the car just before it started moving. The astonished spectators would see a car that appeared to come to its owner on command.

Just a few of the other enhancements invented and installed by Mr. Struck included a power mechanism for raising and lowering the folding top, a lighted writing desk for the passenger door, a drinking water dispenser (with a silver cup), and a rudimentary navigation system with a map that unspooled from one roller onto another as you drove. To keep the myriad additional instruments in the cockpit (each lighted, of course) from distracting or blinding the driver at night, Mr. Struck devised a mechanism that extinguished the instrument lights for nine tenths of each mile and switched them back on for the remaining tenth. The driver could watch the road and still periodically check his gauges.

In the mid–1950s, Henry Struck began in his customarily careful way to select his Cadillac roadster's next owner. It took three years for the choice to be made, and the car was transferred to owner number two in 1958. That lucky designee was a gentleman named William Locke, and Mr. Struck gave him a thorough introduction and training regimen to familiarize him with the intricacies and capabilities of this most unusual motorcar. From

The working model. In the course of applying for patents for his inventions, Mr. Struck constructed a cutaway model of the roadster, complete with an articulated figure of an operator. In earlier times, patent applications required an accompanying model of the device for which protection was sought (courtesy William Locke).

Opposite: Henry Struck explains the instrumentation. The proud engineer and inventor is shown in 1958 pointing out the features of the cockpit (courtesy William Locke).

Engine compartment, passenger side. Looking over the top of the front fender, one sees the extensive additional plumbing, wiring, valves and servos utilized by Mr. Struck to automate various functions. The engine is almost concealed (courtesy William Locke).

time to time thereafter, Mr. Locke corresponded with Mr. Struck at length on the fine points of adjusting and maintaining the various elaborate systems.

Some months after he relinquished his personalized V-16 Cadillac, William Struck passed away. Without his detailed knowledge and familiarity with the systems and their operation and upkeep, it became impossible to sustain them. Gradually the Cadillac roadster reverted to its factory configuration. Around 1960, Bill Locke, who was starting a family and sensitive to financial concerns, succumbed to the persistence of a collector and restorer from Ohio named Russell Strauch. He put a price on the roadster that he thought would be high enough to put Mr. Strauch off, but the price was accepted and the deal was done.

Russ Strauch had the car for some time and sold it to a gentleman in North Carolina. Along the way, it received a restoration. Around 1985, noted collector Steve Nanini of Tucson, Arizona, purchased the car and turned it over to a talented and knowledgeable restorer, the late Wayne Merriman, to rectify various issues with the engine, transmission and so forth. Mr. Nanini showed the car and won a number of prestigious awards, including first in its class at the Pebble Beach Concours d'Elegance.

Today, this beautiful roadster graces a private collection in the Southwest. Although it no longer performs the clever stunts its first owner taught it, the car is a factory-authentic exemplar of its breed.

17. A West Coast Classic

In late 1959 or early 1960, Norman Taunton of Galt, California, purchased a 1930 Cadillac Series 4330 imperial sedan from Phelps Chamberlain of Berkeley. Mr. Chamberlain stated at the time that he wanted a smaller car and that the Cadillac was "too big" for him. That V-16 is one of four survivors of the Series 4330 body style that I have been able to identify (the other three are my own car, another car in New Jersey, and one in New Zealand). All that Mr. Taunton remembers about the prior history of the car he bought was the statement by Mr. Chamberlain that the car was "a Planters Peanuts car out of San Francisco." He's not sure whether Mr. Chamberlain meant that the car was a company car or that it was associated with Planter's in some other way. Mr. Ted Raines, who has known and owned V-16 and V-12 Cadillac automobiles, and who knew Mr. Chamberlain, reports that Mr. Chamberlain had acquired the car from an expert mechanic named Bob Kipps of Menlo Park. Mr. Raines had heard the car may have been originally purchased by Spreckels Sugar people.

When Mr. Taunton purchased the car, it bore the deep blue paint that it wears today. It had been repainted in 1947, and Mr. Taunton recalls being told that it was a Chrysler paint color. He thinks that he might have been given a can of the same paint to use for future touch-ups. As it turned out, Mr. Chamberlain's search for a "smaller car" concluded with his purchase of a Pierce-Arrow.

Mr. Taunton and his wife drove the Cadillac from the Sacramento area down to Los

Opposite: **Happy owner of a V-16 roadster. William Locke poses with his car shortly after succeeding to its ownership. The photograph was taken by the photographer for the Auburn-Cord Duesenberg Club at a club function in Auburn, Indiana (courtesy William Locke).**

Stately yet graceful lines of this body style are evident from this view. Accessory trunk is fastened to the folding luggage rack. Handle for right rear door appears to have been moved to the front door, perhaps to replace a broken front handle (courtesy Ione Taunton).

Angeles and back several times and participated in car club tours without any breakdowns or mechanical difficulties. Consistent with the assumption that the car was sold new in San Francisco, the gear ratio of the rear axle was very low (the better to climb hills with). Consequently, the car was not very fast (Norm Taunton said he could take it comfortably to perhaps 55 miles per hour). But it was smooth and powerful. Once the Tauntons drove the car to Harrah's Club in Reno, Nevada, back when casino magnate Bill Harrah was known far and wide for his enormous collection of fine old automobiles and his extensive restoration facility. Mr. Harrah had arranged a driving tour for a number of classic car owners to enjoy. The Cadillac took the mountains between Sacramento and Reno in stride. The destination of the tour was the town of Genoa, where a fine picnic lunch had been set up ahead of time for the tour participants. Mr. Taunton noticed that a number of fine old classics (including Lincolns and Packards) overheated on the way, their owners having paused by the road with the hood up to let the engine cool. His V-16 stayed calm and happy. One of the other drivers, Mr. Jack Nethercutt of the Merle Norman cosmetics company, approached Mr. Taunton and said that he wasn't offering to buy the Cadillac, but he didn't have one in his collection and would like to know how they drive. Would Mr. Taunton be interested in swapping cars for an hour? Mr. Nethercutt was driving a Marmon V-16 at the time. The deal was done, and the drivers swapped their rides for the agreed hour. Mr. Taunton found the Marmon to have "lots of power" but it was quite noisy in the engine and drivetrain. That appraisal tallies with other accounts by people who drove both cars.[1] The Marmon, of course, had aluminum cylinder blocks (cast integrally with the crankcase, and containing hardened steel cylinder liners) and aluminum heads. Cadillac used cast iron for cylinder blocks and heads.

The photographs of the Tauntons' car show how well cared for it has been over the

Engine compartment. Large chrome-plated item next to spare tire is one of two vacuum fuel pumps. On early 1930 cars the entire vacuum tank was chromed. Later cars' tanks had painted midsections. To the right of the vacuum tank on the firewall is an aftermarket oil filter. Small rectangle between oil filter and rear end of valve cover is the oil level indicator. The distributor, with plug wires attached to posts on the top of the distributor cap, is a 1932 through 1937 item, although it will work on a 1930 or 1931 engine (courtesy Ione Taunton).

years. The radio knobs and buttons to the right of the instrument panel are not what would have been installed in 1930 but a later addition that Mr. Taunton did not recall when I spoke with him. The wind wings are a practical addition, and look to be a correct Cadillac option. Mr. Taunton said that the trunk did not have fitted luggage when they purchased the car. The passenger compartment boasted a polar bear–skin rug.

The engine still gleams majestically. The distributor cap (with plug wires out the top of the cap) is from a later model year, and the oil filter is an aftermarket replacement. The vacuum tank has a chrome-plated body because this was an early 1930 car (engine number 700163). Later in the year, Cadillac began painting the body of the vacuum tanks with black enamel. To the left of the oil filter is the oil level indicator (missing the little red ball on the end of the vertical wire) which Cadillac moved to the left side of the engine under the manifolds after engine number 702502.

Mr. Taunton performed a particular service to V-16 owners by contracting with a vendor to reproduce the decorative panel that surrounds all of the gauge faces on the instrument panel. The original was a flat piece of brass onto which was etched a black background with a fine white cross-hatch overlaid pattern. A black border surrounded each opening for a gauge, and a label with white letters on black identified the spark advance and choke knobs. Mr. Taunton had 100 reproductions made from sheet aluminum, going back and forth with the vendor until he got the cross-hatch pattern to mimic the original. He still has a stack of letters from delighted Cadillac owners who were able to restore the original appearance of

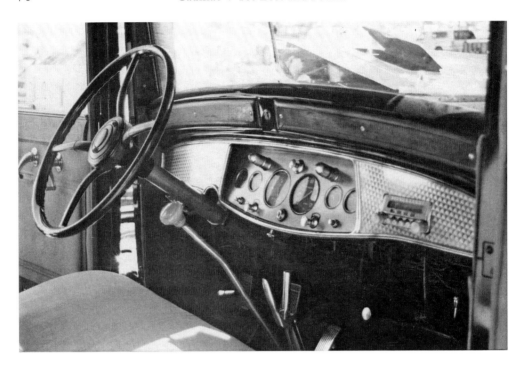

View of driver's compartment. Radio installation is a late addition. Although a radio was offered by Cadillac in 1930, the installation on the instrument panel consisted of a large knob (for tuning the station), a small knob (for volume) and a key lock (because radios were novel, and the batteries they required were expensive) (courtesy Ione Taunton).

their V-16 dashboards, and he told me that "Cadillac Jim" Pearson bought the rest of the panels from him.

In subsequent years, the Tauntons parted ways and the 1930 Cadillac V-16 stayed with the wife and son, who care for it today. Mr. Taunton has owned several V-16s over the years (including a 1934 sedan that he described as "almost scary" due to its size, a full twenty feet in length, and styling). Even today, he'd like to acquire another Cadillac V-16.

Mrs. Taunton sold the car in 2008 to another V-16 owner, Mr. Craig Watrous of Fair Oaks, California. She had known Mr. Watrous, and when the time came to find a new home for the Cadillac, he was a natural choice. Mr. Watrous took the car to Ted Raines's garage, and the two set about completing a re-wiring job that had been started, replacing a broken axle shaft, and getting the car back on the road.

Upon Mr. Watrous's sudden and unexpected death in 2009, the dark blue Cadillac passed back to Mrs. Taunton.

18. The Head Chef's Coach

Around 1954, Richard W. Colpitts, a lover of old cars in Windsor, New York, found out that a Cadillac V 16 Series 4375-S seven passenger sedan was for sale 150 miles away in

Livonia Center, New York. He drove there and purchased the car, and he was told the following tale. The seller had been a meter reader for the gas company in the Delhi (New York) area. In making his rounds, he had noticed a large old car in the garage of one of his customers. One day he stopped to ask the woman who lived there about the car. He asked her if it was for sale and she said yes, so he bought it. She told him that her husband had been the head chef of the Waldorf Astoria Hotel in New York City. When he wasn't cooking, he would drive the Cadillac to the train station "to pick up gangsters and prostitutes and bring them back to the hotel." She added, somewhat ominously, that her husband "had come up missing." The meter reader advertised the car for sale, and Mr. Colpitts purchased it.

In 1958, Richard Colpitts sold that V-16 sedan to his son Donald, then a sophomore in high school. Don drove the car regularly to and from school and extracurricularly. Sometimes he would take a date and two other couples to one of the three drive-in movie theaters in the area. That sometimes occasioned howls of protest from cars parked behind the over-six-feet-tall Cadillac. The couple in the jump seats effectively blocked any remaining view through the Cadillac's rear window. After blowing their horn, the other car would seek another spot.

In August of 1961, this Cadillac helped inaugurate the new Penn-Can Highway (now Interstate 81). It and Richard Colpitts's 1922 Auburn touring car were the first two cars to cross the New York–Pennsylvania border on the new highway, and a photo appeared in the local newspaper.

After high school, Donald Colpitts took the car to shows, kept it out of anything resem-

Open passenger door invites. Minimal age-related wear is visible on the door trim panel. Decorative wood panel features walnut burl and ebony inlay (courtesy Donald Colpitts).

On display with the hood open. Cream-colored wheels work well with the black color overall. Accessory metal spare-tire covers and heron radiator ornament are splendid accents (courtesy Donald Colpitts).

bling inclement weather, stored it in a heated garage, and generally babied it. In the late 1970s, he had the car re-painted black with light cream-colored wheels. In 1991, circumstances moved him to sell.

Brian and Shirley Hughes of Middlesex, England, are quite adept at restoring old cars. Between them they have remanufactured the old "composite" automobile bodies (hardwood framework with sheet metal panels formed and hung on the framework) for a range of fine classic automobiles. They've also tackled the daunting task of upholstering and trimming the interiors of these cars. Brian had long wanted to own a Cadillac V-16, but they never thought they would have that privilege. Then in 1991, between trips to the massive annual car show/swap meets in Carlisle and Hershey, Pennsylvania, the Hugheses attended the Dutch Wonderland Auction and saw the Waldorf chef's car. At that time the odometer registered 63,620 miles. When Brian Hughes approached the owner, Mr. Colpitts was still smarting from a man who had bid on the Cadillac and immediately disappeared. Mr. Hughes was intent on negotiating a deal, though, and he persisted for several hours until a purchase was finalized.

The Hughses shipped their new treasure back to the UK and have enjoyed it ever since, although in recent years they haven't driven it much. They still love to admire the big Cadillac and acknowledge their good fortune to own it.

The build sheet for engine number 701098 shows that body number 264 (of 501 built) was shipped from the factory on April 1, 1930 (although paradoxically it was registered in New York State as a 1931 model). The car was finished in a subdued but distinctive fashion. The paint was black overall, except for the lower panels of the doors and body, which were "Alpenstock Green," and the body pinstriping, which was a light cream color. Few options were reflected on the build sheet—wire wheels, fender-mounted spares, Goodyear 7.00" ×

19" tires. The gearing for the rear axle was specified as 4.75 to 1, rather than the standard 4.39 to 1 ratio. Cadillac recommended the 4.75 gear set only where uphill driving would be encountered regularly.

Today the big sedan remains largely original. The interior is nearly new. Except for a missing horn trumpet, the outside is nearly new as well. There has never been any rust. Both Don Colpitts and the Hugheses describe it as a car that drives beautifully. This automobile's story is an example of what by rights should have befallen each Cadillac V-16—respectful use followed by a dignified and honorable retirement.

19. California Dreamin'

When I was a junior in high school, my family took a vacation trip to Southern California from our home in Albuquerque. It would be the first time I had been there since my infancy. I was born in Santa Monica but only because my father was doing his medical internship at the hospital there. My parents were both confirmed East Coasters in those days and they couldn't wait to leave the Golden State.

When I heard about the planned trip, I immediately researched auto museums that I might be able to persuade my father to take us to. The most likely candidate was the Briggs Cunningham Automotive Museum in Costa Mesa, and I put in a plug for it right away.

As it happened, we did stop at the museum, and it had a splendid assortment of fine, nicely cared for old cars. There was at least one Duesenberg, several Mercedes-Benz specimens and representatives of the Rolls-Royce marque. Of course, the 1950 Cadillacs that Mr. Cunningham campaigned at Le Mans were both present—"Le Monstre" with its aerodynamic body, and the almost stock coupe that looked like a normal luxury car, but for the leather hood tie-down straps and the racing numbers painted on.

But the car that caught my eye and held me like a magnet until it was time to leave was the very first Cadillac V-16 I had ever seen in person. I had seen pictures and assembled plastic models, but I'd never seen an actual car. This one looked to be showroom perfect to me. It was a 1930 roadster with a copper-bronze body and black fenders. Built without fender-mounted spare tires, this one had its spares on the back over the gas tank. And the wheels were thick-spoked wooden "artillery" wheels with black sidewall tires. Not by any means the flashiest example of the breed, this car had no Pilot Ray lamps or spotlights, although it did sport chrome-edged wind wings on either side of the windshield. But to me, this car was a heavenly apparition.

I craned over the velvet ropes arranged to keep curious museum guests at a safe distance. I peered into the engine and passenger compartments and inspected every visible bit of the exterior, mentally comparing everything with the models I had assembled and the pictures I had seen. The taillight housings echoed the shape of the headlights (in contrast to the round ball-shaped taillights on the models). I noted how the radiator hoses connected to the engine and the way that the ignition wires poured from the side of the distributor to disappear beneath a painted plate covering the valley between the cylinder banks. And the surface of the running boards had a series of rubber strips edged in chrome running fore and aft to provide secure footing for those entering or leaving the car. And the radiator ornament,

1930 Cadillac V-16 Series 4302 roadster as it appeared when exhibited in the Briggs Cunningham Museum. It has since been meticulously restored to the specifications of the original owner's purchase order. After the museum was closed the cars were sold (courtesy Robert and Brigitte Thayer).

too small to clearly discern on the models, was a revelation: a slender woman leaning forward from the rim of the radiator cap, hands clasped behind her head, hair and scarf billowing back in the breeze.

The most unexpected detail was a small rectangular plate attached to the left side of the decorative sheet metal piece that covered the fuel tank. The wording was easy to make out. The name of Inglis M. Uppercu, an entrepreneurial Cadillac dealer in the New York City area, was prominently proclaimed, along with the address of his New Jersey branch. As I recall, the engine number and body number of the car were also included. I was accustomed to contemporary car dealers plastering their names on the flanks of their merchandise, but this was the first I'd seen of that practice in the early 1930s.

Eventually, it was time to leave the museum, and I had to tear myself away from my vigil. With one last long glance, I followed the family out the door and on back to our motel. My first sighting of a V-16 had met my expectations and increased my desire to see more of them and even own one someday, God willing.

Over the years that followed, I would get to peek at a 1934 V-16 convertible victoria wrapped in a protective cloth cover. I saw several V-8 Cadillacs from the 1930s and even owned a 1931 cabriolet for a while. But I wouldn't take a long look at another V-16 until

Seen from the rear. Rear mount spare tires mean no folding trunk rack, and any touring luggage must be carried inside. Access to rumble seat is by three step plates on rear bumper and up the right rear fender (don't trip on the taillight!) (courtesy Robert and Brigitte Thayer).

Exquisitely correct engine compartment. Visual impact was intentional, with everything finely finished and carefully organized. As much as possible, wiring and plumbing are concealed, and whatever is exposed is decorated (courtesy Robert and Brigitte Thayer).

2004, when I saw two at the *Washington Times*'s annual old car show in McLean, Virginia. And I wouldn't ride in one, drive one or hear one run until I acquired my own V-16 imperial sedan in 2005. Along the way I heard that the Briggs Cunningham museum had been closed at the end of 1986, and that the cars had been sold off. In the course of writing my book *The Cadillac That Followed Me Home* I tried to trace and locate the 1930 V-16 roadster I'd stared at, but all I could determine was that it was not one of the former Briggs Cunningham museum cars that the Miles Collier collection bought up. I did receive a picture of the car from the Miles Collier collection staff. Experienced V-16 restorer Marc Ohm related a rumor he'd heard that the car was purchased by someone in Florida and that it had been given a thorough restoration and painted black.

Then one day I saw pictures of a 1930 Cadillac V-16 roadster on conceptcarz.com, the website operated by Dan Vaughan. This car had two rear-mounted spare tires, wood-spoke wheels, black sidewall tires and glass wind wings with chrome-plated edges. Most intriguingly, it also had a small rectangular plaque on the side of the fuel tank cover, and although the pictures weren't clear enough to read the little plaque, the top line of the lettering was consistent with the name "Inglis M. Uppercu." I got in touch with Dan Vaughan, who told me that the photos were from the exclusive 2006 Amelia Island Concours event in Florida, and that at the time the car was owned by Robert and Brigitte Thayer of Atlanta, Georgia. The write-up on the conceptcarz.com website (apparently taken from materials available at the concours) read as follows:

> Mr. Floyd E. Becker, of Roseland, NJ, placed the original order for this car on January 27, 1930. The order specified a V-16 engine (452 cubic-inch displacement, 175 HP and 320 ft-lbs torque),

The roadster as it appears today. The Thayers have returned it to the paint scheme that Floyd E. Becker ordered in January of 1930. Absence of fender-mounted spare tires lends a lean and graceful look to this big car (courtesy Robert and Brigitte Thayer).

20 inch wood spoke wheels painted the same color as the body, two rear-mounted spares, 3.92:1 rear axle ratio, special door pockets, windshield wings and special seats. The total price was $5,896.40, and included two spare coils, condensers and points. A complete restoration was completed in June 2001, with 3,392.5 man-hours of labor.

One of the things I had learned about the 1930 and '31 Cadillac V-16s was that the standard wheels were wooden (not that one could tell that fact by looking at the cars that survive today—all but a minuscule number have wire wheels). The standard wheels were simple "artillery" wheels. But the wooden wheels on the Briggs Cunningham car (and the Thayers' car) are actually another optional type of wheel. These were 20-inch wheels (as opposed to the standard size of 19 inches) and they had "demountable rims." That meant that when a tire wore out (or blew out), the operator would jack up the wheel, loosen six clamps, and remove just the rim (with the tire) from the wheel itself (which could stay on the car). The spare tire and the rim on which it was mounted would then be attached to the wheel and the clamps tightened down. Later, the old tire and rim would be separated and the tire repaired or replaced.

In June 2008, I was able to speak with Mr. Thayer and learn more about the car and its history. He had spoken with the son of the original purchaser, who had traveled to Detroit with his father in 1930 to take delivery. The son explained to Mr. Thayer some of the car's idiosyncrasies. Mr. Becker had been a tall man, so at his request a hand brake lever as long as the gear selector was installed. The driver's seat bottom cushion was extended to the front by two inches for thigh support, and raised two to three inches higher than standard. The

Gleaming and inviting driver's compartment. Open cars frequently had a ribbed rubber mat on the floorboards instead of carpet, due to potential weather exposure. Mr. Becker specified shatterproof glass for the accessory wind wings. His son notes that the seat was special-ordered with larger dimensions for added thigh and shoulder support for his tall frame (courtesy Robert and Brigitte Thayer).

back cushion was two inches higher as well for shoulder support. Mr. Becker had believed that it would be easier to change a flat tire if the spares were mounted on the back of the car instead of in fender wells, and he thought that wood wheels would ride more smoothly than wire wheels and so equipped his Cadillac V-16.

The roadster changed hands two or three times after it left the museum. By the time Mr. Thayer purchased the car, its condition had declined to the point where a full restoration was justified, and he entrusted it to RM Classic Cars in Canada. What the Thayers have now is a 100-point prize winner that has taken its class at the prestigious Pebble Beach Concours d'Elegance.

So, I had caught up with the car from the museum. I think it's great that the car is, if anything, better cared for in its present home than it had been when I first saw it. It certainly made an impression on me back then that became a life-long passion.

20. David Holtzman's Car

David Holtzman acquired his car in 1972 or '74. It's "pretty much all original" and the paint is still pretty good. As on my own car, the pinstriping has been rubbed off except for a few out-of-the-way spots. The body style is Series 4330-S, five-passenger sedan without divider window. He does not want to restore it, preferring to leave it in original condition.

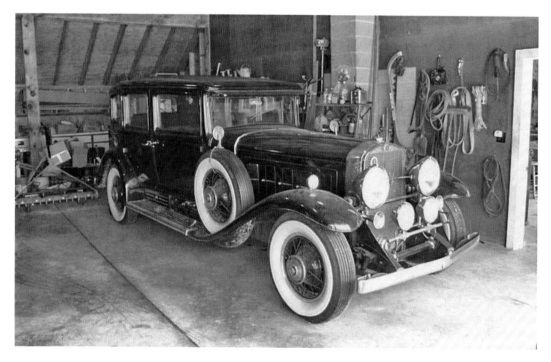

"Pretty much all original." Some stone scars and wear under the fenders, but otherwise, this car looks like it did when it was new (courtesy David Holtzman).

(Brian Joseph of Classic and Exotic Service, Inc., whom Mr. Holtzman calls "the best restorer in the country," comes to visit once a year and to try to persuade him to consider selling or restoring the car.) The interior is still serviceable, although the edge of the driver's seat is frayed and the front carpet is missing. The car is currently garaged in Vermont.

Mr. Holtzman doesn't really know the early history of his car. He bought it from the late Jim Pearson, known in old car circles as "Cadillac Jim." Everyone knew Gaylord Pearson, Jr., as Jim, and he lived up to the "Cadillac" nickname. According to Mr. Holtzman, he was "crazy-smart" and he knew everything there was to know about old Cadillacs. He remembers strolling with him at the 1962 Indianapolis Grand Classic and watching as he advised owners about backwards-fitted door handles and all manner of other details. During the late 1940s and early '50s, working on his hunch that old Cadillac parts would become scarce and valuable, Jim went around the country, stopping at Cadillac dealers and buying up their old parts for very little money. He lived "car-and-parts poor," at one point living with his wife and children in one half of a two-car garage (the other side was filled with meticulously sorted and inventoried Cadillac parts). But he had multiple examples of all the parts you could need for a V-16 (for a price), in varying degrees of preservation (priced accordingly) and neatly organized, some in velvet-lined drawers. Before his early death from lung cancer, he owned and drove many of the finest Cadillacs built.

Getting started. This photo was taken during an effort to get the car running again after sitting for some time. Open compartment below lower edge of right front door reveals the long narrow battery. Accessory trunks for these cars were secured to the luggage rack by unique clamps that tightened down with wing nuts (courtesy David Holtzman).

Truly impressive "face" of the 1930 Cadillac V-16 is nicely finished with Pilot Ray lights. These accessory lamps were styled to mimic the Cadillac headlights, just the way the fender-mounted parking lights were. Between the lights, horns, mirrors and emblems, a symphony of circles greets the oncoming viewer (courtesy David Holtzman).

Mr. Holtzman met Cadillac Jim in the early 1960s and got to know him well. He learned never to haggle with him over his prices. No, Jim's prices weren't cheap. But he had the genuine item, and both of you knew it. In the early 1970s Mr. Holtzman set his eye on a lovely well-preserved V-16 Series 4330-S sedan. He told Cadillac Jim, "I want that car," and Jim gave him a price. Mr. Holtzman couldn't afford it at the time and balked, but Cadillac Jim told him not to worry—just pay $1,000 whenever he could until he paid for the car. Jim convinced Mr. Holtzman to add a set of correct Pilot Ray accessory driving lights to the purchase for an additional $1,000. It took Mr. Holtzman two years to complete the acquisition.

David Holtzman said that he wanted to drive the car back home from Kansas City, Kansas, to Michigan. Jim told him it would run fine, and he set off. The roof of one of these sedans is a treated fabric covering stretched over some padding laid on a lattice of wood slats. In those days, the automobile manufacturers hadn't solved the puzzle of stamping a one-piece steel roof for a closed car, and the fabric insert was a more cost-effective technique than welding together and finishing a series of steel plates. The fabric on the roof of Mr. Holtzman's newly-purchased Cadillac was dried and cracked with age and outdoor exposure, and Jim had given him a roll of new material so he could have the roof resurfaced when he got home. But wouldn't you know it, Mr. Holtzman had gone about 200 miles when he and his Cadillac encountered a massive thunderstorm. And as he crossed a big bridge, a gust of wind peeled the top fabric right off of the car and into the river below. Mr. Holtzman was left looking at the weather through the rafters.

The storm subsided as quickly as it had come up, and Mr. Holtzman pulled off the road when he reached the next town. He unrolled the new material and stretched it across the open top of his car, securing it in place with carpet tape. With this temporary repair in place, he continued on his way.

The next challenge was the discovery that the packing around the water pump shaft had failed. As long as the engine was running, the pump's suction prevented any loss of coolant, but as soon as the engine stopped, the leaking resumed. Although Mr. Holtzman resolved to keep the car going as long as possible, fatigue eventually won out, and he asked a gas station owner's permission to park at the side of the station and sleep. When he awoke, he refilled the cooling system and got back on the road, eager to make it home.

But the fates weren't through with the car and its driver. The car began to run a little rough, accompanied by a clattering noise from the upper part of the engine. Mr. Holtzman stopped and placed a phone call to Cadillac Jim and explained what was going on. Jim told Mr. Holtzman to take the valve cover off, and pull up the loose valve by the stem. He followed the phoned instructions, buttoned up the engine and finished the trip home.

Mr. Holtzman bought the car just to drive every day. At the time his office was just down the street from his home, and he intended to use the big Cadillac to travel back and forth. He hung onto the car, and as it turned out, he never put many miles on it.

Where Jim Pearson got the car is not certain. According to the build sheet, it was originally shipped to West Virginia, but not much else can be determined. Original equipment included a trunk that is still with the car (but missing the luggage it came fitted with). Two years ago, Mr. Holtzman saw an ad for a set of luggage that was the right size and number for his trunk, but he was too late to buy it. Mr. Holtzman does not regret letting Mr. Pearson persuade him to buy the Pilot Ray lights. These rare accessory lights replicate the shape of the headlights and point in the direction that the wheels are steered (the advertising slogan was "Pilot Ray lights the winding way"). He also added a Cadillac hot water–type heater, but only installed the front seat portion, though that's enough to heat the car since there is no imperial division. There is also a Kelch heater (or at least the register head that sits in the floor), such as my own car once had.

I asked Mr. Holtzman for any general advice or things to be aware of with these cars. He said, "When it runs good, it's very easy to drive when rolling (hard to turn when it's standing still). The power brakes help. The V-16 engine has so much torque, if you just get it rolling in first, shift to third and mash the accelerator pedal, it pulls out real smooth."

Cadillac Jim had a trick he would do with his V-16 cars that took advantage of the engine's enormous low-end torque and the design of the chassis and drivetrain. He would decelerate in third gear to a very slow speed. Then he would retard the spark, so the car would run at an easy walking pace. Then he would open the door, climb out of the car, shut the door and walk alongside, with his hand through the open window holding the steering wheel, casually guiding the car along. Once his guest was suitably impressed, he opened the driver's door, climbed back in and took the wheel. Then, as he returned the spark control to the fully advanced position, he mashed the accelerator pedal to the floor and the car would move out and accelerate with the smoothness of a turbine engine. (Of course, the usual "Closed course, trained driver, don't try this at home" caveats apply. But it tells a lot about how tractable and flexible these multi-ton old cars really are.)

Cadillac Jim lived an old Cadillac lifestyle. One of his front teeth was prosthetic, and for fun he had a dentist attach a tiny Cadillac V16 emblem to the false tooth. Just the thing to make an impression at a car show. Some of the cars he owned were astonishingly unique,

David Holtzman and his Cadillac V-16 participating in a "cruise-in" event in Vermont, sponsored by *Hemmings Motor News* **on August 19, 2010. Afterwards, Mr. Holtzman said that his car "never ran better." This picture ran in the November 2010 issue of the magazine (courtesy** *Hemmings Motor News***).**

like the big V-16 sedan that had been equipped with railroad wheels. He would meet Mr. Holtzman at the airport driving a Cadillac V-12 sport phaeton. Later in his life he sold some of his cars and bought a big Bluebird travel camper that he would load with parts and take to Hershey and other car shows. By this time the lung cancer was advanced, and on the way back from his last Hershey trip with his son driving, he died.

Living in Michigan with the car in Vermont has not helped David Holtzman keep up with the car's need for exercise and maintenance. And the needs of children (and later grandchildren) competed for time and attention. In the late '00s, however, Mr. Holtzman brought his Cadillac back to running condition, and he is very pleased with the way it drives. He's been spotted and photographed at cruise-ins and other venues enjoying his beautiful unrestored classic.

21. A North Country Convertible

The Cadillac factory installed engine number 702619 in a Series 4235 convertible coupe. For the 1930 and 1931 model years, two distinct styles of V-16 convertible coupes were offered. Series 4235 had the curved lower edge of the body, the so-called carriage sill characteristic of the style numbers beginning with 42. It had a one-piece, gently sloping windshield, complemented by the gently angled back panel of the convertible top. The graceful lines of this large car conceal its size and weight and give it an almost jaunty appearance. With the same wheelbase as a seven-passenger limousine, and standing six feet, one inch tall, this is not a small car. And yet it doesn't suffer from that resemblance to an aircraft carrier (a normal-sized two-person "greenhouse" sitting on an acre of body) that bedevils some of the large two-passenger classics. By contrast, the straight sill counterpart (Series 4335), with its upright, two-piece V'd windshield and its more vertical top profile, is a good deal more formal.

Both convertible coupe styles are two-passenger cars with a rumble seat to accommodate two additional riders. The 4235 cars are referred to as "Detroit" cars and their 4335 siblings are called "Pennsylvania" cars, reflecting the consensus among most historians that the V-16 bodies with V-shaped, two-piece windshields were manufactured at the Fleetwood Metal Body Company's original plant in Fleetwood, Pennsylvania. That facility was vacated after General Motors's Fisher Body Division purchased Fleetwood, and consolidation of Fleetwood personnel and facilities was complete in January of 1931.

On the Series 4235, the slender, functional landau irons (which lock the rear half of the folding top in the "up" position) seem to reach forward, implying smooth, effortless movement even when the car is standing still. The curve of the lower edge or "sill" of the body softens what had always been a straight horizontal line where body met frame. In the future, the frame would be entirely engulfed and concealed, but for now it was only partially overhung. A continuous beltline molding runs from the radiator shell across the hood, cowl and door, dipping to make room for the top well, and following the curve of the rear deck to its end. For a closed convertible coupe, it has a decidedly sporting appearance.

Series 4235 convertible coupe. Canted windshield, long landau irons, curved lower body "sill," and radiator-to-tail beltline molding give this large car a fleet and graceful air (courtesy Jim and Brenda George).

A Series 4335 convertible coupe captured at Pebble Beach. This profile view shows the upright character of the passenger compartment, and the sweeping character line along the top of the hood and down the side of the cowl behind the spare tire (courtesy Joseph Scott).

This particular car was sold new in Minneapolis, Minnesota, wearing a two-tone brown finish. The name of the original purchaser is not known, but from 1961 through 1967, Mr. Elmer Fransen owned it, and in 1968, the iconic "Cadillac Jim" Pearson acquired the car. Mr. Pearson's associate Sonny Elliott recalls the car as a "real good original," well cared for and complete. It was spared the periods of neglect and deterioration that many automobiles endure before an eventual rehabilitation or restoration. In 1983, a close friend of Cadillac Jim's, Bud Tinney of Grand Rapids, Michigan, bought the convertible. Mr. Tinney restored the car, painting it black with pale gray leather upholstery and a black fabric top. In 1997 he sold it to Los Angeles newspaper magnate Otis Chandler.

In 2002, Mr. Chandler sold three of the thoroughbred cars from his collection at the annual auction held in concert with the Meadow Brook Hall Concours d'Elegance. There was a Duesenberg, a Darrin-bodied Packard, and the 1930 V-16 convertible coupe. The lucky purchaser of the Cadillac was Mr. Jim George of Haymarket, Virginia, who owns it today.

Mr. George has not been able to determine the identity of the original owner of his car. What he does know is that it was shipped from Detroit across Lake Michigan to Milwaukee, Wisconsin, from which point it was diverted to Minneapolis. One has to marvel at the optimism or the wealth of the man or woman who paid the substantial price for such a lovely convertible with a rumble seat and no heater in the land of serious winter snows and frigid weather. The part of the year during which such an automobile would not be practical

Opposite: Driver's compartment. Engine-turned panels flank instrument cluster. Gauges are set in a recessed bay, offset against a fine white cross-hatch pattern on a black background. V-16 exclusive feature is green-tinted dial numerals, hashmarks and pointers (courtesy Jim and Brenda George).

Polished aluminum, gleaming chrome, enamel and porcelain. The V-16 engine was designed to be enjoyed visually as much as it was engineered for smooth running and powerful performance (courtesy Jim and Brenda George).

transportation would be pretty large in that part of the country, especially in light of the sort of roads and highways available in 1930. The purchaser was likely a well-to-do gentleman with other vehicles for use in cold, wet, slushy or otherwise intemperate circumstances. The big gleaming convertible would come out of its berth in the carriage house only when the sun was shining and the weather was fair.

22. Brought Back from the Dead

Pete Sanders, of McLean, Virginia, trained well before he restored this car. He had restored a V-12 Cadillac, a car that shares many construction details, common parts and other similarities with the magnificent V-16s. He put the word out that he was looking for a V-16 and heard about a car that was for sale. He contacted the owner, Sonny Elliott in Kansas City, Kansas, but it took a few months to finalize a deal. In June 1999, he bought the car.

As Mr. Elliott related the history to me, the car was shipped from the factory to Kansas City, where it may have been displayed in the 1930 auto show. Reportedly, the first owner was Dr. John R. Brinkley. Dr. Brinkley was a very colorful figure in Kansas during the '20s

Grover Phillips and his Madame X sedan in 1941. Later Mr. Phillips would convert this seven-passenger sedan into a pickup truck. Still later, it would be returned to passenger car configuration, but this time as a five-passenger town sedan. Ultimately it would become an award-winning show car (courtesy Sonny Elliott).

and '30s, famous for pioneering the use of radio to market his patent medicine services. Dr. Brinkley appears to have traded the car in, and a gentleman (remembered only by the given name Frank) who operated a rental fleet of touring cars and limousines for dignitaries and special occasions obtained it. In 1937, Frank sold the Cadillac to a fellow named Grover Phillips, telling him about Dr. Brinkley's prior ownership. Mr. Phillips owned the car from 1937 into the mid–1960s. There is a photograph of Mr. Phillips standing next to the car in 1941, by which point it was an old-fashioned used car, albeit a stately and impressive one. Sometime later, Mr. Phillips converted the big Cadillac into a pickup truck, removing the rear doors and the back half of the body. At the time he performed this drastic surgery, his wife asked him if he thought he was doing the right thing. He spent the rest of his life trying to find another body for the car.

After Mr. Phillips's death, classic Cadillac collector "Cadillac Jim" Pearson obtained the car and kept it until about 1991. For a significant period of time it sat outdoors, unprotected. Mr. Pearson traded the V-16 pickup to Fred Weber in St. Louis, Missouri, who undertook to replace the wooden framework for the rear portion of the body. The doors and rear window frame had been kept with the vehicle, but the metal for the part behind the doors and around the back had to be remade. When it came from the factory, this Cadillac was a seven-passenger sedan, Series 4175-S. Since he was going to have to remanufacture the rear half of the car's body from scratch, Mr. Weber chose to re-create a body style that he liked better, the close-coupled "town sedan" (style number 4161-S) and he had the work done by Mr. Stan Francis of Golden Restoration in Denver, Colorado. Once the pickup had been converted back into a passenger car, in the latter half of the 1990s Mr. Weber consigned the car to the Leake Auction in Oklahoma, where Mr. Elliott purchased it. Mr. Elliott reattached the carburetors, and he had gotten the car running again by the time Mr. Sanders sought to buy it.

When the truck arrived with his purchase, and Mr. Sanders saw the car for the first time, the effects of its exposure to the elements were apparent. When he fired up the engine, he shut it off after about 30 seconds, depressed to see so much smoke. The massive frame had been bent, and the chassis and rear axle assembly were severely rusted, with deep pitting. Many of the parts that weren't missing had been damaged or corroded over the years out in the open.

Another car collector might well have passed up this vehicle as too far gone. But Mr. Sanders went to work on it. Since the hardwood framing that gives the body its strength and integrity had been recently replaced, he was that far ahead of the game. But it took him a year and a half to rebuild the engine, which had never been rebored. The crankshaft and connecting rods were in good condition, and all that was really needed were new pistons and rings. Overall, twenty-seven months of intense work were spent transforming the car into a showpiece, after which he took it on the concours circuit. A few years later, he brought the Cadillac to the AACA Hershey Fall Meet and sold it in the car corral, but the sale fell through. Today, he's very glad he got to keep the car.

Several explanations have been offered to explain the origin of the name "Madame X" for 4100 Series V-16 cars—that the raked windshield was inspired by the profile of the woman in John Singer Sargent's famous painting titled "Madame X," or that Cadillac chief stylist Harley Earl had impressed by the stage play by that name, or that Mr. Earl had been attracted to an actress in the cast. Regardless of where the name came from, it is permanently associated with a group of closed-bodied early thirties V-16 Cadillacs that share certain unique features not seen on the other closed V-16s. These include slender windshield pillars

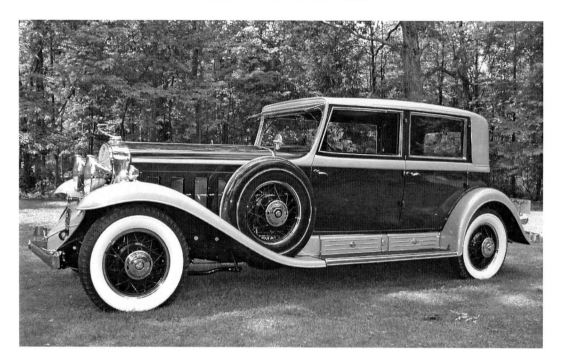

Graceful and stylized lines of the Madame X town sedan. This is exactly what a Series 4361-S town sedan would have looked like new. Slender windshield and door pillars, together with chrome window reveals and the daring rake of the windshield itself, give the car a lightness and grace unexpected in a three-ton automobile (courtesy Pete Sanders).

and door window pillars, thin bright-metal reveals around the door windows, and a windshield raked back at an angle of 18 degrees from vertical, rather than the standard models' 7-degree angle. The hood did not have the so-called LeBaron Sweep character line that arced from the forward edge across and down the top panel and into the cowl of the 4300 Series cars. Nearly all Madame X models were sedans, although there were a few coupes described in factory literature as having a "Madame X style windshield." The distinctive styling attributes made these cars appear significantly lighter and more graceful than their non–Madame X stablemates, despite nearly equal curb weights.

Pete Sanders's car bears engine number 702232. Mr. Sanders has restored the engine and its bay to pristine showroom condition. Even the radiator hoses are the original fluted type (available as a reproduction). The completely chromed vacuum tank is characteristic of a car built early in the 1930 model year. After May of 1930, the body of the vacuum tank would be painted with black enamel.

The 4161-S body style was a "close coupled" sedan accommodating five passengers (including the driver). The companion series (4161 without the "S") had an imperial division with roll-up divider window (only one was built and it is not known to have survived). A Series 4161-S was typically an owner-driven car, and it had a built-in trunk for touring. A folding luggage rack would accommodate an additional trunk, if the owner desired.

No more than 324 Madame X cars were built in 1930 and 1931, meaning that they accounted for only about ten percent of V-16 production during those years. The few that survive bear witness to a robust spirit of innovation and a desire to provide the customer with a superb selection of products to choose from.

23. Photographer's Model

It is rare for the contemporary owner of a Cadillac V-16 to have a photograph of the car when it was new. For one thing, photography was not the casual, everyday activity it is today. With a digital camera, or even a cell phone, we think nothing of snapping a picture of an interesting event, an item in a store that we might come back to buy, or a friend leaving on a trip. In years past, one had to load film in the camera, set it up for exposure, focus and film speed, perhaps load a flashbulb, and set a tripod or other steady mount for the camera. Afterwards, the exposed film had to be developed. Cameras and photographic supplies were expensive and the process took a while. It is rarer still to have a picture of your car (when new or nearly so) that was taken by one of the preeminent photographers of the day.

James Van Der Zee (1886–1983) was an African American photographer working in the New York City area beginning in the early 20th century. His studio portraits, street scenes and occasion photography, often shot with daring experimental methods, captured and gave enduring vibrancy to a period in history known as the Harlem Renaissance, and his work is exhibited and prized today, both for chronicling an exciting and fascinating era, and for the technical creativity he displayed. One of Mr. Van Der Zee's best known images is "Couple in Raccoon Coats, 1932." It is an outdoor portrait of a young man and woman taken on 127th Street in New York City's Harlem neighborhood. They are both wearing long furs and fashionable hats. He is seated in a 1930 Cadillac V-16 roadster with the passenger door open. She is standing in high heel shoes next to the running board and both are looking into the camera. Taking some distance from the couple, Mr. Van Der Zee has brought into the composition the entry staircases and parlor windows of the brownstone row houses, as well as nearly the entire length of the Cadillac.

The trappings of opulence in this scene are at odds with the time the picture was taken (well into the Great Depression) and the conventional understanding of the area's demographics. The image challenges the viewer to admit the possibility of opportunity and prosperity where he might not expect to find it.

Of the subjects in the photograph, it is fairly certain that the car survives today. Mr. Bud Tinney of Grand Rapids, Michigan, is currently restoring a 1930 Cadillac Series 4302 roadster with engine number 700694 and body number 19. The build sheet called for a two-tone color scheme of black and "Tokio Ivory." The body of the car was to be black, with ivory on the rear deck and extending along the moldings along the tops of the doors to the cowl. The side vents on the hood and cowl were likewise ivory, as were the tops of the fenders for an attention-getting contrast. The wheels were to be black with chrome spokes, as seen in the picture. By the time Mr. Van Der Zee photographed the car, the fender tops had been resprayed black. But the rear deck, door molding, and hood vents are still clearly a contrasting light color. Consistent with the proposed provenance, Mr. Tinney received the car with the same paint combination seen in the picture. And consistent with the build sheet, he found ivory underlying the black paint on the upper surfaces of the fenders.

Jim Pearson, known as "Cadillac Jim" and introduced in more detail elsewhere in these pages, sold the ivory and black roadster to Mr. Tinney shortly before Jim passed away in the 1990s. Unfortunately, not much is known of the car's intervening history, or who pur-

An iconic image. James Van Der Zee used ingenious techniques to create a fascinating visual record of the Harlem Renaissance. Here, the soft focus and textures of the house fronts in the background seem to make the shiny car and the people feel closer to the viewer than they are. The composition almost draws you in to speak with the couple. What would they tell you? (*Couple in Raccoon Coats*, 1932, James Van Der Zee, © Donna Mussenden Van Der Zee).

chased it new. But one moment in its early days is immortalized in black and white. And in time the car will display the same gleaming elegance it showed in that image, so many years ago.

At this writing, a gallery in New York City has a signed and dated original print of the Van Der Zee photograph available for purchase at a price of $35,000.

24. Raising Cane

It's generally agreed that the flashiest, most extravagant V-16 Cadillac the company produced was the Series 4264-B. This was an open-front town car with squared-off rear side and roofline corners, and without rear quarter windows for a distinctively formal and private effect. The rear window was a small, flattened oval of glass high up on the nearly flat back wall of the body. The body sill was unique, in that the sides of the passenger compartment dipped down toward the running boards like an old-fashioned carriage, with a pointed lower front corner nicknamed a "boot toe."

Only six Series 4264-B cars were produced. Three of them had an additional feature that really made this body style an eye-catcher. On those cars, Fleetwood craftsmen covered the outside of the passenger compartment from the beltline down with a hand-worked woven cane appliqué. The base price was an astounding $9,700, an incredible sum in 1930.

Many exclusive European cars had employed decorative cane work, originally utilizing the same material used for chair seats and furniture decoration. It soon became apparent that this was not a very durable finish. Designers quickly developed ways to achieve the same effect, using a thick paint-like compound instead of actual cane. Application was still done by hand, and it was a laborious process of laying down successive stripes of material and waiting for the previous work to dry before continuing.

When General Motors sent half a dozen V-16s to Europe in the summer of 1930 to introduce the Continent to the magnificent new motor cars Cadillac was producing, one of the six was a Series 4264-B with the ersatz cane work appliqué. The cars toured various cities in France, Belgium, Sweden, Denmark, Germany, Austria, Switzerland and Spain. Yann Saunders believes that the cane-bodied Series 4264-B that was part of the tour remained in Holland and was subsequently modified by custom coachbuilder Bronkhorst. He indicates that quarter windows may have been added and that the body may have been extended to accommodate full-sized auxiliary seating (in place of the fold-down opera seats installed by the factory).

None of the six Series 4264-B cars, cane-decorated or plain, is known to have survived. As the most elaborate and expensive of an already elaborate and expensive line of motor cars, it would have been nice if at least one were still around to bear witness to GM's all-out effort to excel in the field of coach-built automobiles.

In the mid–1960s, David Holtzman and "Cadillac Jim" Pearson were convinced that none of the Series 4264-B "razor-edge" town broughams would ever be seen again. But the two of them hatched a plan to convert a surviving town car into an accurate recreation of the extinct breed. In 1962, Mr. Holtzman had purchased from Cadillac Jim a Series 4291 town car, a style with rear quarter windows and rounded body corners. It was a remarkably well-kept specimen with unique design features. In August 1931, Mr. Charles Wellington Watts, a well-to-do businessman, had placed an order with Thackston Motor Co. in Huntington, West Virginia, for a Cadillac V-16 town car for his wife Ouida Caldwell Watts. The car (engine number 703164, body number 14 of 14 built) was shipped from the factory October 8, 1931. Mr. Watts had special-ordered needlepoint medallions for the back cushion of each rear seat, and he had requested that the hood vent doors and cowl side vent doors be chromium plated. The build sheet shows the code for the key to a trunk that was shipped with the car. Other than the chrome trim, the body pinstriping (in a color called "silver leaf") and the red of the taillight lenses and the car's badges, the exterior was entirely black, including the sidewalls of the tires. Mr. Holtzman reports that the mileage was approximately 15,000 when he acquired the car.

The ethics, if you will, of automotive stewardship and restoration have changed over the years. In the first third of the 20th century, the concept of a "classic" or antique automobile worthy of preservation as a historical or artistic treasure was largely foreign to people. Old

Sumptuous owner's suite. Wool broadcloth covers seats and trim panels. Walnut burl with ebony inlay embellishes the door and divider windows. Overhead net is for small personal items The small protrusion below the divider window houses a Jaeger clock and an ash receiver. Silk window shades can be lowered for complete privacy (courtesy Ray Jones).

cars were just obsolete machinery. It was not until the 1940s and '50s that the notion of nostalgic exhibition of primitive motor cars gave rise to some early museums and collections. In the late 1950s and early 1960s, what we now consider grand exemplars of the Classic Era, big Duesenbergs, Packards, Rolls-Royces, and so forth from the late '20s through the 1930s,

The chauffeur's "office." This car demands a chauffeur. Black leather is the sole upholstery material—considered special today, it was regarded as utilitarian in the classic era. The top of the windshield is hinged so the driver can tilt the lower edge outward for a breeze on warm days (courtesy Ray Jones).

were regarded as nothing more than large, outmoded used cars. The stories are well known of, for example, Duesenbergs advertised for a few hundred dollars in 1959. In 1966, a world's record purchase price for an old car was $46,000, paid for a Mercer Raceabout.

When Mr. Holtzman and Cadillac Jim discussed transforming a Series 4291 town car into a Series 4264-B cane-bodied brougham, what they were thinking would be considered outrageous by most classic car enthusiasts today. But in those days, it was a completely inoffensive plan to show modern eyes, in three dimensions, what these long-lost old Cadillacs were like. Moreover, it was a considerably more manageable endeavor in those days before the added costs of complying with EPA and other regulations, massive increases in raw material prices, and the other factors that have driven automotive restoration costs through the roof.

Mr. Holtzman's town car was brought to Detroit and placed in the hands of multitalented designer and car builder Ray Jones. In addition to being an avid and accomplished aviator, Mr. Jones is known for having constructed Bugatti automobiles from factory parts after the company went out of business, and for manufacturing SS and SSK Mercedes cars. Former GM styling director Bill Mitchell bought and drove a Ray Jones Bugatti and a Mercedes.

Mr. Jones and his crew, including Herb Brown and expert mechanic Ron Clark, began working on a project that would take about twenty years and involve a host of well-known people in the auto restoration world, including Brian Joseph and Fran Roxas. Even Dave Holls, former director of corporate design at GM, got into the act, searching GM's photo archives to come up with a picture showing how the cane work on the back of the car was originally done. Without blueprints or a surviving car to work from, measurements and plans had to be extrapolated from a handful of contemporary photographs.

The conversion was carried out with intense attention to detail. Ray Jones offered an example of the level of workmanship. When applying aluminum moldings to the rear of the car, they used screws to attach the moldings. Instead of simply countersinking and filling or covering the screw holes, a cylindrical hole would be drilled that equaled the diameter of the screw head, and with the screw in place, ¹⁄₁₆-inch holes would be drilled in the walls of the larger hole. Then the opening would be packed with lead, like a dentist filling a cavity in a tooth. The reasoning was that if epoxy or a similar compound were used to fill ordinary countersunk screw holes, it might fall out after a period of years.

Ron Clark sums up the approach the men took: "We had to figure out how they did it at the factory, then do it the same way." The rear section of the car's body was basically torn down and re-manufactured to conform to the Series 4264-B design. The formal partition with its roll-up window behind the driver's seat was retained. The doors, too, were kept, but re-shaped. The roof, the rear quarters and the entire back wall of the body were all replaced. Everything was measured, cut, assembled and finished as close as humanly possible to the way that the Fleetwood craftsmen did it decades earlier.

Tasks that posed particular challenges included squaring the rounded door window frames, which had to be carefully worked by hand, the craftsman mindful that a break could not be welded with the wood framing backing up the metal. And converting the hardware for the removable top over the driver's seat was a complicated process. Generally, Mr. Clark found the project interesting and rewarding.

Mr. Jones had an upholsterer named Bruno Gilbert working for him, who had worked in the Fleetwood Body Company when it was still located in Fleetwood, Pennsylvania (before General Motors purchased the company and moved it to Detroit). He was 81 at the time, and he re-created the leather door panels and front seats for the driver's compartment. He also made patterns for the rear compartment door panels, but that work would be completed later.

At one point David Low from the Jo-Han model company came to Mr. Jones's shop to take measurements so that the company could cast a ¹⁄₂₅ scale plastic model of the cane-bodied brougham. As a teenager, I bought and built that model, and fantasized a great deal about owning and driving such a car.

The car was painted Madeira Red, a color from the Rinshed-Mason paint library.[1] Mr. Jones credits Ron Clark with finding an old article in the Detroit Public Library on how the cane work was done in the day, and how to use the specialized tool to apply it (similar to a syringe). The article also had a formula for mixing the paint and paste to form a compound that the tool would extrude to make the canework lines. Mr. Jones called it a scary process—once you started, you knew you had to keep going until you were finished. The job was made all the more time-consuming by the need to wait for the first lines to dry before the diagonal and perpendicular lines could be laid down over them.

Fran Roxas did some finishing work on the car, and his upholsterer Chris Nerstheimer re-upholstered the passenger compartment of the car, using the door panel patterns that Mr. Gilbert had made. Mr. Roxas brought in a craftsman from New Jersey to carry out the caning work. This man and an assistant would arrive at 5:00 p.m. when the shop closed, and they would work into the night on the delicate and complex project. The overall job was completed at master restorer Brian Joseph's shop. Once the transformation was accomplished, the result was stunning. With red body, black fenders and roof, and the signature canework,

How to leave a lasting impression. Seen from behind, the squared-off roof and body corners contrast with the diminutive oval window. Former GM executive David Holls was able to locate factory photographs to enable the team to construct this part of the car. Canework and body lines evoke royal carriages (courtesy Ray Jones).

it was a guaranteed attention-getter. Mr. Holtzman had wanted to have the needlepoint medallions reproduced for the car (the originals were faded), and he says that there was a monogrammed throw pillow as well, for the rear seat passengers.

Mr. Holtzman came to realize that the finished vehicle was really more flamboyant than he was comfortable with. And he said that it didn't run the way it should. He speculated that when the engine was rebuilt the bearings were set too tight, so it wouldn't idle right. Perhaps, he suggested, it required a longer break-in period, or someone to work on the bearings. In 1989, he offered the car at the Kruse Auction in Auburn, Indiana, over the Labor Day weekend.

Restorer and collector Peter Schlacter was the high bidder, but there was no sale. In 1993 at the Barrett-Jackson Auction in Scottsdale, Arizona, the Cadillac was again offered, but not sold. In February 1994, after following the car for several years, Mr. Schlacter was finally able to purchase it privately, and to add it to his collection. Upon acquiring the car, he worked on the electrical and fuel systems, making the magnificent town brougham roadworthy.

Mr. Robert Waldock had attended the 1993 auction in Scottsdale, and he walked past the brougham three or four times, thinking that someday he would like to own such a car. Once his friend Pete Schlacter had become the car's owner, he visited Mr. Schlacter's collection several times and decided he could not live without this unique Cadillac. The two men agreed to terms and 45 days after Mr. Schlacter bought it, Mr. Waldock took over as the car's caretaker. On Mr. Waldock's watch, new carburetor kits were installed, upgrades were made to the electrical system, and other general maintenance work was done at Mr. Schlacter's shop, Peter's Motorcars in Norwalk, Ohio. These efforts have eliminated any operating difficulties and the car runs and drives as splendidly as it looks.

Today Mr. Holtzman finds himself eminently happy with the Series 4330-S V-16 sedan he had bought from Cadillac Jim in 1962. As it turns out, he told me, that was really all he wanted. For his part, Mr. Waldock reports that the cane-bodied brougham "has been a dream to own." He has shown his car sparingly and has won numerous awards with it, not to mention enormous spectator interest. Mr. Schlacter says (and Mr. Waldock concurs), "No matter what the car is parked next to at a show, the cane-bodied brougham is the one that garners people's attention."

Recently (spring 2008) the car has been back on the market. Someone once told me that we don't own these cars—we just take care of them until the next owner comes along.

---

25. Mysterious House Guest

On December 5, 1930, a V-16 five-passenger imperial sedan was shipped from the factory in Detroit to Prather Cadillac-LaSalle Company on the corner of Live Oak and Pearl in Dallas, Texas. The build sheet for engine number 702861 states that the car was a rush order, but the customer's name is not indicated. According to Cadillac historian Mr. Alan Merkel, it was the last of nineteen 1930 and 1931 V-16s shipped to Dallas, and the only Series 4330 five-passenger imperial sedan sent there. Whether it was purchased to provide a suitable inauguration carriage for the incoming mayor of Dallas, or a showy departure coach for his flamboyant predecessor, the Honorable J. Wady Tate, is a subject of pure speculation, as Prather Cadillac-LaSalle Company has been out of business for many years, and the ultimate fate of its customer sales records is unknown.

I have come across some tracks left by Prather Cadillac-LaSalle Company in the historical record. On January 19, 1930, the Dallas *Morning News* carried the following item:

Cadillac V-16
Pre Exhibition
Wins Comment
—

**Magic Smoothness and
Flexibility Reported
For Engine**

—

Visitors to the New York Auto Show displayed interest in the new sixteen-cylinder Cadillac that recalled the enthusiasm aroused when the first American eight-cylinder car was exhibited by Cadillac in 1914. This new automobile, to be called the Cadillac V-16, is the first sixteen cylinder car in this country. It was on exhibition in the Grand Central Palace, the General Motors Salon at the Hotel Astor, and Cadillac's permanent Fleetwood Salon at 10 East 57th Street. The sixteen-cylinder engine alone is on display at the Hotel Commodore.

The Cadillac V-16 will not be available for delivery to purchasers for several months. The two cars which were on exhibition at New York were specially prepared. In Dallas, the Cadillac is handled by the Prather Cadillac-LaSalle Company, Pearl and Live Oak streets.

Outstanding features of the engine are the almost magical smoothness and flexibility; the trim appearance and the capability under all traffic conditions. In design the engine is V-type. The included angle between the two blocks of eight cylinders is forty-five degrees. The valve mechanism is overhead, operated by a single camshaft set at the base of the vee between the cylinder blocks, and assured of absolute silence by a patented automatic valve silencer in collaboration with General Motors research laboratories.

The V-16 power plant is provided with two fuel systems—two vacuum tanks, two carburetors and two intake manifolds. Accelerator control is conventional. Lubrication is full pressure at all bearing surfaces. Crankcase ventilation is thermostatically controlled. Ignition is by Delco-Remy, incorporates two coils, and eight lobed timer with double contact points, two condensers and a distributor.

A common practice of automobile manufacturers was to provide dealers with copy and photos to submit to their local newspapers. Inserted in the news item would be a reference to the dealer that served as indirect advertising. In the example above, the Prather dealership is the beneficiary of this treatment.

On March 12, 1930, another article in the Dallas *Morning News* covered the occasion of a two-day district training institute held by Cadillac at the Prather Cadillac-LaSalle Company to bring twenty dealership service managers from Oklahoma, Louisiana, Kansas and Texas up to speed on the features of the new Cadillac V-16. Identified in a photograph accompanying the article was the service manager for the Prather company. The car shown in the picture was the same body style as my car, but mine would not be built and shipped to Prather for another nine months.

Only 50 Series 4330 cars were built, and I have only been able to account for four survivors, including this one. The companion series without a divider window (Series 4330-S) was produced in larger numbers and is better represented among surviving V-16s.

Subsequent to the shipping date, the historical record is silent regarding this particular car until September 28, 1957, when it was sold out of the estate of Mr. Benjamin Belgard of Brooklyn, New York. The purchaser, Mr. Clarence M. Tolson, Sr., of Southampton, Massachusetts, also purchased a 1937 or 1938 V-16 sedan at the same time. Mr. Tolson's cousin in Connecticut had seen an advertisement and had told him about the cars. Mr. Tolson joined his cousin for the trip to New York to look at the cars, and he bought them for $1,000 each.

Mr. Tolson drove the 1930 Cadillac to Southampton, where it would stay in his personal collection until 1975. On the way there, he stopped at the home of a female relative in Connecticut and loaded some of her furniture into the passenger compartment for the rest of the trip back to Southampton.

The shipping order or "build sheet" for the author's car. The car was ordered entirely in black except for an "Old Ivory" pinstripe. Installation of a Kelch heater and a radio are specified, and Weise 2972 cloth is called for in both front and rear compartments. The delivery point was Prather Cadillac and LaSalle Company in Dallas, Texas, with the instructions "RUSH ORDER" (author's collection).

    Mr. Tolson's son Ronald told me how he and his brother were pressed into service to clean and polish their father's many cars on a regular basis. He told me that the 1930 Cadillac spent nights and cold weather in a heated garage, and during warm days, it might be moved outside into an open but covered area. When I showed the son recent pictures of the car, he told me it looked just as he remembered it, with the exception that the chrome had been redone since he saw it, and that the broken and missing window cranks were intact when he knew the car. The moth holes and other flaws in the upholstery were already there when his

The author's 1930 Series 4330 five-passenger imperial sedan. Only 50 of this limousine body style were built. Only four appear to have survived. Elegance and dignity give the car a timeless presence (author's collection).

father owned the car. He said that the car was driven around the block on occasion, and that it stayed put otherwise.

Clarence Tolson sold the car to another car collector, Mr. Robert Schill of Hinsdale, New Hampshire, on March 20, 1975. Mr. Schill's son Richard told me that his father drove the car home from Southampton, but Mr. Tolson's son told me that Mr. Schill put too much air into one of the tires, and the resulting blow-out forced him to take the car home on a trailer. Robert Schill had intended to restore the car, but, according to Richard, his time and resources were diverted into the restoration of a V-8 Cadillac phaeton, to the detriment of the V-16 limousine. He did have the V-16 engine rebuilt and he repainted the front fenders. Mr. Schill's notes indicate he changed the engine oil three days after he bought the car, at which time the mileage was 7,180. According to his son, Mr. Schill rarely drove the cars he collected.

Around 1990, Mr. Schill sold the car to Mr. James Bradley of Edmund, Oklahoma. When Mr. Bradley purchased it, the engine had been mostly reassembled (except for some of the external components like the manifolds, distributor and carburetors). The fenders had not been bolted back onto the car, but some of the re-chroming had been done. Mr. Bradley bought the car to use as a reference while he and his brother restored a V-16 roadster. Mr. Bradley felt that since the limousine was such a solid original car he could rely on it as a guide for re-assembling the roadster he was working on. He sent the chrome items from the roadster out to be re-plated, together with the parts from the limousine that had not already been done. When the parts came back from the plating company, he put the nicer-

Driver's compartment. Small crank above windshield in front of driver raises windshield glass to allow ventilation (author's collection).

looking pieces on the roadster. When pressed, he allowed that some other parts from the limousine were swapped with the roadster, where, for example, a gauge face looked nicer than the roadster's counterpart. That certainly happened to the speedometer, and possibly to the ignition switch/transmission lock and some other items. Mr. Bradley said that during the time he owned the car he might have driven it as far as five blocks.

Once the restoration of the roadster was completed, Mr. Bradley put the 1930 limousine back together, got it running and otherwise prepared it for sale. In June 1996, he put the car up for auction at the Leake Auction Company's annual event in Tulsa, Oklahoma. Mr. Lawrence Smith of Wichita, Kansas, bought the car and kept it with his diverse collection of classic and exotic automobiles (offered for sale on his website as investment vehicles). By the time I became aware of the car at the beginning of 2005, it had been featured on the Internet with Mr. Smith's other investment vehicles for at least three years. In July 2005 I purchased the car from Mr. Smith.

Mr. Bradley sold the roadster to a well-known collector, Mr. John Groendyke of Enid, Oklahoma. In 2002, Mr. Groendyke consigned the car to be sold by RM Auctions, Inc., in Arizona. According to RM's records, the catalog description of the roadster stated that the odometer reading was 7,241. The roadster was sold to another noted collector, Mr. Ray Scherr of California, and in 2007 it was auctioned by Gooding & Company, selling for a price of $495,000.

Today, the imperial sedan retains a great deal of its originality. The black paint on the body, though polished down to the primer in a couple of spots, is generally as shiny and rich as ever. The interior, though worn and torn in places, is quite serviceable, and was stitched entirely by Fleetwood craftsmen in 1930. The doors close like bank vaults and the chassis is secure and quiet on the road. It's a fun car to drive, very much like driving a brand new V-16 in 1930, and it holds its own in traffic. The fenders have been repainted, the chrome trim replated, the outside glass replaced and the chassis and engine compartment detailed. I've been gradually replacing some missing switches and miscellaneous items, and returning some of the gauges and other parts to working status.

This limousine presents several intriguing questions. First, who would have ordered it from the factory? The declining economy was already taking its toll on the luxury car market by December 1930, and shipments of Cadillac V-16s had declined from a high of 576 per month in March 1930 to 33 in November of that year. And yet someone bought this limousine, as a "rush order," and equipped with a radio (1930 was the first year Cadillacs were wired to accept one) and a heater (specifying a register in the rear compartment only). The upholstery in the driver's compartment was specified to be the same cloth as was fitted in the passenger compartment (instead of the customary leather used in the front for cars with a divider window). Was this just a dealer decorating his showroom with a stunning showpiece to try to perk up sales? Or did a prominent Texan know exactly what he wanted in an elegant conveyance?

Second, why was the car driven so little? Mr. Schill recorded 7,180 miles in 1975. And in 2002, the odometer (now attached to another car) had advanced only to 7,241. The condition of the car's chassis and wear-prone parts is consistent with that abnormally low mileage figure. The successive ownership by collectors from the 1940s on is a partial explanation. But what was going on during the prime of this car's life, when it was new during the early '30s? Was it put into storage and left there?

Third, long ago someone installed snap fasteners across the back of the front seat (two rows, one on either side of the slot for the divider window) and across the back of the rear seat. What was that all about? Was it for seat covers when the car was not in use? Was it to protect the seats from sandy, wet beach-goers in the summer? Or from dusty oil company honchos out in the field?

Much of this car's story can be told, but a significant part of it remains shrouded in mystery. Whether the rest can ever be uncovered remains to be seen. In the meantime, this Cadillac sedan stands as a witness to a time and spirit largely forgotten: a nation buoyed by the carefree optimism of the Roaring Twenties, a classic era of automotive design where cars were proud to be machines *and* works of art, and a certain innocence not yet spoiled by the grim events of the middle and late twentieth century. I'm privileged to make room for it in my home and to do my best to take proper care of it.

26. The Banker and the Countess

In 1869, the first railroad link between the Atlantic and Pacific coasts of the United States was completed, when the Union Pacific and Central Pacific Railroads met in Promontory, Utah. The four men who led the Central Pacific were Leland Stanford, Colis P. Huntington, Mark Hopkins and Charles Crocker. Mr. Stanford's name is memorialized in the name of a major California university. Mark Hopkins's name adorns a prominent San Francisco hotel, and Mr. Huntington planned and established the city of Huntington, West Virginia.[1] Charles Crocker acquired a controlling interest in the Woolworth National Bank for his son William, and added their surname to the bank's name. The Crocker Woolworth National Bank later became simply Crocker National Bank, and it was a fixture in San Francisco life. It was acquired and merged into the Wells Fargo Corporation in 1986.

In 1930, Mr. Templeton Crocker purchased a Cadillac V-16 limousine. The body style that was ordered was a seven-passenger sedan (Series 4375-S), but what was wanted was an imperial sedan (Series 4375 without an "S"). The difference is the roll-up window between the driver's and passengers' compartments, known as an "imperial division." Before the car was delivered to the purchaser, a sliding glass partition was installed (apparently by the dealer) over the back of the front seat, in effect a dealer-installed imperial division. The 4375-S sedan was meant to be an owner-driven car. The 4375 imperial sedan was expected to be driven by a chauffeur, and ordinarily it would have leather upholstery in the driver's compartment (his "work space"). And ordinarily, an imperial sedan would have a fixed front seat—the driver could not move the seat cushion forward or backward to suit his preference. This car has cloth upholstery up front and an adjustable front seat.

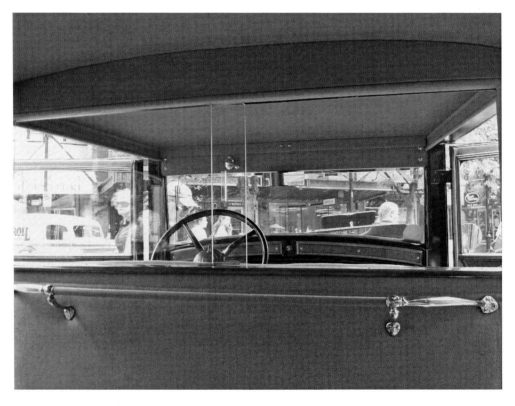

Unusual horizontal sliding divider window. Imperial sedans were distinguished by a glass division between the driver's compartment and the passenger compartment. Usually this was a roll-up window operated by the passenger with a crank on the back of the front seat. Here, a sliding pane arrangement has been installed, and very professionally. Most likely this was accomplished by the dealer after the car was shipped from the factory (courtesy Ted Raines).

Lillian Remillard, Countess Dandini. This lady is one of the most colorful people in San Francisco history (photograph public domain).

Lillian Remillard, Countess Dandini, inherited a brick manufacturing company from her father. The business had been started by two brothers who emigrated from Canada about the time of the California gold rush, and the company provided many of the bricks with which San Francisco was built. The Remillard Brick Company is said to have had a near monopoly on supplying bricks to the western states and the Pacific islands. Following the great earthquake and fire of 1906, the company participated in the rebuilding. Lillian Remillard tutored a young Jack London in French at Oakland High School. She became Countess Dandini as a result of her marriage at age 52 to Count Alessandro Dandini (aged 32 at the time). The count was a handsome man with a big smile and a dapper mustache. He would live to 1991, help to found a scientific research institute in Nevada, spend a year and a half in prison for tax law violations, and take out 22 patents for inventions ranging from solar energy collectors to the three-way light bulb. The marriage lasted only a few years, but the divorcée retained the title until her death at 93. She became the second owner of the 1930 Cadillac V-16 with the sliding glass partition only a year or two after it was sold new. A sensible businesswoman, her practice was to buy her fine motor cars used, permitting someone else to absorb the depreciation a car typically incurs in the first year or two.

Shortly after she acquired the car from Mr. Crocker, the standard rear axle (4.39:1 ratio) was replaced with a 5.06:1 unit. Mr. Jim Weston, a subsequent owner, believes that this was done after a major breakdown in front of the St. Francis Hotel in San Francisco involving a broken axle shaft. A slower rear end ratio was recommended only where steep hills would be encountered much of the time.

The countess used the 1930 Cadillac until 1936, when she replaced it with a 1935 V-12 town car. That car was succeeded by a 1938 Cadillac Series 65 sedan (with a divider window) in 1939 or '40. Jim Weston reported having seen all three of these cars in a shed at the

Wood strips that replace the original rubber treads for the running boards are visible in this photo. A number of V-16 owners over the years have used that technique to restore the running boards. Original design was for the metal base of the running board to be finished in a wood-grained pattern, with narrow parallel rubber strips edged in stainless steel or chrome extending almost the entire length of each running board (courtesy Dr. Dave Mikol).

Remillard Company brickyard in San Jose in the early 1960s. Rats had taken a serious toll on the upholstery of each vehicle. Mr. Weston was told at the time that the '35 town car had been sold but not yet picked up. Mr. Joseph Cali of San Jose purchased the 1930 limousine and gave it a substantial restoration. The rodent damage was corrected, the upholstery and window glass were replaced and the paint redone. The pinstriping was done by the man who painted the Greyhound buses locally. Mr. Cali did all of the mechanical work. He had new hubcaps made out of aluminum, and his wife remade the silk window shades. At that time, they were able to obtain cloth that neatly replaced the original window shade material. One place where Mr. Cali deviated from original specifications was the running board treads, where instead of rubber inserts, he had strips of oak cut to fit. Ultimately, Mr. Cali put more than 2,300 hours into the restoration, and he was able to give Countess Dandini a ride in her old car before she passed away.

Mr. Cali told how he showed the car at the Pebble Beach Concours in 1964 and took first in his class in a closely-decided contest with a Packard owned by the late J. B. Nethercutt. The car took top honors on other occasions, as well. Due to illness in the family, Mr. Cali was unable to keep the Cadillac, and he sold it to Mr. Ed Gunther, also of San Jose. Over thirty years later, Mr. Cali is sorry he had to part with it. Around 1974, Mr. Gunther sold the car to Mr. Weston, who resolved some operational issues to get the car running the way a Cadillac should. He also replaced the 5.06:1 rear axle gearing with the standard (and faster)

4.39:1 ratio. In the late 1990s, Mr. Weston sold the car to Ted Raines of Rescue, California, who owned it for eight or nine years.

The limousine's engine number, 700280, is an early one, and indicates that it was shipped from the factory in February of 1930. The bodies of the vacuum tanks on the firewall are chrome plated, as was the practice early in the model run. After March 1930, the vacuum tanks on V-16s were painted black except for the tops, and Cadillac service personnel were advised that if the need arose to replace the vacuum tanks, the chrome cases should be replaced with the black-painted counterparts.

Former owner Ted Raines told me that after its second owner, this was a "collected" car, meaning that it was cared for as part of someone's stable of fine automobiles. As such, the mechanical and electrical components have been kept as originally designed. There has not been a need or desire to replace, substitute or update, as is sometimes seen with cars whose owners had to keep them running, regardless of the availability of authentic replacement parts or dependable service for obsolete technologies. For example, the vacuum fuel delivery systems are functional and correct, with no aftermarket electric fuel pump. The stock carburetors have not been switched with Carters or Solexes or Detroit Lubricators, and the decorative braided fuel lines from the vacuum tanks to the carburetors have not been replaced with rubber hoses or copper tubing.

Until 2007, when it was acquired by Dr. Dave Mikol of Southfield, Michigan, this Cadillac was entirely a West Coast car. After assuming ownership, Dr. Mikol rebuilt the transmission and sorted out some other issues. The willingness of the Cadillac-Johnson car-

Well-conserved engine. Some of the porcelain coating remains on the exhaust manifold. Enameled Cadillac crests on the knobs between the cylinder banks are outlined in real gold (courtesy Ted Raines).

buretors to drip fuel from time to time provided a measure of challenge, but installation of properly lapped stainless steel needle valves and brass seats should have smoothed that wrinkle.

In August 2009, Dr. Mikol consigned the car to RM Auctions, Inc., to be offered at their Vintage Cars at Meadow Brook auction. The estimate in the auction catalogue was $100,000 to $125,000, but the V-16 limousine brought a price of $126,500.

27. Lone Star Legacy

Gray County, Texas, is situated in the eastern part of the Panhandle, that squared-off northern protuberance of Texas that nestles into the corner created by the strip of Oklahoma that reaches over to New Mexico. Halfway between Amarillo to the west and the Oklahoma border to the east, Gray County had been farm and ranch country. In the 1920s, oil discoveries were coming in rapidly in the Panhandle, and Gray County found itself in the thick of things. Toward the end of the decade a couple who'd been making a modest living out of ranching suddenly found themselves with piles of oil money. One of the first things they did was what countless other suddenly-wealthy folks did—they went out and bought the nicest Cadillac they could. They purchased a black Series 4361-S V-16 town sedan and carried on what had become a cultural tradition in that part of the country.

Joe B. Bowers, Sr., was born in about 1871 in Bell County, in central Texas, northeast of Austin. He moved to Roberts County in the northeast Panhandle, and for several years served as the county tax assessor. He married Lizzie Humes there, and around 1911, they purchased a ranch in neighboring Gray County, south of Pampa, and settled there. Oil was discovered on the ranch in 1927, and the "Bowers Pool" made them the wealthiest family in Gray County. Mr. Bowers ordered a new Cadillac V-16 town sedan and in April 1930, his car was shipped from the factory.

Engine number 700892 powered the car and it bore body number 78 (of a total of 258 V-16 town sedans built in 1930 and '31). The car was all black with gray wool upholstery, and it had the accessory metal covers fitted to the fender-mounted spare tires. This was a dignified and proper car for a man of means. It was not a flamboyant roadster or phaeton that Mr. Bowers purchased, or an ostentatious limousine or town car. Just a self-respecting family car, albeit a very dear one built to the most demanding standards.

Good fortune does not always last, and sometimes it runs out rather abruptly. Barely four months after they bought their special Cadillac, Lizzie Bowers passed away on August 21, 1930. Her husband died on September 30 of the following year. At some point subsequently, their children relegated the V-16 to a perch atop blocks in a barn on the Bowers Ranch. There it remained until some time in the 1950s, when the family donated the dormant vehicle to the Panhandle Plains Historical Museum in nearby Canyon, Texas.

When the museum took possession of the car, the interior had been badly damaged by moths, and a careful reconstruction was undertaken. One source at the museum told me that the paint only required cleaning and some wax to look fully presentable, while another said that the car was repainted and some of the chrome pieces were replated. Either way, it's a very well preserved original car that most likely has all of its original innards configured

The Bowers family Cadillac. This car is in very impressive original condition. Accessory wind wings and metal spare-tire covers were optional equipment. Over the years, the radiator ornament has lost part of her trailing scarf (courtesy Panhandle Plains Historical Museum and Bill Green, curator emeritus).

exactly the way Cadillac arranged them a little over 80 years ago. The odometer reads 43,615 miles, a figure that has remained unchanged for the past twenty years or so. Somewhere over the years, the goddess on the radiator cap lost the scarf that should be fluttering in the breeze behind her head. A retired curator of the museum told me that the car used to be taken out on special occasions and driven in parades. It hasn't been run or driven in a long time, and part of the reason is that the museum building doesn't readily permit removing or replacing a big old motor car without extensive preparatory work.

Today the Bowers's car sits in an exhibit designed for it, and serves to tell modern folks what life was like for a small but significant segment of the rural Texan population during the early part of the last century. As such, the museum considers this Cadillac to be a very valuable asset, and displays it proudly.

28. Two for the Road

Jack Wade, Jr. of New Orleans, Louisiana, has owned two Cadillac V-16s since the early 1960s. One has been a source of driving pleasure and adventure for him and his family, and the other is still waiting for him to install a new engine to replace the original one prior owners crippled and discarded. The stories of these cars follow here.

Part I: A Series 4330-S Fleetwood Sedan

In the spring of 1962, Jack Wade, with his close friend Walt Jones, drove his 1941 Buick coupe to Lake Jackson, Texas, to purchase a 1930 V-16 Cadillac Series 4330-S five-passenger sedan. The car bore engine number 702765 and body number 408. Among its distinguishing features was a heater (the hot water variety) with the appropriate trade name of Hades. Jack had seen the car advertised in the *Horseless Carriage Gazette,* the magazine of the Horseless Carriage Club of America. He and another prospective buyer had competed for the sale, and the other buyer had failed to come up with the money. Once the papers were signed, the seller told Jack and Walt about the owner of a steel company in Houston who would sell a box full of parts for the car for $75. So before taking the car home, they located the steel company, bought the parts (which included two complete carburetors in excellent condition and a distributor cap, among other items) and loaded them into the trunk of the '41 Buick, about 10:30 p.m. the night before beginning the long trip home (almost 400 miles).

The retrieval of the old Cadillac began in a straightforward manner, but "issues" soon arose. The engine seemed to want to run on the left-hand cylinders alone. But when the radiator stopped up completely on U.S. 90, not far from Beaumont, it was clear that the sedan would have to be towed the rest of the way. Using a chain to tow the car into Beaumont, Jack and Walt then rented a tow bar and the little Buick coupe hauled the big Cadillac the rest of the way to New Orleans. Stopping at a filling station on the Airline Highway around midnight, they started the Cadillac again, and it fired right up. Because the car was equipped with exhaust cut-outs on both exhaust pipes, and because both cut-outs were stuck wide open, the rest of the journey home was a noisy one, and definitely not what the neighbors expected.

Contrasting color scheme shows off the lines and curves. GM's Art and Colour Section and its Fleetwood Body Company put a lot of visual interest into even the workaday sedan bodies. Except for doors and window frames, the body uses aluminum from the beltline up (courtesy Jack Wade).

Jack Wade and his car in New Orleans. Jack Wade and his 1930 Series 4330-S five-passenger sedan, seen during the days when he drove the car regularly (courtesy Jack Wade).

Before advertising the car in the *Horseless Carriage Gazette,* the seller had hauled it to Houston from Pecos, Texas. He had shown Jack a registration certificate for the car from the early 1950s with an address in Tulsa, Oklahoma. (Jack later tried to look up the former owner, but the address on the old title no longer existed.) The seller told Jack that at one time the car had been sold to pay for its own fuel bill. When Jack bought it, it had old undersized tires (6.25" or 6.50" × 19", where the car was supposed to ride on 7.00" or 7.50" × 19" tires), and those old tires somehow carried the heavy car all the way from Houston to New Orleans. According to the truck scales he crossed coming into New Orleans, the Cadillac weighed 6,800 pounds.

The sedan now has about 86,000 miles on it, and Jack estimates that his family has put about 7,000 or 8,000 of those miles on the odometer. It is hard to believe that this sedan was originally purchased as a parts car for the roadster.

Part II: A Series 4302 Fleetwood Roadster

In early 1961, Jack, who then lived in Lake Charles, Louisiana, "was working big in the oil industry, onshore and offshore." In the course of his work, he heard about a 1931 V-16 roadster sitting at a trade school in DeRidder, Louisiana. This car had been built with engine number 703053 and body number 92. It was shipped in May of 1931, at a time when the Great Depression was really beginning to take hold of the nation. The effect on the market for grand luxury automobiles was severe, and according to notations on the build sheet, the roadster was moved from one dealership to another in the New York and New Jersey area until it was finally sold. Flash forward to the 1950s, when a fellow at Chennault Air Force

Base in Lake Charles drove it there from Oklahoma. This particular gentleman managed to immobilize the car, causing it to throw a connecting rod through the side of the engine. He brought the car to a mechanic in Lake Charles to be repaired and abandoned it. The mechanic, in turn, sold the roadster to the trade school. A few weeks later, he had second thoughts and tried to buy the car back, but the trade school wouldn't oblige him.

The trade school used the Cadillac as a teaching tool, discarding the broken V-16 engine and installing a high-performance DeSoto hemi V-8. The mechanic who had sold it to the school clued Jack in to its existence, and he set about trying to talk the trade school owner out of the car. The owner got the idea that Mr. Wade might sign on to teach chemistry at the school (he had minored in chemistry at Tulane University). Eventually, Jack was able to buy the car (declining the hemi engine to save money), and without becoming a chemistry teacher.

Loading his young family (wife, three-year-old son, and infant twin daughters) into the '41 Buick, he drove up to the trade school at night, hooked up a tow bar and quickly found out that the car would not readily steer itself through the narrow streets and tight turns in DeRidder. So Jack was obliged to ride in the roadster's driver's seat and steer until they got out onto the highway, with Sue, his wife, driving the '41 Buick. The truck scales only read 4,250 pounds when this engine-less V-16 rolled through. After they got the roadster home, he disassembled the rear end, bought new bearings and catalogued the many missing parts. Trips to junkyards in and around the Lake Charles area failed to turn up the original wounded engine, so he began looking for a replacement.

In the fall of 1961, the Wades drove from Lake Charles in the '41 Buick to attend a combined Veteran Motor Car Club of America and Cadillac-LaSalle Club meet in Kansas City at Country Club Plaza (one of the first shopping centers in the United States, built in 1922). It was there that they met Jim Pearson ("Cadillac Jim," as he was known). The day after the meet, Mr. Pearson had the Wades over to his home. The house was a modest structure built of cinder blocks. Outside was a veritable "Cadillac junkyard" with several Cadillac V-16s just sitting there. Cadillac Jim offered to buy the Wades' recently-acquired roadster, sight unseen, for several times what they'd paid for it. But the deal struck that day was Jack's purchase of a box of castings for handles and trim items, which he paid for by trading a pair of metal covers for fender-mounted spare tires. Two of the castings, cleaned up and plated, are now on Jack's V-16 sedan.

Later the Wades got to see Cadillac Jim's own V-16 roadster, which he happily let Jack and Sue take turns driving, while Jim rode in the rumble seat. Afterwards, he drove the Wades back, with the couple occupying the rumble seat.

Jack's sedan and the roadster have been garaged for some 40-plus years now, and both survived Hurricane Katrina with no ill effects. Before the hibernation began, Jack and Sue used to drive the Series 4330-S sedan regularly in highway traffic along the coast of the Gulf of Mexico. Among other trips, the car has gone to Biloxi, Mississippi, and back, and it has driven across the Lake Pontchartrain Causeway (a 24-mile bridge on which you don't want to have to stop). On the occasion of a local car club meet at Lafayette, Louisiana, a bar in the commutator in the generator came out. Removing the metal strap that covers that end of the generator, Jack was able to pry the brushes away so that they would not catch in the open space in the commutator. The brushes were held out with a short piece of wire, and the Wades drove the 140 miles home on the battery. On the way home, the Wades found themselves driving on the edge of a hurricane. The smoked glass sunshade over the top of the windshield began to work its way loose in the wind, and Jack was obliged to pull over, remove it and stow it inside the car. It remains in his office, needing new brackets before it can be reinstalled. The Visionall wiper worked well through the rainstorm.

The annual Spring Fiesta Parade is part of a New Orleans tradition that celebrates blooming azaleas, offers tours of the fine old homes in the French Quarter, and involves a great deal of partying and good times. The Wades attended many parades with the Cadillac sedan, and their enjoyment was threatened on one such occasion by the failure of the car's clutch linkage. The pedal fell to the floor useless, and there was no way to disengage the clutch to shift gears. Taking advantage of the V-16's tremendous pulling power, and a trick that Cadillac salesmen used to employ to impress prospective V-16 buyers, Jack was able to drive the car home. With the car in third gear, and the engine stopped but the ignition switched "on," the driver can simply press the starter pedal. The powerful starter turns the engine over, the car starts moving, the engine catches, and away you go. Jack just left the car in third, and whenever he had to stop (at a traffic light, stop sign, etc.) he switched the car off. When he could proceed, he switched the ignition on and pressed the starter pedal. Arriving home, he drove right up the driveway and into the garage in third gear. One of the latest fuel-conserving features on some modern cars is a feature called "Stop/Start." The U.S. government's fuel economy website (http://www.fueleconomy.gov) explains the concept as follows: "Stop/Start technology conserves energy by shutting off the gasoline engine when the vehicle is at rest, such as at a traffic light, and automatically re-starting it when the driver pushes the gas pedal to go forward." As the old saying goes, "Everything old is new."

Jack has three loose V-16 engines from which he should be able to assemble a running powerplant for his roadster. One engine that came from Ohio had been "torn to pieces" with several broken cylinders. Its engine number is 700416, and as an early engine, the oil level indicator is located at the rear of the V between the banks of cylinders. Cadillac later moved it to the left-hand side of the crankcase, reportedly so that servicemen and owners could view the oil level without having to unlatch and lift the substantial hood each time. The second engine, found by Walt Jones, was literally winched out of a junk pile in a New Orleans salvage yard in 1964, having languished there since World War II. Jack has disassembled this one, having to knock the pistons loose with a block of wood and a hammer. He's had the cylinders sleeved and he's bought new pistons for it. The third engine has a number of broken stud bolts from an unsuccessful restorer's earlier efforts to take it apart. But it came with extra parts, including carburetors and a distributor.

With major efforts being expended in constructing a large building which includes two-story living quarters and workshop on the north shore of Lake Ponchartrain, and cleaning this property of major Hurricane Katrina damage, Jack has been very slow in getting the venerable Cadillacs back on the road, but he is optimistic he'll do so soon.

29. Old Red

It's not uncommon in the company of car guys to hear stories of the cars they owned, worked on or wished after in younger days, and that they would love to have today. Less often, you hear of the people who let a car go and then many years later managed to find and reconnect with (or even repurchase) the same automobile. Then there are the folks who hang on to that "special car" through their adulthood, and the car becomes part family member, part plot device for the narrative of the owner's life, catalyzing events and giving rise to myriad adventures. The car can even become a sort of personal trademark, and an aspect of the owner's very identity (like Jay Leno and his '55 Buick Roadmaster).

Paul Schinnerer of Long Beach California served in the navy in World War II, and spent his twenties during the post-war hot rod craze in Southern California. That was the time when many returning GIs hopped up passenger car engines and planted them in anything from junked pre-war Fords, Willyses and Chevies to surplus aircraft fuel tanks, and took their rods to dry lake beds and the like to see how fast they could run. In 1949, Paul's one-year-younger brother Al and two fraternity brothers came upon a junked car that had a lot of potential, and they bought it for $75. It was pretty banged up, but it was a convertible with a sixteen-cylinder engine and it had only 35,000 (actual) miles. The three college boys fitted the wreck with used 18-inch tires and wheels from a V-12, replaced some broken brake drums, and drove the car to Los Angeles.

The car was a Series 4380 convertible sedan, known in the terminology of the day as an "all-weather phaeton." A conventional phaeton was a touring car, a four-door convertible that, like a roadster, had no roll-up windows. In rain or snow, the occupants had to find, deploy and fasten side curtains. An all-weather phaeton, on the other hand, was truly the best of both worlds—open-air motoring in fair weather, snug isolation when things got ugly.

Cadillac records show that this all-weather phaeton was shipped new to a dealer in Chicago, but the original owner's identity is unknown. Somehow the car made its way to

Sad shape indeed. What was once a beautiful Series 4380 Cadillac V-16 all-weather phaeton languishes in a junkyard, having been stolen and rolled. The owner had been using it to launch gliders for research purposes. This is the car's condition when Al Schinnerer bought it and fixed it up well enough to serve as an admirable college frat-mobile (courtesy Paul Schinnerer).

Southern California, and in the 1940s it was owned by John W. Meyer, a Northrop Aircraft test pilot, who used it to tow a glider in connection with the development of the XB-49 "flying wing" project. (The XB-49 never went into production, but a subsequent flying wing design became the B-2 "stealth" bomber that we know today.) The test pilot was involved in an aircraft accident and lost track of the V-16. Meanwhile, the car was stolen, and the thief was killed when he rolled the Cadillac at high speed. The damaged vehicle was left to languish on a farmer's field, where Al Schinnerer and his buddies encountered it.

The nice thing about finding a neglected V-16 was that it usually had a lot of use left in the engine and drivetrain. The cars' thirst for gasoline, for one thing, tended to deter most people from driving them into the ground. When Paul first saw the former glider tow car and got to ride in it, it wasn't much to look at. A makeshift windshield had been installed, since the original one had been destroyed in the rollover, and the hood had been removed to show off the engine. The body was battered, the paint had faded and the upholstery was sad. But brother Al pointed out the Eddie Edmunds intake manifolds with a total of four downdraft carburetors, each topped with a chrome-plated velocity stack. He told Paul that the car could beat any stock Ford. It needed a lot of TLC, in terms of paint, parts, upholstery work and chrome plating, but the smoothness and power made Paul think twice about old cars.

A year later, Paul was able to buy the car for twice what the trio of frat boys had paid, although its condition was somewhat the worse for wear. Paul had seen his brother burn rubber for about 100 feet by racing the engine near full throttle and suddenly dropping in the clutch. In addition to hard use, the Cadillac had been run into a tree, damaging a front

Flirting at the filling station. Paul's brother Al and his fraternity brothers chatting up a pretty attendant at the local service station in 1949. Two chromed velocity stacks can be seen atop the downdraft carburetors on the left-hand side of the engine. Paul would later figure out how to make the engine backfire through those stacks for special occasions. The hot rod Cadillac dwarfs the Model T roadster waiting next in line (courtesy Paul Schinnerer).

fender. Paul took delivery of the vehicle with both front fenders, the hood and the headlights piled in the back seat. Taking the car home, he hid it from his parents until he could figure out how to break the news to them.

Then began a long and laborious process of bringing a neglected and mistreated motor car back to its proper glory. In this endeavor, Paul was sailing uncharted waters. What we now know as "the big classics," the high-end cars from the late 1920s and early-to-mid '30s, were just used cars in 1950. They were considered obsolete, and primitive at best. And if worn, wounded or wrecked, they were just so much scrap metal. Today there exists a broad range of resources for restoring and maintaining veteran automobiles. Original and reman-ufactured parts can be located for almost any production car. And there are specialty outfits that will help replace parts for one-off and custom vehicles. Publications like *Hemmings Motor News* and the want ads in the back of many club newsletters and magazines serve as a sort of monthly nationwide swap meet to find and sell cars as well as hard-to-find parts. And in recent years, the eBay auction website and other Internet resources have become essential assets to car owners, restorers and "wannabes" alike.

There are clubs for almost any make, and even for many specific models, as well as umbrella organizations—the Horseless Carriage Club for brass-era enthusiasts and the Clas-sic Car Club of America for Full Classics, to name a couple. Clubs give access to a pool of knowledge and experience that's invaluable if you want to do a job right the first time, or figure out where to get it done by someone else. Fellow club members provide encouragement that's sorely needed when a project seems overwhelming or endless (or when uninitiated family and friends just don't understand!). And they comprise an appreciative audience to whom you can show what you've accomplished.

All of this infrastructure developed over time, as interest in, and appreciation for, the cars of the past increased. In 1950 Paul Schinnerer was on his own. By his own account he had no idea what he was taking on in terms of hard work and the problems posed by missing or broken parts. Even the local junkyards were unfamiliar with anything as fancy as a V-16 all-weather phaeton. But Paul was a determined young man.

He was also an adventurous and ingenious young man. Being able to drive the powerful and imposing Cadillac between bouts of serious repair work provided a large helping of motivation to continue. He found that, true to what his brother had told him at the outset, he outran every Ford he raced, flooring the accelerator pedal and waiting to shift until he was well past 40 m.p.h. Theron Baganz told me a similar story from the early 1950s of racing the hot new Oldsmobile overhead-valve V-8s, and beating them as long as he didn't shift out of first.

Then there was the pyrotechnic display Paul found he could produce on command, courtesy of the four downdraft carburetors and the exotic manifolds. One can only imagine the restless car-guy experimentation that developed the following technique: Take a specially equipped Cadillac V-16 and, while driving, slow down to about 5 m.p.h. in third gear. Pull out the dash knob to retard the spark. Press the brake pedal with the left foot, and with the right foot, "wiggle" the accelerator. A loud "poof!" noise will be accompanied by flames reaching about five feet into the air. Armed with this new skill, one summer evening just after dark, Paul and some college friends drove the V-16 to a local drive-in frequented by the hot rod crowd. The Cadillac arrived with a noisy, fiery display that sent the patrons running. Once they realized that the car was not blowing up, people gathered around to inspect this fearsome technological wonder.

For twenty years after he purchased the V-16, Paul drove the car enthusiastically, to put it mildly. On one occasion, running with wide-open throttle in low gear, driver and car passed through a pool of water. The sudden return of traction when the car reached dry pavement broke an axle shaft. His friends were treated to rides at speeds of 80 m.p.h. or more. The following vignette in Paul's own words describes a "demonstration ride" that he gave another old car owner near the completion of the V-16's restoration:

> Many of my friends got fast rides in the all weather phaeton at 80 miles per hour. One called recently and reminded me of such an exciting event back in 1959. About that time a young man showed up in a nice original '30 Franklin sedan. He said that the flat out top speed was 52 miles per hour. That called for a ride in the "16." The Cadillac had nice loud pipes. We raced through an underpass, about a quarter mile long below the airport runway with a glorious deafening roar. When we got out in the open, I could see that my friend was shaking and appeared to be a little scared. Back at his Franklin again he felt safe even if its top speed was only a few miles faster than the Cadillac's 1st gear.

In 1952, Paul turned down a friend's offer to buy the V-16 from him for $300. Paul says it was tempting at the time. Instead, the work proceeded. The engine reverted to stock configuration (although Paul uses the later Detroit Lubricator carburetors) and he reports that the performance is almost as good as in the former "hopped-up" state. The hood went back on, all the absent or broken parts were replaced, and the car gradually took on its present lustrous elegance. In about 1960, with the car restored, Paul discovered and became involved with the Cadillac-LaSalle Club (founded only two years previously). Through the club he met a group of fellow old Cadillac enthusiasts living nearby, and it wasn't long before they formed a Southern California Region of the CLC and began organizing and conducting meetings and other events.

Paul at the wheel. After purchasing the car from his brother, Paul has re-installed the hood, but the four downdraft carburetors remain. This "sleeper" car astonished many riders and other drivers as it reached speeds of 80 m.p.h. or more (courtesy Paul Schinnerer).

Stately and sporting. Restored and painted a deep red with dark maroon fenders and molding, the all-weather phaeton combines elegant motoring with open-air excitement. The rather upright windshield maintains a conservative restraint. The top folded level with the tops of the doors gives the big car a lithe presence (courtesy Paul Schinnerer).

The restored V-16 has had an exciting life, being featured in five Hollywood Christmas parades while transporting movie stars, movies (including *My Wicked, Wicked Ways*, about the life of Errol Flynn), TV shows, weddings, car shows and meets. Paul has never been shy about really driving his car (or driving it fast when the urge hits!).

In 1970, the Cadillac was 40 years old, and after two decades of Al's and Paul's antics, the valves were failing and it was time for an engine overhaul. Observing the motto of "If it ain't broke, don't fix it," Paul had never removed the cylinder heads or dropped the oil pan. Upon disassembling the engine, Paul noted that the rod bearings were good, notwithstanding the work-out the car had been given. "Who says," he asks, "that babbitted rod bearings are no good?"

One parade the car participated in during the early 1980s was organized by the Kiwanis Club to honor Jack Northrop, the founder of the aircraft company that bears his name. Mr. Northrop required the help of his daughter and an assistant to climb into the Cadillac's back seat for the parade. No one knew at the time that this car was the same one that Northrop test pilot John Meyer had used to tow his glider back in the 1940s!

Paul Schinnerer and his Series 4380 V-16 Cadillac remain happily together today, and each has become a part of the other's identity. His experience confirms that the overhead valve Cadillac V-16 was and remains a very reliable and durable engine. Paul keeps busy working on the slow but steady restoration of a Series 4260 sport phaeton that he started on some 40 years ago, and sharing his boundless knowledge and enthusiasm with fellow Cadillac owners.

A "Madame X" V-16 sedan. This subset of V-16 body styles sported slender pillars for windshield and doors that gave the car a lighter, airy feel. Madame X sedans cost about $1,000 more than their counterparts in the other series (courtesy RM Auctions).

Sporting elegance. This is Henry Struck's 1930 roadster as restored by Steven Nanini of Tucson, Arizona. Optional equipment on this car includes twin spotlights and wind wings on the windshield pillars, and Pilot Ray driving lights that swivel with the front wheels (courtesy Steven Nanini).

Accessory trunk in later years would merge into the body of the car. But we still call a rear compartment for luggage a "trunk." This elegant unrestored 1930 five-passenger sedan looks great from any angle (courtesy David Holtzman).

Meticulously restored engine. The investment of time and resources has returned the engine compartment to an eye-catching marvel, as originally designed by Owen Nacker. Even the rubber cover for the distributor cap is in place. Note the oil can on the fender ledge next to the firewall (courtesy Pete Sanders).

Most elegant Cadillac ever? Six Series 4264-B town brougham cars were built, three of which had the canework appliqué on the lower rear quarters and back. None have survived, but this re-creation is an impeccable representation of the most expensive car in the 1930 V-16 model lineup. No expense was spared to achieve the same fit and finish that the Fleetwood craftsmen created in 1930 (courtesy Ray Jones).

A profile that commands respect. This is probably the most impressive design for a motor car that Cadillac ever built. It was the pinnacle of the V-16 model lineup in 1930 and 1931 and only a handful were built. This is the high-water mark and end point of the influence of traditional carriage building themes in automobile design. From 1932 onward, the car leaves the carriage behind (courtesy Ray Jones).

A 1930 five-passenger imperial sedan. From the beltline up, the body skin is aluminum. As with almost all cars of this vintage, the metal panels are fastened onto a hardwood framework. The separate fenders and running boards and the shaping of the body are late carry-overs from the days of elegant horse-drawn carriages (author's collection).

Silk curtain opulence. Rear compartment of an unrestored imperial sedan features silk roll-down shades on side and rear windows provide privacy. Lady's vanity unit with built-in Jaeger LeCoultre clock included a hand mirror and cigarette case, in addition to ash receivers. Walnut burl and ebony inlay accent the windows (author's collection).

On the show field at the 2008 Pebble Beach Concours. The Rollston coachbuilding firm converted a standard 1930 Cadillac V-16 roadster into this unique and racy convertible coupe. Very few Cadillac V-16 cars were shaped by coachbuilders other than Fleetwood (courtesy Joseph Scott).

The Series 4355 sedan cabriolet as it appeared in *Automobile Quarterly*. With the car posed in a bucolic setting, the refined dignity of this formal body style stands out. Metal spare tire covers with rearview mirrors are Cadillac accessories. The trunk mounted on the back, however is an aftermarket style. The photograph is from the early 1970s, and the car was a very well preserved and presented original (courtesy *Automobile Quarterly* Photo and Research Archives).

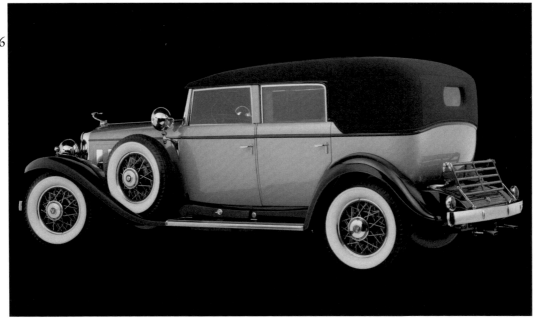

Bodywork by Saoutchik. The French coachbuilder Jacques Saoutchik crafted this sedan body and worked it harmoniously into the Cadillac chassis and front end design. The massive roof line contrasts with the delicate window frames and graceful door handles. The ornate mounting for the spotlight is especially interesting (courtesy Scott Williamson).

Vast opening to the sky on the Saoutchik-bodied 1930 sedan. With the sunroof fully retracted and the windows lowered, the occupants have plenty of light and air. The smoothly handled transition from the passenger compartment through the cowl to the (stock Cadillac) hood is easily seen in this view (courtesy Scott Williamson).

Opposite: The airy openness of a convertible. V-16 enthusiast Paul Schinnerer combined a junked V-16 chassis with an unusual 1930 Cadillac V-8 hardtop sedan body known as a "sedanette cabriolet." With the center pillars folded, the occupants have an unobstructed view to the side, almost like a touring car or phaeton. But the car has a solid roof and can be weather-tight when necessary (courtesy Steven Sherwood).

Exquisite workmanship and materials. Beautifully grained wood and delicate inlay adorn the doors and the interior partition on the Saoutchik-bodied V-16 sedan. Barely visible in the lower left is the paired speedometer and Jaeger chronometer that Cadillac installed in the Series 4260 sport phaetons. Instrument panel and controls are typical of all V-16 Cadillacs. The rest of the interior is bespoke (courtesy Scott Williamson).

Opposite: A restored Series 4302 roadster. The roadster was the least expensive model of the available 1930–31 Cadillac V-16 body styles. Today, they command some of the highest prices. Chromed hood vent doors were a popular embellishment, and a Cadillac accessory "lowboy" trunk can be seen at the back end of the car (courtesy RM Auctions).

No ordinary 1933 Chrysler Custom Phaeton. Powerboat racing champion Lou Fageol engineered and carried out the installation of a Cadillac V-16 engine in this dual-windshield phaeton. The lighter Chrysler chassis and body made this a very quick car (courtesy Paul Schinnerer).

President Herbert Hoover's 1932 Cadillac V-16. This is the car the former president took with him into retirement and kept well into the 1940s. For 1932, Cadillac streamlined and simplified the front "clip." Headlights and parking lights are smaller and bullet-shaped. There is no crossbar between the fenders supporting the headlamps. The radiator is rounded and the grille is built in instead of latched on. Front fenders and running boards form a continuous curve that bends into the rear fenders. The windshield has no sun visor, and the header is rounded off (courtesy Worldwide Auctioneers).

Revealing overhead view. This perspective really shows how long and lean the 1934 V-16 stationary coupe is. The 154-inch wheelbase and almost twenty-foot overall length make this one of the largest production passenger cars built. In spite of those dimensions, the car is proportioned and graceful (courtesy Monty Holmes).

Side view of the 1935 V-16 with accessory trunk in place. The dimensions of the 1934–1937 V-16s are astounding. The car itself is twenty feet long. The radio antenna can be seen suspended beneath the running board (courtesy Louis Barnhart).

Opposite: Mr. Frederick Vanderbilt's car in front of his home. The maroon and black color scheme is elegant and subtle. Maroon had been a favorite of his late wife. Purchasers of 1933 V-16s could choose chrome or painted finish for the headlights, parking lights and radiator shell. Many considered the painted accessories more appropriate, given the nation's financial distress. Here, they are consistent with Mr. Vanderbilt's conservative preferences (courtesy Bud Juneau).

A 1938 V-16 town sedan. The "late series" V-16 cars built between 1938 and 1940 used the same bodies and chassis as the Series 75 V-8 cars. The three spears on the fenders and hood side panels of this car signify the V-16 powerplant within. The town sedan body achieves an imposing presence without being ponderous (courtesy Brad Ipsen).

Unobtrusive to a fault. This is the last V-16 engine Cadillac installed in a production car. In contrast to the 1930–37 overhead-valve engine, the 1938–40 "flathead" V-16 engine sits very low in its bay, and with a 135-degree angle between them, the cylinder banks lie almost flat. Generator, carburetors, air cleaners, manifolds and one of the distributors are all readily visible. The engine itself can barely be seen past the left-hand intake manifold to the lower right of the shot (courtesy Douglas Tite).

30. Paul's Phaeton

In every field of endeavor, be it a business or an organization or a hobby, there are men or women who become identified with the endeavor so closely as to be downright synonymous with it. Sir Edmund Hillary is so connected with mountaineering. Beverly Rae Kimes will always be associated with the history of classic cars and the era that gave birth to them. The world of restoration and conservation of V-16 Cadillacs is no different. The late Jim Pearson, known to the hobby as "Cadillac Jim" (and described more fully elsewhere in these pages), comes to mind.

Paul Schinnerer of Long Beach, California, has been driving, fixing, acquiring, selling showing and otherwise enjoying V-16 Cadillacs for longer than I've been alive. He has owned seven V-16s, as well as assorted other vintage Cadillacs. His first was a 1940 V-8 convertible coupe that he treated himself to when he returned home after serving in the Navy during World War II. Through the years, he has become extremely well acquainted with these venerable machines, and other owners turn to him regularly for advice and help with their own projects. He was a founding member of the Southern California regional chapter of the Cadillac-LaSalle Club and he has been active in other clubs. His maroon 1930 V-16 all-weather phaeton with dark maroon fenders (featured in the previous chapter) that his brother first bought in the late 1940s has paraded movie stars and has graced car shows and other events for decades. What he doesn't know about V-16s probably isn't worth knowing.

Paul's "other" V-16 is a Series 4260 sport phaeton that he calls "the forty-year project."

Work in progress. Still waiting for its upholstery and convertible top, the V-16 sport phaeton draws attention at a car show. Without the spare tire, the flowing lines of the front fender and the body on this body style are even more evident. Openings for the front and rear seating areas are reminiscent of early open-cockpit aircraft (courtesy Paul Schinnerer).

He bought it in 1968 and has been working on it ever since. As these words are written, he has the car running and reassembled, but it still needs to have the seats rebuilt, the upholstery replaced, some of the chrome parts replated and the wire wheels re-shod.

The sport phaeton is one of the flashiest and most desirable of the V-16 body styles. It was a little bit uncivilized and a bit of a throwback to earlier days, not having roll-up windows. In the event of bad weather, either the car stayed in the garage, or the driver brought out and installed side curtains that never seemed to completely shut out the elements. A sudden storm could drench the passengers before the weatherproofing process could be accomplished. But there was nothing better for a sunny afternoon drive with friends. The rear seat occupants could amuse themselves with a duplicate speedometer and a chronometer built into the back of the front seat. And everyone could enjoy the outdoors and something akin to the sensation of flying.

In 1935, a certain green Cadillac V-16 sport phaeton found its way to a used car lot in West Hollywood, California, priced at $150. The proprietor claimed that the car had been the property of movie star (and later World War II naval officer and humanitarian) Douglas Fairbanks, Jr., and a young lad still in high school fell in love with it. (In high school, I would have cheerfully given my eye teeth to purchase a working V-16 Cadillac for $150. But let's return to our story.) Let's hear Mr. G. Thatcher Darwin (when he was retired and living in Laguna Hills, California) tell the story in his own way.

> As nearly as I can recall, I bought the phaeton in 1935. At that time, big cars were a drug on the used car market. That was before the "previously-owned" euphemism and long before they had acquired "collector" status. My late '20s edition of the Pacific Coast Red Book, a forerunner of

Douglas Fairbanks, Jr., and his V-16 Sport Phaeton. When Thatcher Darwin bought his car, the salesman said it had belonged to the movie star. That may have been the case, but the car Mr. Fairbanks is posing with has chrome-plated hood vent doors and stainless steel wheel spokes that don't seem to be present in the old photo of Thatcher Darwin's car (courtesy Roy Schneider).

the Kelley Blue Book, shows that Cadillacs, Packards, and Lincolns lost more than half their value in the first year!

Those of my fellow High School students who could afford cars at all were attracted to Model A Ford Roadsters and the '32 Ford V-8 was the ideal that most of them dreamed of. To me this seemed a false economy. Used big cars cost less, were faster, more comfortable, reliable and with gasoline selling for as little as two gallons for a quarter (!) their higher fuel consumption was not a major problem. My after-school job had allowed me to buy a 314 (1927) Cadillac phaeton, replaced later with a 341 (1929) Cadillac sedan.

My father was an attorney with Farmers Insurance—then only a couple of years old—and, as he could conveniently commute to his downtown office by Pacific Electric trolley, my Cadillacs were, in fact, our family cars.

When I spotted the green V-16 phaeton on a lot in West Hollywood, it was love at first sight; I simply had to have it! The dealer told me that Douglas Fairbanks, Jr. had been its original owner—plausible, although I never had reason to verify the claim. The details of how I negotiated to buy it, how I raised the money and how long it took to consummate the deal are no longer clear in my mind. As best I can recall, the price was $150—an absurd figure for us to contemplate now but consistent with the big-car market at the time!

While my father was comfortable with my owning the V-8 sedan, I knew he would balk and [sic] my owning *two* Cadillacs, so my immediate problem was to keep the whole project under wraps. For some weeks, I parked the phaeton on the street several blocks from home. I would leave for school in the '29 V-8, drive to where I had stashed the phaeton, switch cars, then on to Hollywood High! At a class reunion fifty years later, there were schoolmates who had long-forgotten my name but I was recognized as the "guy who had the V-16 Cadillac!" It was my sole claim to celebrity! Again, I'm unclear about the details but eventually the phaeton seeped into my father's awareness and I could bring it home.

For the next several years the car served uneventfully except for one memorable incident. I was taking my mother and my aunt on a sight-seeing trip up nearby Mt. Wilson. It was a warm day. We had the top down and, on the steady grades up the mountain, the engine began to overheat. By the time we reached a spot where I could turn off the road, strange noises were coming from under the hood and the temp gauge needle was off the dial! I walked around to the front and, without thinking, grasped the flying lady and gave her a half turn. Instantly, a column of boiling, muddy water blew the radiator cap out of my hand and shot high into the air! In a flash, my mother was out the passenger side door and my aunt, who was riding in the back, hit the folded top with one step; her second was to the trunk rack and her third was on the ground! I had never seen two dignified ladies move with such athleticism! It was an amusing family story told for many years after!

Just before the war, I was married and my bride and I moved to an apartment in Westwood Village. I became part of a three-man car pool from there to the Douglas Aircraft plant in Long Beach and on my days to drive, my companions referred to the Cadillac either as the "Fresh-Air Special" or the "Pneumonia Express," depending on the weather.

Some time after the war, Colonel George Van Deusen found out I had the car and was anxious to buy it. He was the Commanding Officer of the Air Force Base in Tucson and would frequently phone or fly up in a T-33 to persuade me to sell it. This went on for several weeks. I didn't want to sell it and tried gracefully to turn him off but he was very determined and apparently assumed I was just holding out for a higher price The matter came to a head one night when he arrived at my door, unannounced, and said, "Look—let's stop fooling around—here's a check that I've signed but left the amount blank. Write in whatever amount would satisfy you!"

Well! I had never faced such a challenge before and for a moment I was completely nonplussed! Then I realized that this was an opportunity to get him off my back for good. I took the check and, after some quick calculation, thought of a figure, then doubled it and handed the check back. I was sure this would end his interest in the car. He just looked at it and said, "When can I pick up the pink slip?"

Immediately I regretted having fallen into his trap but having accepted his challenge, it would have been too embarrassing to back out. In any case, the amount was far above the car's market value at the time. My trusty V-16 phaeton and I had come to the parting of ways!

I should explain that, somewhere along the road, I had cut two inches from the top of the windshield and lowered the rear two inches by installing blocks between the springs and axle housings. At the time, I was unconcerned with preserving the car's original configuration—I just thought the changes made it look better!

Fast-forward to the summer of 1968. Paul Schinnerer noticed an ad in the back of the July issue of *The Self-Starter*, the monthly newsletter of the Cadillac-LaSalle Club. It was actually two ads placed by the same person.

> *1931* Cadillac Phaeton body mounted on 1939 V-16 chassis running gear and motor. Over drive is installed behind stock transmission. 8.20 × 16 wide white walls with less than 2,000 miles. Also....

> *1931* V-16 chassis for above body, less engine, hood and front fenders. Radiator and grill are good. Six wheels and tires. 1931 V-16 starter, generator and distributor present and good. Large wooden trailer body on 1931 chassis. Not used since 1955. George H. Van Deusen, USAF, 210 Eureka, Peterson Field, Colorado, 80912 All items are in N.H.

Not used since 1955. It seems the colonel didn't use the sport phaeton he bought from Mr. Darwin for long. Colonel Van Deusen was, at one point, the head of North American air defense. He was something of a hot rodder, and pictures taken when he owned the Cadillac show smaller headlights in place of the iconic thirteen-inch V-16 lights, and 16-inch wire wheels in place of the nineteen-inch stock wheels. And in any event, he put the phaeton's body onto a late-series V-16 chassis (how strange that must have looked!) and converted the 1931 chassis into a trailer. The ad listed some missing major parts (which implied, of course,

On the flightline. Before Col. Van Deusen undertook massive modifications to the car, he took this shot in the midst of Army Air Corps. P-51 Mustang fighter planes. Note that the enormous 1930–31 V-16 headlights have been replaced by smaller (sealed beam?) units (courtesy Paul Schinnerer).

that various other parts would be absent, as well). But Paul Schinnerer had accumulated an assortment of V-16 parts, including front fenders, running boards, headlights and three engines. If he answered the ad, he was certain that the project he would be undertaking would be more manageable than his all-weather phaeton (that car had been rolled and wrecked before his brother acquired it).

Paul sent away for pictures and was pleased with what he saw. He found out that the trailer body contained two Rolls-Royce Merlin engines (manufactured under license by Packard) for P-51 Mustang fighter planes. The cost of purchasing the lot and for shipping from New Hampshire to California was $6,000. That was more than the factory price for a new 1968 Cadillac Sedan De Ville, and where the money would come from was a good question.

Where Mr. Schinnerer worked as an electronic technician, the newly-hired shop manager quickly lent him the money. His name was Jack Howard, and he was the grandson of Charles Howard, the pioneer West Coast Buick distributor who had owned the illustrious racehorse Seabiscuit. Charles Howard was also the man who took a new Cadillac V-16 roadster to the Murphy Body Company and had them fashion a custom phaeton body for it (not long ago, that car sold for the very respectable price of $1,056,000).

Paul Schinnerer sold off the aircraft engines to Norm Taunton of Galt, California. Mr. Taunton (who appears elsewhere in these pages) had a friend with a P-51 Mustang who was happy to obtain spares for his airplane. Then Mr. Schinnerer divested himself of the 1939 V-16 parts and returned the '31 body to its chassis. The restoration thus begun continues today.

Thatcher Darwin's account continues:

Fast forward now to sometime around the middle of 2004.

I ran across a photo in the *Los Angeles Times* of a lovely, completely restored V-16 Convertible Sedan along with its owner a Long Beach resident. I was reminded that somewhere I still had a few V-16 parts left and, thinking that they might be of use to the owner, I called the *Times* in an effort to contact him. It was the paper's policy, of course, not to give out addresses or phone numbers but they agreed to give him my number so he could contact me if he chose. Soon I got a phone call that began my warm friendship with Paul Schinnerer.

Fairly early in our exchange of e-mails and phone conversations, I learned that Paul was restoring a second Cadillac V-16—a Sport Phaeton! My antenna went up about ten feet and, after further correspondence, I asked the sixty-four-dollar question. Did his phaeton have a lowered windshield and blocks under the rear axle housings? BINGO! I had found my old car!

Paul was in contact with Mr. Darwin many times after that initial phone conversation, and in 2009, he succeeded in getting the former owner to come by and see the car. Upon seeing his old sport phaeton for the first time in 57 years, Mr. Darwin just stood there for a long while, saying "Oh ..." In trade for a large collection of spare parts that Mr. Darwin had kept from when he owned the Cadillac, all he asked was the promise of a chance to drive the car, once its restoration was complete. As Mr. Darwin tells it:

Paul has offered me a ride in my old car when the restoration is complete but I've told him, "No!— On that momentous day, I intend to drive it!"

Sadly, G. Thatcher Darwin passed away in 2010, before the completion of the sport phaeton's restoration. He was a fine fellow and will be missed.

It seems very likely that Douglas Fairbanks, Jr., was, in fact, the original owner of the sport phaeton. The build sheet shows that it was shipped new to the Don Lee Cadillac

Two owners meet. At the wheel, G. Thatcher Darwin, who bought the Cadillac V-16 sport phaeton for $150 in 1935 from a used car lot in West Hollywood. Standing next to the car, Paul Schinnerer, who bought the car, a trailer and two Merlin aircraft engines in 1968, and who has been restoring the Cadillac ever since (courtesy Paul Schinnerer).

dealership in Los Angeles on July 19, 1930. (Strictly speaking, it's a 1930 model, although the 1930 and 1931 Cadillac V-16s are almost completely indistinguishable.) And there is a photograph of Mr. Fairbanks standing next to a V-16 of exactly the same body style, with his right foot on the running board and his hand on the inside door handle. Mr. Darwin believed that the photograph confirms what was told to him when he first bought the car at that West Hollywood used car lot in 1935. But definitively documenting celebrity provenance is a tricky thing at best, and this case may never be pinned down with absolute certainty.

Meanwhile Paul Schinnerer continues his work bringing this magnificent Cadillac back to its proper glory.

---

31. Senator Glass's Limousine

There is a mystery photograph I have wondered about for over 40 years. I first saw it in a book I borrowed from the Albuquerque Public Library in 1966 when I was 14. The book was *Famous Old Cars*, by veteran boat racer, auto enthusiast and writer Hank Wieand

Senator Glass's 1930 Cadillac V-16. This photograph was likely taken during the 1950s. It appeared in a book about old cars in 1957 where it was described as showing Senator Carter Glass's V-16 limousine, without identifying the man standing next to the car (author's collection).

As a public servant. This photograph was taken between 1918 and 1920, when Carter Glass served as Secretary of the Treasury under President Woodrow Wilson. In 1920 he would be appointed to the United States Senate.

Bowman, and I hadn't seen it since. But I remembered the photograph because it showed a V-16 Cadillac limousine, and that was the kind of car I had decided was the best car in the world to have.

The Cadillac in the photo is a Series 4375 seven-passenger limousine, of which 438 were built. It has fancy octagonal rearview mirrors mounted on the spare tires. Many of these elegant and comfortable cars failed to survive the wartime scrap drives, obsolescence, neglect and the depredations of the elements. This one made it at least as far as the mid–century year in what looks like very good shape. One of the horn trumpets is a little cockeyed. And someone has added an anachronistic bumper guard to the front ensemble. The heron radiator ornament seems to have had its wings clipped, but otherwise, everything appears to be in order.

The caption in the book identified the car in the photo as follows: "V-16 Limousine was custom finished for the late Senator Glass of Virginia, at a reported $14,000. Photo courtesy H.D. Chisholm." That could only be Senator Carter Glass, co-sponsor of the Glass-Steagal Act, the depression-era legislation that separated investment banking (the sale of stocks, bonds and mutual funds) from commercial banking (loans, savings and checking accounts). That separation has largely broken down today, but in the 1930s it was a big deal. Senator Glass began his career as a newspaperman, editing a paper in his native Lynchburg, Virginia. He entered the United States Congress as a representative, appointed to complete the term of a deceased member, and he was re-elected eight times. He spent two years as Secretary of the Treasury under President Woodrow Wilson before being asked to fill a vacant Senate seat, where he served from 1920 until his death in 1946.

The car in the photo carries a 1950 North Carolina license plate. The gentleman with his foot on the running board is certainly not Senator Glass. Perhaps he is H.D. Chisholm, but no one seems to know for sure who he is. He wasn't identified in the book, and the vendor from whom I purchased a print of the photograph had no information about him either. The vendor had received his copy of the photo with a large collection of material, and on the back of the picture was handwritten "Senator Glass."

I've often wondered what became of Senator Glass's limousine. If it survived, and the engine number could be determined, a look at the build sheet might provide some interesting information about the car and its history. Maybe there are relatives of the senator in Lynchburg who recall his fancy Cadillac (or who have pictures or other references to it). It's another one of those tantalizing bits of stories left behind by the big old classic cars that once roamed the land in impressive numbers.

32. Bull

Depending on which source you consult, you will find that movie actor Richard Arlen was born either Sylvanus Richard Van Mattimore or Cornelius Richard Van Mattimore. During World War I he served with the Royal Canadian Flying Corps as a pilot, ferrying planes to the front, but he didn't see combat. After the war he held several jobs before moving to Los Angeles and working as a motorcycle messenger. The tale that is told in various forms is that he was injured in a wreck outside one of the major movie studios and was given a first acting job on the basis of his good looks, or because a director felt sorry for him. In any event, he became a Paramount Studios regular and something of a star in the silent films of the 1920s. When the talkies replaced silent motion pictures, Richard Arlen was one of the fortunate actors to make the transition. He would go on to perform in dozens of feature films from the '20s into the 1970s, but he is probably best remembered for his role as a pilot in the William Wellman picture *Wings*, which won the Best Picture *Oscar* at the first-ever Academy Awards presentation, May 16, 1929.

On June 6, 1930, the Cadillac Motor Car Company shipped a Series 4260 V-16 sport phaeton to the Don Lee dealership in Los Angeles for purchase by Richard Arlen. Here again, legend steps in to inform us that Mr. Arlen arrived at the dealership to find the irrepressible Mae West sitting in the car, saying that if he didn't buy it she would. He bought the phaeton and used it for a number of years.

According to the "build sheet" for Mr. Arlen's Cadillac, it came with the body painted a color called "pastel," while the fenders, the chassis and the beltline molding around the car were "talina brown." A "red bank red" pinstripe added a jaunty flair. Fender-mounted spare tires were the only optional equipment ordered from the factory, but the rear axle ratio that was specified (4.75:1) was one that Cadillac recommended for cars likely to be driven in hilly areas.

As the 1930s progressed, Richard Arlen's career failed to take off as he might have hoped. In 1935 he left Paramount and sought performing work on his own. In 1939 he signed on with Universal Studios to do action pictures, and in 1941 he returned to Paramount and appeared in adventure films for its Pine-Thomas unit. In the late 1930s, the V-16 sport phaeton was sold and came into the possession of a man named Brinkerhof in Bishop, California.

Mr. Brinkerhof appears to have owned the car for something over twenty years, keeping it in a garage most of the time and bringing it out for the town's annual Fourth of July parade. At some point a gentleman who had just been to Bishop, California, stopped in at the Picture Car Company and spoke with its owner and operator Jim Brucker. Mr. Brucker had started the Picture Car Company as a stable of vintage automobiles and other vehicles available for rental to the movie studios for use in pictures set in earlier decades of the twentieth century. The visitor told Mr. Brucker about having recently ridden in a 1930 Cadillac in Bishop, but he couldn't remember the address of the owner. With the help of a call to directory assistance, Mr. Brucker was able to find his way to the car in question, strike a deal with the owner and place a deposit on it. Mr. Brucker and his son Jim Jr. returned in a few days with the balance

Ready to tour. Another prized Cadillac accessory is the "low boy" trunk mounted to the car's luggage rack by means of special hook clamps. The trunks were frequently sold with fitted suitcases (typically two or more flat cases and a hatbox). The trunks are hard to find today—the suitcases even harder (courtesy Dr. Edward Dauer).

of the purchase price. They were just in time, as another collector was on the phone trying to buy the car for a higher price. But since the Bruckers were there, the owner agreed to sell to them. Jim Jr. drove the Cadillac the 280 miles back home. He was just a teenager at the time and it was a big deal to him.

The first motion picture that the V-16 phaeton was used for was *The Carpetbaggers*, a 1964 release based on the 1961 Harold Robbins novel of the same name. Paramount is said to have paid $4,500 (not far from the base price of a new 1963 Cadillac) to have the car modified with "unborn calfskin" upholstery and boot for the folding top, a white paint job, western revolvers for door handles, a bucking horse for a radiator mascot, and a big set of steer horns mounted to the front of the radiator. In the movie script, the car would be owned by a character named Nevada Smith, a former gunslinger turned cowboy star played by Alan Ladd. The "westernized" Cadillac would only be on screen for a few moments, but it picked up the nickname "Bull," and the name stuck.

In the 1970s, the car was auctioned and made its way through a number of owners including "Cadillac Jim" Pearson. Donald E. Mayoras bought the car in 1985 and decided on a full restoration, entrusting the task to Stone Barn Automobile Restoration in Vienna, New Jersey. The leather interior was re-done by Sharpe Brothers Automobile Upholstery in Elyria, Ohio, and completed in 1992. The car is now a bright red with tan leather upholstery and light beige top material. Subsequent to its restoration, Bull won top honors with the

On the set. Alan Ladd poses for a publicity photo with the 1930 Cadillac V-16 sport phaeton on the Paramount studio back lot. Both actor and automobile are in costume for the movie. Steer horns, six-gun door handles and other western embellishments to the Cadillac are visible (courtesy Roy Schneider).

Bull as it is today. The 1930 V-16 Sport phaeton is now part of a private museum in Florida. Restored to a "T," the car carries noteworthy Cadillac accessories: metal spare-tire covers with integral rearview mirrors; "Pilot Ray" driving lights that pivot with the front wheels; and twin cowl-mounted spotlights (courtesy Dr. Edward Dauer).

Antique Automobile Club of America, the Classic Car Club of America and other organizations, and at the prestigious Pebble Beach Concours d'Elegance.

Today, Bull is a featured exhibit at the private Dauer Museum of Classic Cars in Sunrise, Florida. Their website is www.dauerclassiccars.com.

33. Mogul Mobiles

When a fine motor car is delivered to an important or well-known purchaser, there is a certain newsworthiness to the event, and both the car dealer and the celebrity owner can get some publicity "mileage" out of the occasion. Not ignorant of this phenomenon by any means was Don Lee, who served as Cadillac's exclusive sales agent for the State of California from 1919 until he died of a heart attack in 1934 and his business empire (which by then included custom coachbuilding and radio stations) passed on to his son Tommy. During Don Lee's tenure, when one of his dealerships sold a new Cadillac to a movie star or other notable, a photographer would be on hand for the delivery to record the event. This photograph is from just such an occasion.

The cars are 1930 Cadillac V-16s. On the left is a Series 4335 convertible coupe, a two-passenger car with room in the rumble seat for two additional folks who like fresh air. Next to it is a Series 4130 Madame X Imperial sedan, and an early one, too, since it has the nearly upright, split windshield, instead of the one-piece, dramatically raked windshield. Madame X cars had enhanced styling features and cost $1,000 more than their non–Madame X counterparts. The limousine has two-sided whitewall tires, while the convertible coupe's tires are blackwalls, and the unusual matching ornaments on the radiator caps were not among the optional items offered by Cadillac. To accommodate the desire of many customers to personalize their cars, Don Lee displayed and offered for sale many alternative radiator ornaments at his Los Angeles location.

The lady is Frances Marion, a prolific screenwriter and author who worked as a war correspondent in World War II. Born Marion Benson Owens, she married four times, and the man standing next to her was her last husband. By the time this photo was taken, she had been writing for important motion pictures that featured well-known actors for nearly two decades. She would keep working in the movie industry until after World War II, receiving two Academy Awards. Her later life activities included writing stage plays and novels. She had two sons with her third husband (1920s cowboy star Fred C. Thomson, who died unexpectedly in 1928), and she passed away in 1973 at the age of 84.

The gentleman has a sadder story. George W. Hill was born in Kansas in 1895. As a young teenager, he became a stagehand for pioneering movie director D.W. Griffith and developed into a talented cinematographer and director. He directed top-ranked stars and his films were highly regarded. Frances Marion and George Hill were married in 1930, but

Happy Birthday. Screenwriter Frances Marion and MGM director George Hill pose for the camera with their respective 1930 V-16 Cadillacs. He gave her the limousine and she gave him the convertible coupe. Note the matching accessory radiator mascots (author's collection).

Same car, a little later. This car is the same one George Hill stood next to. The license plate is different, and the tires show worn treads and scuffed sidewalls. But the same pointy-winged ornament sits atop the radiator and the chromed hood vents and unique spare tire covers match those on the car in the other photograph. The car is parked in front of a home that still stands, in much the same condition today (author's collection).

their marriage only lasted about three years, ending in divorce. Mr. Hill was seriously injured in an automobile accident, and not long afterwards (some think because of his injuries) he took his own life at his Venice Beach home in August 1934.

This elegantly composed shot catches the newlyweds in a happy moment in 1930. The story that accompanies the photograph is that she presented the convertible coupe to him as a birthday gift, and that a few days earlier, he had given her the limousine for her own birthday. Perhaps that's the title to the convertible coupe that she's handing to him. The exact details may have been a bit different, as her birthday is recorded as November 18, and his as April 25. Perhaps one of the cars was actually a wedding gift, and the other a birthday present. In any event, it seems clear that these are "his and hers" love tokens as only the Hollywood elite had the means and the inclination to exchange.

Curiously, Frances Marion's V-16 limousine shows up in another photo from about this time, in front of a house in Beverly Hills, with another gentleman standing next to the car and a 3- or 4-year-old boy sitting on the spare tire.

34. A Million-Dollar Cadillac

In 1961, Norman Taunton of Galt, California, was newly married, and he and his bride were taking their honeymoon, traveling in a 1929 Ford Model A roadster. When they got to San Francisco, the Tauntons purchased an unusual 1930 Cadillac V-16. The car had been sold new through the Don Lee Cadillac agency in San Francisco and had left the factory as a roadster. Cadillac was very wary about allowing anyone other than the Fleetwood Body Company to design and build bodies for the V-16 chassis. The factory wanted to keep control of the build quality, image and public impression of the epitome of General Motors Corporation's entire product line. Moreover, the many and varied offerings in the Fleetwood catalog, combined with the willingness to make changes to suit the owner's tastes, should, as the GM executives saw things, obviate the need to use an outside coachbuilder.

In 1930, Mr. Charles S. Howard, who owned the famous racehorse Seabiscuit, was the California distributor for Buick. He wanted a Cadillac V-16, but he wanted to have it his way. Instead of trying to convince Cadillac to part with a bare chassis that he could take to a custom body maker, he simply ordered the least expensive model in the lineup (a Series 4302 roadster) and when the car was delivered, he took it to the Walter M. Murphy Company of Pasadena, California.

The Murphy company built high-quality custom bodies on a wide range of chassis, including nearly a quarter of all the Duesenberg J's and their supercharged variants. It was formed in 1920 by the nephew of William H. Murphy, who in 1902 had brought Henry Martyn Leland in to appraise the assets of the failing Henry Ford Company, of which William Murphy was a director. Mr. Leland persuaded the board not to close the company but to produce cars with a Leland-built engine. The company name was changed to the Cadillac Automobile Company and Mr. Leland and his son became president and vice-president. So, by choosing the Walter M. Murphy Company to build a body for his new car, Mr. Howard was, in a sense, keeping it in the family.

The car that Murphy built for Mr. Howard was a distinctive four-door convertible, a style known at the time as an "all-weather phaeton." It had a flat windshield with a 22-degree rearward slant, and unusually slender (for the time) windshield pillars and posts between the side windows. The Murphy Company had developed a version of the "Clear Vision" system that Swiss coachbuilder Georges Gangloff had originated. Sturdy aluminum forgings replaced the customary wood-based, metal-covered pillars, and allowed the structural supports for the window glass and roof to all but disappear, in terms of obstructing the driver's range of vision. On an open car, the visual effect of lightness and grace was even more pronounced.

Mr. Taunton had seen an ad in the *San Francisco Chronicle* for the all-weather phaeton. The ad indicated that the car could be seen at the Cadillac agency in the Stonestown neighborhood of San Francisco (Fazackerly Cadillac, later replaced by a pet superstore). Mr. Bob Gillespie was in the midst of a divorce, and he was offering for sale the Murphy-bodied V-16 Cadillac, an Alfa Romeo sports car and a small airplane, each of which could be had for $3,000. Mr. Taunton saw the Cadillac in the basement of the Fazackerly dealership, and decided right away that he had to have it. He didn't care for the Alfa and he knew nothing about airplanes. The Tauntons quickly arranged to borrow the necessary funds and they bought the V-16.

Mr. Taunton states that the car was in excellent shape when he acquired it. "You wouldn't believe," he says, "how nicely the doors shut." The paint was not the greatest—the dark green finish had some nicks and scrapes—but the upholstery, and the car generally, were entirely sound. Even with an all-aluminum body, the big Cadillac weighed 6,200 pounds. His purchase of this particular car caused some consternation among the West Coast car collector community. It seems that the man in charge of the classified ads in the *Chronicle* at that time was accustomed to tipping off some of his acquaintances ahead of time when interesting cars were about to be advertised in the paper. When this particular interesting car came on the market, that fellow was on vacation, and the person who substituted for him simply put the ad in the paper and that was that. Mr. Taunton saw it and bought the car before the folks who had been waiting for it to be offered. There were some hard feelings for a while afterward.

Even in the early 1960s, classic car owners were faced with the same dilemma posed today by a well-preserved motor car—leave it the way it is (the way the factory made it, give or take what the years have done), or undertake a restoration (and to one extent or another, remanufacture the car). For Mr. Taunton, events forced the issue. A drunk taxicab driver ran a red light just as the custom V-16 was passing, and the cab hit the Cadillac's right side, damaging the rear fender and the running board. As long as bodywork and painting were now unavoidable, Mr. Taunton decided to do the whole car.

Mr. Taunton removed the dark green paint (which was not the original color) and he found underneath it a cream color for the body with lilac fenders. He stripped and sandblasted the frame, treated it to prevent rust, and repainted it. The body was amazingly sound with no rust whatsoever. An interesting and unique feature was the gearshift knob, which was fashioned out of mother-of-pearl. Jack Nethercutt of the Merle Norman cosmetics company offered to buy that knob from Mr. Taunton on several occasions.

At some point, the Cadillac had received larger wheels to accept 20-inch tires, instead of the stock 7.00" × 19" tires. Mr. Taunton wanted to run 7.50" × 19" tires (in a midyear change, Cadillac had switched from 7.00" to 7.50" tire width, and had changed the width of the wheel rims to match). He also wanted to add the stainless steel spokes that were offered as an option in 1930. He was able to obtain a set of wheels with the correct 19-inch diameter, but they had the narrow rims. He removed the spokes and then split the rims, welding in a ⅝-inch piece to widen them for the wider tires. Then he sought the assistance of Mr. I.E. Burnside in Stockton, California, who had worked for the Murphy company, to help with the fabrication of stainless steel spokes for the six wire wheels, and "lacing" or attaching the spokes to the hubs and rims. They took the assembled wheels to a sports car garage in Sacramento to be properly trued up and balanced.

Mr. Burnside was an older man who still had some of the specialized tools he had used when he was employed by Murphy, such as the hammer that was used to make the distinctive "peened" surface finish on the outside door handles. Mr. Taunton recalls a tale of Mr. Burnside saving the Murphy factory from burning to the ground. Leaving work late one evening, he had noticed some liquid running off the curb and into the gutter. Curious, he smelled the stuff and found it was gasoline. He called the fire department, and they determined that a large tank in the building had begun leaking a considerable amount of flammable material. The problem was rectified and disaster was averted.

Mr. Taunton sold the Murphy-bodied Cadillac in 1968 to friends in Santa Barbara. The mother-of-pearl gear shift knob seems to have disappeared from the car some time afterwards. Jimmy Brucker acquired and intended to restore the car, but never got around to beginning the process during the ten years he owned it. He sold it to another California collector, who undertook and completed the restoration, and also showed the car.

As restored, the car was red and maroon with a tan convertible top. Mr. Taunton describes it as a high quality restoration. Around 1985, it was sold to John Mozart, who kept the car and made small improvements until 1991, when he sold it to Jim King of Berkley, Massachusetts. Three years later, it was sold to John J. McMullen.

Mr. McMullen repainted the car a combination of maroon and gloss black, and extensively refreshed the older restoration. He showed the car at the most prestigious concours events, and it took consistently high awards. In June of 2007, Mr. McMullen placed a selection of his cars up for auction with RM Auctions, Inc. This car, lot number 238, brought the stunning price of $1,056,000.

The informative description provided by RM for the auction bidders includes the ownership history and a listing of the impressive honors the car has reaped at exclusive shows. It also reveals that shortly before he died, Mr. Franklin Q. Hershey, one of Murphy's best designers, was able to see the car again at the 1997 Pebble Beach Concours d'Elegance (where the car was awarded first place in its class). When Pebble Beach featured Cadillac V-16s in August, 2008 the current owner (Mr. Paul E. Andrews, Jr., of Fort Worth, Texas) showed the sleek Murphy-bodied phaeton amid a field that included, among others, a Rollston-bodied 1930 roadster, a 1938 fastback limousine built for then-president of Cadillac William Knudsen, and Cecil B. DeMille's own 1930 town car.

Mr. Taunton told me that he regrets having decided to take the Cadillac apart to make it into a high-point car. He also disclosed that it once had small, removable rear quarter windows that no longer appear to be with the car, judging from the recent photographs. These would have allowed the car to look like a traditional touring car or phaeton, while main-

The Murphy-bodied 1930 Cadillac V-16 convertible sedan. This is the car after its first restoration, painted two red shades. Previous owner Norm Taunton stated that there were removable rear quarter windows, and these seem to have parted company with the car over the years (courtesy John Mozart).

In its present plumage at the Pebble Beach Concours d'Elegance. The car now sports a red and black combination, and fillers using top material have been fashioned to fill the rear quarter window apertures (courtesy Joseph Scott).

taining the weatherproof qualities of a car with roll-up windows. It would be interesting to know what became of those items that were properly part of the Murphy design.

Many of the big classics have gone through wild and wide variations in terms of what people paid for them at different times. During the '40s and '50s, they were nearly all available for very little money, because they were almost universally considered impractical, out-of-date and superfluous. This Cadillac is certainly an example of that price volatility, and if there have been other cars of its make for which higher prices have been paid, they are few indeed.

35. Rollston Convertible Coupe

When I joined the Cadillac-LaSalle Club in the summer of 1968, I received the current issue of the club's monthly newsletter, *The Self-Starter*. Named after part of the reason for Cadillac's second award of the Dewar Trophy by the Royal Automobile Club of Great Britain, the newsletter consisted of twenty pages stapled at the corner and punched on the side for filing in a ring binder. It was filled with features, letters and ads for parts or whole cars. The June 1968 number filled one page with a photograph of a somewhat battered 1930 Cadillac V-16 convertible coupe with unusual fenders, windows and top. Someone had rolled the car down a driveway just to the street, clearly for the purpose of taking its picture. The three-quarter front elevation viewpoint emphasized the unique attributes of this particular Cadillac. And the tire tracks in the soft ground, the bare branches of the background trees and the snow remaining on the ground were in stark contrast to the warm summer weather I was experiencing at the time in Albuquerque.

Unlike the stock 1930 Cadillac configuration, the fenders of the car in the picture were partially skirted, a treatment that Cadillac didn't employ until the 1933 model year. The windshield was seriously chopped, leaning back farther than on any body style that the factory offered in 1930. The windshield glass was narrower, top to bottom, than the stock dimensions.

Cadillac offered two convertible coupe body styles in the V-16 line that seated two passengers with rumble seat accommodations for two more. One style (Series 4335) had a nearly upright windshield, split vertically at the center of the cowl and gently V'd. The other style (Series 4235) had a single-pane windshield with a slight rake to it. The side windows on each of these body styles had vertical rear edges, while the side windows on the car in the photograph were trapezoidal—the forward edges sloped rearward, while the back edges sloped forward.

The photo in the newsletter was accompanied by a plea for information about the car:

A MYSTERY CAR This is a picture of what appears to be a 1930–31 V-16 customized and slightly botched convertible coupe. We do not know who took the picture, who the owner is, or who did the customizing—particularly the Duesenberg-like topwork. Do you? Have you ever seen or heard of the car before? Can you add any information or clues to this mystery???? Please write your editor if you can tell us anything about this car.

The condition of the convertible coupe was disheveled, at best. The headlights, horns, hubcaps, parking lights and taillights were all missing, as were the radiator stone guard, the cover for the battery box, the spare tire and the handle for the golf bag compartment. The right front fender had been buckled over the wheel, and the paint (as well as could be determined from the low-resolution black-and-white photograph) was rubbed thin, down to bare metal in some spots. The door handle drooped at a 45-degree angle and the top fabric was lumpy and possibly torn. This once-racy damsel really needed some intense T.L.C.

As one who had recently discovered and fallen in love with the Cadillac V-16 motor cars, I found this photo intriguing, evocative and captivating. What I wanted most of all was to find a Cadillac V-16 for sale whose condition was rough enough to be affordable, but good enough to be restorable with the modest resources I had available. That was a tall order, as there just weren't many V-16s of any stripe in or near Albuquerque, and the prices of these big classics had already begun to move smartly upwards. The same June 1968 *Self-Starter* I was reading contained an advertisement for a 1930 V-16 dual windshield phaeton that had just undergone a complete restoration and had never been shown. The asking price was $25,000. The price of my parents' recently-acquired 4-bedroom house had been only $10,000 more than that, so a restored car was out of the question. An unrestored car, say, one like the unusual convertible coupe in the photo—well, that just might work. So I dreamed.

When the September issue of *The Self-Starter* arrived in the mail, it contained an answer to the editor's plea for information on the mystery car. Peter Hinrichs of Mequon, Wisconsin, had submitted the following:

In paging through the June issue of the Self Starter, I was quite surprised to come across a picture of my 1931 Cadillac V-16 Convertible Coupe on page 14. As long as the car was called a MYSTERY I would like to clear that mystery up.

I had always wanted a 1930 or 31 V-16 so when one was advertised in Chicago, I grabbed it.

Somewhat the worse for wear. An exquisite and unique custom-bodied Cadillac V-16 had sunk into obscurity when this photo was taken. But an avid Cadillac enthusiast undertook to restore it and discovered its distinguished design heritage (courtesy Bortz Auto Collection).

Now the fun began. Of course we had to find out who the body builder was to restore it. Should we restore it the way it was or should we do it like the original Cadillac appeared in 1931.

After many months of getting nowhere, even with the Cadillac Motor Division, we decided to start the restoration and do it as it was. Incidentally, we could only find a Fleetwood tag on the car but we knew from close inspection that the car was done after it was delivered by a reputable custom coach builder.

To say the least, it was quite a relief when we finally came upon the solution. In disassembling the auto we took off the bronze cast windshield and low and behold after close inspection we found the name ROLLSTON July 1932 stamped on the bottom side of it.

The car is now being completely restored by Dick Braund in Elroy, Wisc. He has done a lot of work for Bill Harrah in Reno. When done it will be a perfect example of a one of a kind (I hope) V-16 Convertible Coupe by Rollston.

I was glad that the car was being properly looked after and not neglected, but I was disappointed that the possibility (however slim and outlandish) that I might conceivably have been able to acquire that car had just dried up. Life is not always fair.

Just a few years ago, while exploring the World Wide Web, I came across photos of a V-16 Cadillac that looked strangely familiar, and upon closer examination, it was clear that they depicted the restored incarnation of the shabby specimen I had seen in the club newsletter years before. It was poised on a show field with a light and dark green color scheme (see photograph in color section), and the racy lines that Rollston craftsmen had added to a stock Cadillac gave it a feline grace and lightness uncommon in a 6,000 pound automobile.

After the 2008 Pebble Beach Concours d'Elegance, I found out that a successful businessman in Nevada was listed as the present owner of the Rollston-bodied V-16. He acquired it from John Mozart (a noted collector who has owned another custom-bodied V-16, the Murphy-bodied convertible sedan that Charles Howard, owner of the legendary racehorse Seabiscuit, commissioned on a V-16 roadster). Mr. Mozart had acquired it from the Paine Collection.

The fellow in Nevada doesn't have any information on the car's early history, and neither does Mr. Mozart. Mr. Mozart was certain, however, that the had started life as a complete Fleetwood V-16 roadster. The Rollston Company had extensively modified the car to give it the appearance of a full custom-bodied job. From the beltline down, for instance, the body appears to be stock Fleetwood. But upon examination, one sees that the forward edge of the door opening (and hence the door hinge pillar) has been moved at least three inches toward the front of the car, no small operation with these wood and steel composite bodies. The doors, apart from being wider than standard V-16 roadster doors, have roll-up windows and they swing from three external "barrel" hinges. On a V-16 roadster, the top edges of the doors are rolled and they flow into the rear edge of the cowl, which shades the instrument panel in the manner of the open cockpit of an early airplane. On this Rollston job, the door top edges are straightened and there is a corner where they meet the trailing edge of the cowl.

When contacted about a 1938 V-16 Cadillac he had owned, Joe Bortz of Chicago disclosed that the Rollston-bodied convertible coupe had been the first classic collector car he ever owned. He had answered an ad in the *Chicago Tribune* in 1964 or '65 and purchased the Rollston-bodied Cadillac for $1,800. Mr. Bortz was about 24 at the time, just finished with college, and interested in unusual old cars. The only place he knew to look for them was in the Sunday *Chicago Tribune* in the classified antique and classic car ads. The paper was delivered to subscribers on Sunday morning, but it was printed up the preceding afternoon. On the way out to the suburbs on Saturday evening, the delivery trucks would stop at certain locations and drop off the Sunday papers. One of those was a rib house called Town & Country, at the corner of Ridge and Clark Streets in Chicago, and Joe Bortz would stop by there on Saturday around 5:00 p.m., order some ribs while waiting, and pick up a Sunday *Tribune*. As he waited for his ribs, he would look through the ads for any especially worthwhile cars. Each Sunday there would be from 5 to 20 antique cars (mostly Model A Fords and the like). If he saw something, he'd go to the pay phone and call the owner. One Saturday he saw an ad for a "1930 Cadillac V-16 convertible." That struck him as a naïve ad, because open cars of that era are usually described more specifically—convertible sedan, convertible coupe, convertible victoria, etc. So he immediately called and found out that the car was at a farm in Barrington (about 50 miles from where he lived) and the owner wanted $1,500 for it. He ran upstairs and asked if his rib order was ready. When told it would take another 15 minutes, he paid for the ribs, told the clerk to give them to someone, dashed home, grabbed his checkbook and raced out to see the Cadillac (doing 90–100 m.p.h.). The location was a gentleman's farm with a house, a barn and a yard. The owner who met him was an older man. Sitting on the front porch of the house was a dealer Mr. Bortz knew named Dave Levin. The owner said that Mr. Levin wanted to buy the car but he had told him there was a nice young fellow coming out to see it and he was going to let the young man look at the car first and see if he wanted to buy it. They entered the barn, lit by a single dim bulb overhead. The V-16 emblems told the story and Mr. Bortz, thoroughly impressed with the Cadillac, bought it on the spot. Mr. Levin left fuming.

The car was in the same rough condition portrayed in the 1968 issue of *The Self-Starter*.

Mr. Bortz wanted to get the car running, and he was referred to a fellow named John Troka. After World War II, Mr. Troka had become heavily involved with brokering Duesenberg automobiles, and he must have bought and sold dozens of them during his lifetime. He was 75 or 80 years old at the time Mr. Bortz got in touch with him. He had moved to Arizona for his asthma, but for some reason he had returned to the Chicago area, still plagued with asthma. He had an arcane method for coaxing reluctant automobile engines to start. With a squirt-type, small, hand-held oil can filled with gasoline, he would walk around the car and squirt gas into any opening in the engine—carburetor, air cleaner, whatever. His trick worked on this V-16 and it started and ran.

Mr. Bortz was somewhat new to the old car hobby when he acquired the Rollston-bodied Cadillac, and accurate information about classic cars was not nearly as readily available in 1965 as it is today. When he compared his car to available photos of Cadillac V-16 roadsters and convertible coupes the remarkable differences—the low, raked windshield, the skirted fenders—made him think that someone had taken a standard Cadillac car and had attempted to personalize it the way that hot rodders and West Coast customizers were doing with Fords and Chevys. Thinking that he would have to either undo or live with an amateur customizing job, Mr. Bortz did not hang on to the car for long. He recalls selling it for $5,500 and using the money to go on and acquire other unique older cars. Today he is known for rescuing and restoring some of the most unusual cars ever built—the concept cars and "dream" cars the manufacturers use to tease us, gauge our interest in styles and technology, and let us know what sorts of things they're planning to offer us in the future.

In 2011, I was able to reach Peter Hinrichs, the man who had been so surprised to see a photo of his car in the Cadillac-LaSalle Club newsletter back in 1968. He had left Wisconsin and was living in Florida. He described the restoration as complete and thoroughgoing—"You could eat off the frame." In 1977, after Mr. Hinrichs had seen to the restoration of the Rollston V-16, he had shown it at a Classic Car Club of America event in Wisconsin. Persuaded that it was an authentic Classic and eligible to be judged under the CCCA's standards, the judges awarded the car third place and 97 points. Subsequent health difficulties led Mr. Hinrichs to part with the car.

So, with old cars, things are not always as they first appear. What looked to some like a battered old used car that someone had clumsily tried to personalize turned out to be a unique example of the work of one of the finest custom coachbuilding firms of the Classic Era. It's too bad we don't know who ordered the car and why he chose the modifications he did. But it is wonderful that it has survived and has been carefully restored.

36. Chariots for the Princes

In the late 1800s, a minister from Philadelphia, Pennsylvania, named Charles Taze Russell started attracting a group of followers who became known as the Bible Students. He published a magazine that is still distributed today, and that is familiar to people who encounter door-to-door emissaries of the Bible Students. The movement took on a legal structure with the incorporation of the Watchtower Bible and Tract Society, and it spread to many different countries on the strength of the missionary zeal of its members.

Minister Russell died in 1916, and he was succeeded by a lawyer named Joseph Franklin Rutherford. Rutherford was truly a self-made man. Raised on a farm in Missouri, he was permitted to attend college so long as he paid for a laborer to take his place. He paid for his studies in the law by selling encyclopedias door-to-door and by working as a court stenographer. He clerked for a judge, became an official court reporter, and at the age of 22 was admitted to the bar. During his legal practice, he acquired an appointment as a Special Judge in Missouri state court. On at least one occasion, he sat as a substitute for a judge who was unable to preside, and on that basis and thereafter, he became known as Judge Rutherford.

In 1906, Judge Rutherford was baptized, and the next year, he became legal counsel for the Watchtower Society. He was 47 when he was elected the second president of the society, and until his death in 1942, he led the organization through a tumultuous and dramatic period of its history. Many of the doctrines and practices that are now associated with the society, including the name Jehovah's Witnesses, were originated by Judge Rutherford, as was the magazine *Awake!* that Witnesses distribute together with *The Watchtower*.

Judge Rutherford lived quite comfortably. From 1930 on he spent his winters at a mansion in San Diego named Beth Sarim, which was intended to house the soon-to-return righteous men of old—such as David, Gideon, Barak, Samson, Jephthah, Joseph and Samuel. And he owned two 1930 Cadillac V-16 motor cars.

At the society's Brooklyn, New York, headquarters was kept a Series 4380 all-weather phaeton. In San Diego, the judge had at his disposal a Series 4335 convertible coupe. With its split and V'd windshield it is the two-passenger counterpart to the all-weather phaeton. (There exist in society publications from the period photographs of Judge Rutherford standing with each of these Cadillacs, but unfortunately those images are not clear enough for reproduction here.) At this point it is difficult to ascertain whether either or both of these cars have survived to the present date. I inquired to the Watchtower Society to see if information could be obtained about the cars and the circumstances of their disposition by the society. A short letter dated October 19, 2009, from the Christian Congregation of Jehovah's Witnesses disclosed that there are no records of what became of either of Judge Rutherford's V-16 Cadillacs. The letter pointed out (and enclosed a reprint from a 1937 issue of *The Golden Age* in support) that "the Cadillac cars used by Judge Rutherford at San Diego and Brooklyn ... were gifts of friends."

---

37. The Baker's Dozen

George Ackerle was a baker by trade, like his father before him. As the owner of Ackerle's Bakery on Broadway in Camden, New Jersey, he was known as "The Danish Pastry King." He was also a serious old car guy. In the middle of the last century, if you lived in Camden or in any of the nearby counties and states, George Ackerle was the first guy you called when you had an old car to sell. The yard behind the bakery was filled with cars of all makes from the '30s, '40s and '50s. Over time Mr. Ackerle acquired some high-end classic cars, as well. These he kept in a separate building in Deptford, New Jersey, variously described as an old bus garage or a former car dealership. In the late 1980s, twelve of those cars were sold, including a 1930 Cadillac V-16 series 4355 imperial cabriolet.

Cadillac built 52 Series 4355 imperial cabriolets. The style designation denotes a five-passenger limousine without rear quarter windows. The areas where the quarter windows would have been are spanned by decorative versions of the landau irons that were designed back in the horse-and-carriage days to keep convertible tops erected. Inside, the front and rear seats are augmented by fold-down opera seats for occasional guests. The roof and upper rear quarter panels are covered in leather, and even though the rear portion of the roof is not collapsible (as the styling implies it should be) the design is eminently elegant and distinguished.

The car Mr. Ackerle owned is engine number 701758. According to Cadillac records, it did some traveling in the northeast United States before it found an initial buyer. In the first half of 1930, Cadillac V-16s sold very well. The stock market crash was a recent event, and no one really knew how pervasive and enduring would be the financial difficulties it precipitated. Many expected an imminent recovery. In the middle of the year, though, buyers for these and other exclusive luxury cars became increasingly scarce, and sometimes a V-16 was shipped, only to go unsold until it was sent to another or yet another dealership or distributor. Such was the case with this formal five-passenger limousine. It was shipped on May 26, 1930, to Brooklyn. Over a year later, on June 19, 1931, the car was diverted to Manhattan. Then on September 28 it went to Atlantic City, New Jersey. It's not clear how the car eventually came into Mr. Ackerle's possession.

A photograph of this stately car appears in the June 1971 issue of *The Self-Starter* (the monthly magazine of the Cadillac-LaSalle Club) with text indicating its ownership by George Ackerle. Then in fall 1973, a full-page color portrait appears in *Automobile Quarterly*. This time, the owner's name is given as Charles Ackerle. The photograph was used to illustrate an article explaining that humorist James Thurber's short story "Mr. Pendly and the Poindexter," could only have been referring to a Cadillac V-16. The Poindexter of the title is a pseu-

Mr. Ackerle's car in *The Self-Starter*. This photo and a caption appeared at page 12 of the June 1971 issue of the Cadillac-LaSalle Club's monthly newsletter. The car is missing the chrome trumpet horns that were standard on 1930 and 1931 Cadillac V-16s (courtesy Cadillac-LaSalle Club).

donymous 16-cylinder car that the hen-pecked Mr. Pendly and his wife consider purchasing at a Columbus Avenue showroom in New York City. The unnamed author of the article presents Mr. Thurber's short story in its entirety (with the accompanying cartoon work), and then proceeds to explain how, because of the timing of the story's creation among other factors, the Cadillac V-16 is the only car that could have been in Mr. Thurber's mind.

In the *Automobile Quarterly* photograph, the big car is posed in a park. The folding luggage rack is deployed and occupied by an aftermarket trunk of a style similar to what Cadillac offered as accessory equipment. The fender-mounted spare tires sport the decorative metal covers with rearview mirrors from the factory option list. It's hard to tell whether one is looking at a brand-new car, a well-preserved older one or a nice restoration.

The same photograph as was used in the *Automobile Quarterly* article would in May of 2005 grace the cover of *The Self-Starter*, again illustrating an article not directly dealing with this particular motor car. Comparing the cover picture from *The Self-Starter* with the image from the *Automobile Quarterly* article, it is clear that the latter was retouched somewhat. In the *Self-Starter* cover shot, the photo betrays some chipping or flaking of the paint on the forward edge of the front passenger-side door and in the area where the two doors meet.

Subsequently, in early 1988, the Cadillac was a featured player in two articles in *Cars & Parts* magazine. The first article, in the February issue, broke the news of the purchase and extrication from long-term storage in a New Jersey warehouse of a collection of twelve

Still stately after all these years. This is a body style that commands respect and admiration no matter what angle it's seen from. Although a new owner might want to correct the disintegrating paint, discolored window glass and slight rust rash on the chrome parts, the car is incredibly solid, complete and sound for being over eighty years old. Chrome and paint would be a significant outlay, but there's so much one would not have to do (photograph courtesy of a previous owner).

classic cars (including half a dozen Cadillacs as well as some Packards and Ford products) by a gentleman from Downingtown, Pennsylvania. The name of the seller was not mentioned, but I assume it was one of the Ackerles (or an agent or executor for one of them). In any event, the text and photos by Bob Stevens depicted this exciting "barn find" and showed the emergence into the open air from its gloomy dormitory and onto a flatbed truck of this particular noble Cadillac limousine. In the photos, the paint chipping hinted at in the *Automobile Quarterly* photo had advanced noticeably on the front door, and had shown up as well toward the back of the rear door and the lower rear quarter of the body. The same aftermarket trunk is further evidence that this is the same car. And the article refers to the *Automobile Quarterly* piece, connecting the car with the one shown there. Amazingly, the car claimed only 9,890 miles on its odometer at the time.

In the March 1988 issue, *Cars & Parts* continued the saga of the purchase of the Cadillac V-16 imperial cabriolet and the other cars from the New Jersey warehouse. Photos of the Cadillac, inside and out, accompanied the text. The fine condition of the V-16's interior was duly noted (and partially explained by plastic covers over the door panels and seats). Most entertainingly, the article related and illustrated the ultimately successful efforts to get the long-dormant Cadillac running again.

Chauffeur's compartment. This car is unusual in that it has a divider window between driver and passengers, but the front compartment is upholstered in cloth and not leather. That generally indicated that the owner intended to drive the car as well. When the driving was left to a chauffeur, the front compartment was generally done in leather, considered a more utilitarian trimming at the time. Here, the cloth was long ago covered with clear plastic. Note the delamination of the windshield safety glass (photograph courtesy of a previous owner).

Fast-forward to the present, and it turns out that this magnificent Cadillac is still in original, unrestored condition. Sadly but understandably, the paint condition has progressed inexorably. And the safety glass shows the effects of age on the plastic interlining material. But the interior is still marvelously close to the way it left the hands of the Fleetwood craftsmen in 1930. And it runs well and remains a serenely low-mileage car. This is an automobile that could knock the judges off their feet in the historic preservation class of any car show.

In the fall of 2011, restorer and dealer Manny Dragone of Westport, Connecticut, acquired the cabriolet from an old car enthusiast in Westminster, Maryland, and showed it among several other exotic "barn finds" at the Fairfield County Concours d'Elegance in Connecticut. In October, he brought it to the AACA Hershey meet and offered it for sale. Maria Camelio, of Lanham, Maryland, became the next and current owner of this distinguished Cadillac.

38. Charm City Convertible

During the 1970s, Mr. Harry Corson operated a service station on the Merritt Parkway, a limited-access roadway that runs from Greenwich to Stratford, Connecticut. He owned a 1931 Cadillac V-16 Series 4380 all-weather phaeton, but the car was in pieces and stored at his building. In 1978 or '79, classic car collector Ray Bowersox of Milton, Pennsylvania,

Sensuous lines and elegant bearing. From this angle, the use of curves and flowing surfaces give this large car pleasing proportions. Exposed "barrel" door hinges were favored by custom coachbuilders of the period (courtesy Charles Gillet).

found out about that automobile. Mr. Corson had planned to restore it, but a divorce interrupted those plans and he was forced to sell. Al Prueitt, founder of the famous restoration facility Al Prueitt & Sons, Inc., made the purchase for Mr. Bowersox, and he described the partially disassembled car as a "basket case." At his shop in Glen Rock, Pennsylvania, a complete restoration was undertaken.

In 1930, when the Cadillac V-16 was introduced, the availability of roll-up windows for convertibles (whether for two-door or four-door cars) was still a recent development. For most of automotive history to that time, an open car was just that—open to the weather and the world. The side curtains that owners hurriedly unfolded and tried to install and button down in the event of a rainstorm or other turn of the weather left a great deal to be desired in terms of keeping the car's occupants dry and warm when Mother Nature wanted to ride with them. In the early 1800s, the name of the Greek sun god's son, Phaeton, was applied to a sporty four-wheeled carriage drawn by one or two horses. In the first part of the twentieth century, the name was passed on to a four-door open car that was flashier or sportier than a common touring car. When Cadillac began building four-door convertible cars with roll-up windows that kept the weather out and cozy heat in, instead of being called four-door convertibles, they were given the much more colorful designation "all-weather phaetons."

Al Prueitt set to work on a car that was about eighty percent complete. He recalls some surface rust (on the fenders, for example) but says that otherwise the car was solid. The major parts were generally present and in pretty good shape, but there were a lot of missing trim pieces and miscellaneous items. Many pieces had to be reproduced, including the valence

Ready for open-air driving. With the convertible top lowered, the car appears more reserved than a sport phaeton. The nearly upright windshield frame and the horizontal lower body sill keep things calm and dignified. Lowering the top is a fairly involved process, best done with help (courtesy Charles Gillet).

panels between the inboard edges of the running boards and the lower edges or "sills" of the body (the doors for the battery compartment and the tool box attach to these panels).

While he was rebuilding the seats in the car, Mr. Prueitt had occasion to speak with George Winling, a friend of his who had worked in the upholstery operation of the Fleetwood plant in Pennsylvania when the bodies of the first V-16 Cadillacs were being built, trimmed and fitted at that facility. Mr. Winling told Mr. Prueitt his timecard number and where to look on the seat springs for the timecard number of the worker who had originally assembled it. Sure enough, Mr. Winling's own timecard number could be seen on the springs for the very all-weather phaeton Mr. Prueitt was restoring.

The Cadillac was completely taken apart, down to the bare frame, and meticulously renewed and put back together with all possible attention to detail. The restoration took about four years, and it brought the car back to showroom-new condition. Mr. Bowersox showed the car at classic gatherings, but soon decided to sell it. It seems that neither he nor his wife cared for the way the car handled and drove.

One afternoon over lunch Mr. Prueitt and his friend Mr. Charles Gillet of Baltimore, Maryland, found themselves discussing V-16 Cadillacs. Mr. Gillet somewhat wistfully allowed that he had never owned one. After a pregnant silence, as Mr. Gillet recalls, Mr. Prueitt remarked that he knew where he could get one. Mr. Prueitt brought Mr. Gillet and Mr. Bowersox together, and a sale was completed in 1987. Since then, Mr. Gillet has cared for the V-16, and shown it quite successfully.

The car was delivered new to Cunliffe Cadillac in Baltimore, in October of 1931, but the name of the original owner is not known. Originally painted black with an ivory pinstripe, the car is now a lovely midnight blue with pearl gray pinstripe and contrasting belt molding.

An appropriately elegant setting. The convertible is parked next to a 1932 Cadillac town car with Roman revival architecture as a backdrop, where the aristocratic bearing of this body style really shines (courtesy Charles Gillet).

The blue canvas top completes the ensemble, and on the inside, the light gray leather upholstery is nicely accented by the burled pecan window garnish pieces. It is a testament to the quality of the original restoration years ago, and the level of care bestowed on the car since then, that it continues to take top honors at car club events (it has won the Antique Automobile Club of America's James Melton Memorial Trophy twice over the years).

39. A Coachbuilt Cadillac with a French Touch

Cadillac went to great lengths to control the public image of the V-16 cars. That effort extended to greatly restricting the practice of purchasing a bare chassis from an auto manufacturer and taking it to a custom body builder of the customer's choice to be completed according to the customer's (and the outside designer's) inspiration. Cadillac's position was that the range of body styles available from the manufacturer through the in-house coachbuilder Fleetwood, coupled with the stated willingness to accommodate each purchaser's individual desires, should have obviated the need to go elsewhere. No doubt the manufacturer also preferred to have the customer's money go to a single destination, rather than lose business to an unrelated company. Nev-

ertheless, several V-16s were bodied by firms other than Fleetwood, and each of these is an interesting variation on the theme.

One of the V-16s that was sent on a promotional tour of Europe in 1930 was a sport phaeton, Series 4260, with engine number 701554. It was purchased during the tour, and it spent decades in France before returning to the United States. By some sequence of events, this car came into the hands of M. Jacques Saoutchik, a highly respected French designer and coachbuilder known for attractive and attention-getting creations, some of which, in later years, carried the streamlining concept to extravagant length.

M. Saoutchik removed the phaeton body and replaced it with a sedan body, with a fabric-covered top, that emulated a convertible. What became of the original Fleet-

Mark of distinction. The Saoutchik firm's trademark badge appears on the lower cowl in front of the driver's door (courtesy Scott Williamson).

wood phaeton body is not known. The hood, fenders, gas tank cover and rear seat instruments, at least, were incorporated into the new design, but the rest may have been junked.

According to Marc Ohm, who later worked on the restoration of this car, at one time in its history it was an actual convertible sedan. (In fact, there is some evidence that the unique Saoutchik body once adorned a different chassis altogether—it has a set of holes for mounting bolts in places that don't match up with the Cadillac chassis attachment points, and several wooden shim blocks are required to secure it to the V-16 frame.) Although as the car exists today the top cannot be lowered, there is a cleverly-designed sunroof built into the top of the car that can slide open to uncover both the driver's and passengers' compartments. A small window in the sliding panel lines up with the car's rear window when the sunroof is in the open position.

The car's lighting equipment included twin Stéphane Grebel cowl-mounted spotlights for the driver and front passenger, and the headlights were huge Marchal units. A bright metal beltline runs from the radiator shell all around the car, and the upper edges of the doors are smoothly rounded. The car has the interior room of a limousine, and both a speedometer and a chronometer for the rear-seat passengers.

The earliest history of this custom-bodied Cadillac is incomplete. At some time prior to 1955, the car came into the possession of the Marquis of Goulaine. The chateau of Goulaine in France's Loire Valley has been home to the family of the Marquis of Goulaine from medieval times. King Henry IV (1553–1610) made the estate a marquisate, and but for the period from 1788 to 1858, the chateau has been owned continuously by the family. The break in ownership likely spared the estate from the depredations of the French Revolution and its aftermath.

In 1955, the marquis sold the Cadillac to Hubert Le Gallais, a brewer, who showed the car at various meets in and around Paris. It received significant work at the "Francis" workshops in Paris around 1964 (as described in the August 6, 1964, issue of the French enthusiast publication *Auto-Journal*). Cadillac historian Yann Saunders, who visited M. Le Gallais in the early 1970s and photographed the car, reports that at that time it was dark blue with a dark brown roof.

M. Le Gallais moved to Brittany and ran a restaurant (Le Pave Du Roy in Ploemeur). At the urging of Serge Pozzoli, editor of the magazine *Fanatique de l'Automobile*, he sold the custom V-16 in 1979 or 1980 to a nephew of the late Prince Henri, Count of Paris (and Orleanist claimant to the French throne). M. Le Gallais received, in return, a Rolls-Royce and some cash.

In the 1980s, the Saoutchik-bodied Cadillac made its way to the United States to be restored by Fran Roxas for Fred Weber. At that time, the body was transferred to another Cadillac V-16 chassis, this one from a Series 4330-S five-passenger sedan (engine number 700979) that had been ordered originally for Cadillac chief engineer Charles F. Kettering (who had been responsible for many of Cadillac's electrical and engineering breakthroughs). Subsequently, the chassis on which the Saoutchik body had previously been mounted is said to have been reunited with a sport phaeton body (such as it bore when it was new).

Some consideration was given to converting the Saoutchik body to a convertible sedan, but that plan proceeded only as far as detaching the roof. Plans changed, the top with its sliding sunroof was reattached, and the restoration proceeded. The paint scheme was changed to a silver-blue color for the body and a dark blue for the fenders, wheels and top. The Marchal headlamps were replaced with Grebel lights, apparently to match the spotlights on the cowl. The hood vent doors were chromium plated (an option Cadillac offered at the time, but not, apparently, part of Jacques Saoutchik's design).

In the 1990s, Chicago-area real estate developer Bernie Glieberman purchased the car at a Kruse auction and kept it for several years. He told me that his use of the car was generally limited to lending it to friends for their children's weddings. Yann Saunders saw the car during Mr. Glieberman's ownership at the June 1993 Cadillac-LaSalle Experience at the Gilmore Museum in Hickory Corners, Michigan. It took a class award at Pebble Beach in 1991 and was awarded Best in Class at the Meadow Brook Concours in 1995.

In 2000, the Cadillac was offered at a Barrett-Jackson auction and bids reached several hundred thousand dollars without a sale. In 2001, it was sold at another Barrett-Jackson auction for a reported $126,000. New owner Elliott Dolin showed the car at Pebble Beach in 2002 and it took 3rd place in the 1930–1936 V-16 class. On August 18, 2007, it sold at the Gooding & Company Pebble Beach Auction for $462,000. Then in 2011 it was offered again, this time at RM Auctions' May 21 sale in connection with the Concorso d'Eleganza Villa d'Este at Como, Italy. There it brought a price of €307,500 (at the time equal to approximately $431,000).

One previous owner believes that Saoutchik built the car originally as a convertible sedan, and that someone else may have built the roof with the sliding cover. There is a tag on the top with the name of a company in Paris. Another explanation for that tag is that Saoutchik designed the special top, but contracted with another firm to install it.

The car we see today, then, has a "composite" history. The Saoutchik body was likely first mounted on a distinguished European marque (Minerva? Hispano Suiza?) and most probably as a convertible sedan. Early on, it was remounted onto the chassis of the European Tour V-16 phaeton, and the convertible top was replaced by the sunroof-equipped fixed top. Finally, it was mounted onto the chassis of "Boss" Kettering's V-16. The European Tour V-16 phaeton

Next best thing to a convertible. The full-length sunroof is open with the panel neatly concealed, and the "B" pillars between the door windows are folded down out of sight. The setting is the reviewing stand at the 2002 Pebble Beach Concours d'Elegance, where the car took third in its class (courtesy Bobbie'dine Rodda).

chassis, in turn, was converted back into a sport phaeton, and what became of the body from the Kettering V-16 is not known. In its current configuration this car has won awards at the Pebble Beach and Amelia Island Concours d'Elegance. As of spring 2013, the car is in Finland.

Each of the Cadillac V-16s that went to outside custom body manufacturers gives us a tantalizing glimpse of what might have been created had Cadillac not been so cautious about outside body makers. We have other individual samples from Pininfarina, Murphy, Waterhouse, Kellner, Rollston and Van Den Plas. It would have been interesting to see how these companies would have designed for other body styles. Based on their work for other fine cars, firms like Brunn, Locke, Willoughby, and LeBaron, to name a few, might have turned out some very interesting designs indeed for Cadillac V-16s.

40. Styled in Sweden

Very few of the Cadillac V-16 chassis built by General Motors were sold without a Fleetwood or Fisher body installed. Unlike other luxury automobile manufacturers, Cadillac took great pains to keep the coachbuilding in-house. The brass wanted to keep control over the image and esthetics of GM's top-of-the-line flagship. And not inconsequentially, they

Well maintained and original. This engine and its compartment show the patina of an original, unrestored car. Remarkably, the porcelain on the exhaust manifold has not cracked at all. Long red-orange hoses are for an accessory heater. The horn-shaped object next to the engine and just behind the radiator could be the air intake for a Kelch heater (photo courtesy of Björn Bellander, http://www.bjornsstory.se).

wanted to apply any profit margin realized from the body construction and installation process to pay down the immense capital outlay required to realize the V-16 project. But there were a handful of bare chassis that went to custom builders, and they represent some of the most interesting and tantalizing examples of the breed—interesting because they are unique and tantalizing because they hint at what might have been if wider access had been permitted.

Swedish automobile dealer Hans Osterman obtained a 1930 Cadillac V-16 chassis and contracted with the Gustaf Nordbergs Vagnfabrik firm to construct an elegant and exclusive body for the car. In one of the few instances where Cadillac released a bare chassis V-16, engine number 702073, installed in chassis number 7–2041, was shipped to Stockholm on June 25, 1930. The result of the work by the Nordberg craftsmen was a formal landaulet–town car with a raked windshield (not unlike those on the Madame X Fleetwood styles) and a leather-covered roof. The driver's compartment was open, with a fabric covering that could be put up for inclement weather. And the portion of the passenger compartment top behind the rear quarter windows could be folded down for open-air touring.

Hans Osterman was a pivotal figure in the automotive business in Sweden, and in addition to Cadillac and LaSalle, his dealership sold Chevrolets, Buicks and Minervas. The custom-bodied V-16 was apparently built on speculation, in hopes that a wealthy industrialist or socialite visiting the Osterman showroom would decide that it was just the sort of carriage they needed for touring, visiting or entertaining. But the Great Depression that settled in upon the United States hobbled Europe's economies as well, and those who could afford the

In the "Marble Halls." The Nordberg-bodied 1930 Cadillac V-16 landaulet posed in the Osterman showroom in Stockholm. This magnificent motor car did not find a home until 1935, when the publisher Vitus Pettersson purchased it. Raked windshield is reminiscent of Fleetwood's Madame X designs. Chrome ribs on rear fender are similar to those seen on Duesenberg and other top-tier marques (photograph by Olle Ljungstrom, courtesy Yann Saunders).

Driver's side view. Again seen in the Osterman showroom, this automobile's regal lines agree with the architectural details of the setting. The framed Cadillac and LaSalle poster in the background features the V-16 emblem (photograph by Olle Ljungstrom, courtesy Yann Saunders).

In the Sparreholm Museum. This is a recent photograph of the landaulet. The spare tire appears to be one of the original tires (traces of the same tread pattern as seen on the car in the showroom photograph) (courtesy Björn Bellander, http://www.bjorns-story.se).

finer things in life became more reticent about showing the fact. The landaulet–town car graced Osterman's "Marble Halls" for a number of years.

One day in 1935 a gentleman visited the Osterman premises. He may not have been dressed for the occasion or in a manner likely to impress the sales staff, because he was directed to the used car area. At length he found his way to the Cadillac showroom on the second floor, inquired about several cars and settled his attention upon the big V-16. The salesman he spoke to was Wille Kindwall, who would subsequently become an important Ford dealer. The man told Mr. Kindwall he had a friend in Copenhagen with a similarly styled car, and asked the cost of the car he was looking at. A price was given by Mr. Kindwall with no expectation that a sale would ensue. The man then identified himself as Vitus Pettersson, a prominent book publisher in Malmö, and he offered to buy the car if the Osterman company would take out ads in his publications. A deal was soon struck and the car found a home.

Mr. Pettersson kept the big Cadillac until 1968. At that time, Helge Karinen traded him a used Pontiac and some cash for the V-16, and it has been in Mr. Karinen's care ever since. Mr. Karinen owns the historic Sparreholm Castle west of Stockholm, as well as the car museum there that now houses the V-16 landaulet in addition to other truly special vehicles, including some that were once owned by Swedish kings.

41. Restoration Interrupted

During the late 1920s and early 1930s, the automotive model year generally followed the calendar year (Packard's being a notable exception). That would remain true until 1935, when Franklin Roosevelt would persuade the industry to move the annual unveiling of new models from January to the preceding November in order to help generate increased retail sales activity in the fall and to stabilize auto industry employment. In the early '30s, the yearly introduction of the new cars was almost a choreographed ritual. The first round, beginning in early November, was the Salon, held in a prestigious hotel or comparable venue, at which the custom coachbuilders displayed their latest designs and rolling artworks. This was an invitation-only occasion for those with the means to acquire a custom-built motor car. In January, the National Automobile Chamber of Commerce presented the National Automobile Show, open to the general public, where the manufacturers made their full presentation of new products. This two-step was performed, in turn, in Chicago, New York, Los Angeles and San Francisco. In New York, the auto show was generally held at the Grand Central Coliseum. In Chicago, the site was the Drake Hotel. Manufacturers would also stage separate displays for dealers and select prospects at other locations in conjunction with the auto show.

In the early winter of 1930, a Cadillac V-16 Series 4260 Sport Phaeton was built, earmarked for the Chicago phase of the 1931 show circuit. Bearing engine number 702889, it was, by the estimation of some Cadillac historians, the second of the 1931 V-16s. It's worth recalling, however, that from the introduction of the V-16 in the beginning of 1930 through the end of 1931, bodies, chassis and drivetrains were the same design, with only minor running changes and improvements made now and then during that two-year period. (By contrast, the 1931 V-8 cars received a significant freshening from the 1930 models, to look like slightly smaller V-16s. And the V-12 cars were all new for 1931.) It wasn't until 1932 that the V-16 models were restyled (for example, more streamlined bodies and fenders, redesigned dash and controls, sleeker bullet-shaped lights, integral radiator shell and grille) and given significant engineering changes (including mechanical fuel pump, Detroit Lubricator carburetors, adjustable shock absorbers and improved chassis design). So whether a V-16 is a 1930 or a 1931 model is interesting, but not outwardly apparent.

This car's build sheet has some very interesting notations. There appears to be a reference (partially obliterated by the hole punch) to a special order from General Motors' Art & Colour Studio ("A&C SPEC. 10/29"). That implies a company-originated design and color scheme. The sheet directs that the finished automobile be shipped to the Chicago branch office, with the further instruction "TAG HOTEL STEVENS EXHIBITION HALL EXHIBIT—SHIP BY JAN 15 SURE." The date and time stamp on the sheet indicates, though, that the car was received at the factory loading dock on the January 17, just a bit late. The dates for the NACC Chicago show that year were January 24 through 31. We might venture that Cadillac or its local branch had a display at the Hotel Stevens before or during the show, perhaps for invited guests and important customers.

The phaeton's build sheet further shows that the body, fenders and moldings were painted Florida Grey. The hubs and rims of the wheels were Glacier Green, and the spokes were stainless steel. The pinstriping ("body stripe") was gold leaf. The interior was trimmed in Navim Green leather manufactured by John Reilly Co. The convertible top was covered

Much of the restoration process is done, but many finish and detail items remain. The upholstery, door panels and top are considerable jobs. Many smaller parts (such as the ignition switch and the controls for the steering wheel hub) included with the purchase remain to be assembled and installed. Nevertheless, this project is manageable and well worth the effort (courtesy Ross Morgan).

with Jonarts waterproofed cloth style 1 T 1531, and the side-mounted spare tires wore Burbank cloth covers to match.

This gray sport phaeton with green wheels and interior was no doubt an elegant feature of Cadillac's display at the Hotel Stevens in Chicago. What happened after the show is left to speculation. In the absence of specific information, we can imagine that the car was offered for sale by the Chicago branch, and that it found a buyer. But who the purchaser was and how long he or she kept this sport phaeton is not known. The next thing we know is that it came into the possession of Los Angeles Cadillac dealer and car collector LaRue Thomas. Mr. Thomas had another V-16 sport phaeton like this one that he restored and kept. He sold this car to another well-known collector. At some time in the 1980s, the collector began a restoration that involved at least a partial disassembly of the automobile, even if the body may have remained on the frame. He repainted the car red—body, fenders, chassis, running boards, wheel hubs and rims. The wheel spokes are stainless steel as originally specified. In order to paint the chassis, fuel tank and suspension parts, it is most probable that the fenders, running boards, gas tank cover and the splash apron below the radiator were removed. These have all been reinstalled, as have the headlights, radiator, hood and windshield.

Twice in recent years, the car has been listed on eBay, and each listing has been accompanied by many photos showing the status of the reassembly process, and the many parts still waiting to be put back into place—parking and tail lamps, hood vent windsplits, horns, bumpers, trunk rack brackets, door handles and so on. Some pieces (including the taillights and trunk rack fittings) needed to be re-plated. Some reproduction castings (such as the

Engine looks ready to run. But there are no fuel lines to the carburetors and the ignition coils are not in place. Open exhaust manifolds mean noisy running even if you did start it. Otherwise, it's a beautiful sight (courtesy Ross Morgan).

On arrival in Australia. In a warehouse awaiting inspection, the sport phaeton sits among other cargo items. Assorted parts are stowed in the passenger compartment, including a spare tire cover and seat frames (courtesy Ross Morgan).

bracket that mounts the light switch to the end of the steering box) would have to be machined and finished before they could be used. The new wiring was only partially hooked up and tucked away. And the interior required re-upholstering in quality leather, and a new top to be sewn and fitted with suitable materials.

From the array of images available for viewing, one could easily conclude that everything was there, in one condition or another. But an automobile, even an eighty-some-year-old example, is a very complex mechanism, and when taken apart it's awfully hard to keep track of every single part. When the parts that inevitably go missing are specific to Cadillac V-16s, that poses a financial and logistical problem.

From what was apparent in the photographs, the paint was presentable, but for serious show standards, it would have to be repaired at least, and likely would have to be redone. In the latter case, why not return to the original? Chrome plating will cost money, as will the top and interior. Only a detailed inventory of the loose parts, compared with a careful analysis of what remains to be re-installed could tease out the list of missing items. These can be had, but at a price.

Once assembled, however, this will be a fabulous motor car, elegant with the top up, dashing and flamboyant with it down. Rear-seat speedometer and chronograph for the passengers' entertainment add to the period flair. And there are buyers for sport phaetons in top condition. The trick is to buy well enough to allow for the remaining work.

In early 2011, Australian Cadillac enthusiast Ross Morgan purchased the sport phaeton, after asking Long Beach, California, resident Paul Schinnerer to inspect it for him, and see if its condition was consistent with what the available photographs seemed to indicate. Mr. Morgan already owns a 1934 V-16 aerodynamic coupe, and he has become an ardent fan of these cars. It will be fun to follow his progress as he completes the reconstruction of this fine phaeton.

42. In the Land of the Rising Sun

One doesn't easily imagine a car as long and large as a Series 4375 7-passenger imperial sedan traveling the crowded streets and highways of Japan. But at least one such vehicle resides in that country at the Toyota Automobile Museum in Nagakute. It wears gray paint with light blue fenders, window frames and hood cove panels, and it carries engine number 703181 (although that is not the original powerplant).

During the past century a Pennsylvania automobile mechanic-turned-hotelier named Eugene Zimmerman (1909–1991) assembled an automobile collection that rivaled (and in some respects surpassed) the much better known Bill Harrah collection. Beginning in 1966, Gene Zimmerman's cars were displayed in his "Automobilorama," located at the junction of U.S. Highway 15 and the Pennsylvania Turnpike. That museum was a bit of roadside Americana *par excellence*. Mr. Zimmerman also operated his Holiday West motel at that location, one of three Holiday motels he built in the Harrisburg area, named well before the Holiday Inn chain arose and became a familiar trademark to millions of travelers.

One of the cars in Mr. Zimmerman's museum was a 1930 Cadillac limousine, and a souvenir postcard from the Automobilorama bears its likeness. The postcard shows a car

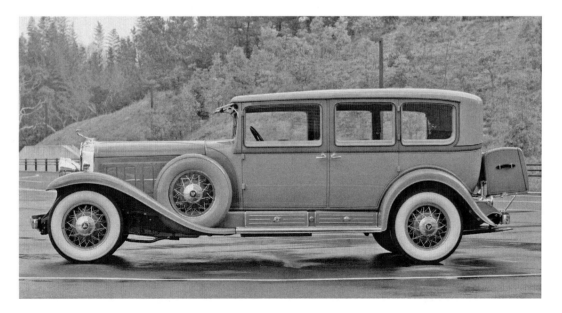

Seven-passenger imperial sedan owned by the Toyota Automobile Museum. The proportions and lines work to keep a large car from being overwhelming (courtesy Toyota Automobile Museum).

with dark paint and some features that depart somewhat from stock configuration, which served to help identify it later. For example, the headlights are slightly smaller than they should be. The 1930 and '31 V-16 cars had the largest-diameter headlights Cadillac ever installed on its cars. The 1931 V-12 and V-8 cars bore a similar front ensemble, but scaled down slightly. The headlights on the car in the postcard are from a '31 V-12 or V-8. They are less easily discerned because of the angle at which the photo was taken and the size of the image, but it is possible to see that the domes over the vibrator mechanisms for the horns are hemispherical, instead of the roughly cylindrical shapes of the originals. The spare tires are protected by painted metal covers consisting of a circular band that covers the sidewall from the tire bead to the tread, and another piece that covers the tread. Finally, the black rubber tread strips of the running boards have been replaced with narrow wooden slats, something a number of restorers resorted to in the decades before Steele Rubber Company reproduced the correct rubber items, complete with molded-in attachment studs.

From the mid–1960s until 1973, Mr. Al Prueitt, now scion of the family that operates the esteemed Al Prueitt and Sons, Inc., automobile restoration business in Glen Rock, Pennsylvania, was employed by Gene Zimmerman. He had met Mr. Zimmerman in 1964 at the annual Hershey, Pennsylvania, AACA meet (then as now a mecca for old car enthusiasts). Mr. Zimmerman immediately offered him a job, but he declined, saying that he was doing well (as an engineer with the Atomic Energy Commission). But Gene Zimmerman persisted, visiting Mr. Prueitt in Tennessee, until he convinced Mr. Prueitt to go to work for him managing his collection.

While on a business trip (or possibly at a convention) in Chicago, Mr. Zimmerman discovered a 1930 Cadillac V-16 limousine stored in a garage, and he decided to buy it. Two weeks later, he dispatched Mr. Prueitt to Chicago to pick up the car. The Cadillac had not been out of the trailer for more than 30 minutes before Mr. Zimmerman "blew the engine." Mr. Prueitt recalls that the engine from a 1933 V-16 convertible coupe was installed in place of the damaged powerplant. There must have been yet another switch along the way, because the engine that is in the car today is from a 1931 car. In the 1980s, Mr. Zimmerman retired to Fort Lauderdale, Florida. The Automobilorama was closed and most of the cars were sold. The 1930 V-16 limousine was one of several cars that Mr. Zimmerman was able to take with him to Florida. It wasn't running at the time, and he asked Al Prueitt to come and get it started so that he could offer it for sale. The Cadillac V-16 limousine was put on the auction block first at the Leake Auction in Tulsa, Oklahoma, where it didn't sell, and later at an auction in Fort Lauderdale, Florida. The auctioneer at the Florida auction was a man from Chicago, now deceased, who can no longer tell us who bought the car. In any event, at some point after leaving Mr. Zimmerman's possession, the 1930 V-16 limousine appears to have found its way overseas.

Having seen an interesting entry in Yann Saunders's remarkable Internet resource the (New) Cadillac Database that indicated that the Toyota Automobile Museum had a Cadillac V-16 limousine on display, I wrote to the museum, requesting photographs, information and anything they might have on the car's prior ownership. The curator of the museum, Mr. Koji Yamada, was kind enough to send me a disc with many images of the car. Unfortunately, he knew nothing of its history, except that the museum had acquired it from an automobile brokerage firm in the United States. Cadillac records show that the car that was originally built around engine number 703181, was shipped in October 1931 and was very close to the end of the 1930–31 model run. Without knowing the original engine number of this particular car, however, we cannot be sure when it was built, where it was originally sold or other details like the optional equipment it was ordered with.

I'm not sure, looking back, what made me compare the Toyota museum's car with the one that had once graced Gene Zimmerman's collection, but it quickly became apparent that they were the same car. The headlights are the smaller V-12/V-8 units, as can be seen with a side-by-side comparison with a different 1930 Cadillac V-16. The running boards have the wooden replacement treads, just like the Zimmerman collection car, instead of the original rubber strips with wood graining on the metal surrounding the tread strips. And the spare tire covers are the two-piece painted metal design that is apparent in the postcard from the Zimmerman museum. Like the car in the postcard, the spare doesn't have a locking hubcap. There should be a removable key-operated plug where the V-16 emblem is. But the real tip-off comes from the license plate. The Toyota museum's car still wears a Pennsylvania historical plate with the number E030. This was one of the historic plates assigned to cars in the Zimmerman Automobilorama collection.

In 2009, I had the pleasure of speaking with Frank Pinola, who, until his untimely passing in 2010, was the director of the Cadillac-LaSalle Club's Central Pennsylvania Region (which he had founded some 20 years earlier). Mr. Pinola told me that he had obtained a block of historic vehicle plates for Gene Zimmerman's cars, numbered sequentially from E000 through E099. He only recalled one Cadillac V-16 in the collection, and said that he thought it had come from Massachusetts, though he couldn't recall when Mr. Zimmerman acquired it.

So, at best there is a partial history for this stately giant. But as with each of these cars, it would be fascinating to know who went to the dealer and ordered the car new, who excitedly waited to be notified that it had arrived from the factory, who climbed behind the wheel and drove off in regal splendor in a car that few could afford, many yearned for and everyone noticed. But now visitors to the Toyota Automobile Museum in Nagakute, east of Nagoya and between Tokyo and Osaka, can see a beautiful example of fine American engineering, artistry and craftsmanship from another era.

Pennsylvania Antique Historic license plate number E030. The late Frank Pinola told the author that he obtained a series of these plates, including this one, for Gene Zimmerman's collection (courtesy Toyota Automobile Museum).

43. Demolition Derby Veteran

In the late 1950s, big American classics were largely disregarded and ignored, except by certain specialized constituencies. The few aficionados who appreciated the style and craftsmanship of these conveyances were a minority among the car fancier confraternity. At another end of the spectrum was a different kind of car fancier. A uniquely American pastime called the "demolition derby" arose in the '50s to take dirt track automobile racing to a sort of illogical conclusion. Outdated, derelict, unwanted vehicles were stripped of glass and items that might fly around in the passenger compartment, and drivers drove them into each other until only one vehicle remained operable. A stock car race track in the Chicago area held demolition derbies every week. A young man named Karl Kahlberg was there because his father performed welding work for the stock car racers. The cars demolished in the derby would be taken to a scrap metal facility and crushed into compact blocks of metal. Some of the cars that passed through that violent race event were once-proud large classics from the early '30s, and young Karl was moved to rescue some of them before they fell into the scrapper's hands. His father had a large tract of land, and he was able to stow these relics there.

One of the cars that was rescued in this fashion was a 1930 Cadillac V-16 coupe. Officially a Series 4376 two-passenger coupe with rumble seat, it has the two-piece V windshield characteristic of the cars produced at the Pennsylvania Fleetwood plant (and seen on the first Madame X cars), and the chrome reveal moldings around the side windows that the

The wrecked fender has deformed the right side of the hood. Note generic truck marker light on fender. On warm days the driver of this car could have swung one or both windshield panes out (hinged at the top) to take in the breeze (courtesy Karl Kahlberg).

A once-elegant motor car humiliated. Young Karl Kahlberg rescued this damaged V-16 coupe from a trip to the crusher. Only 98 Series 4376 coupes were built, and on January 1, 1930, the price for one was $5,950 (courtesy Karl Kahlberg).

Direct and glancing blows to the front of this car have buckled both fenders and pushed the left one into the hood. Amazingly, the car survives today and has been restored (courtesy Karl Kahlberg).

Madame X models sported. The strict understanding of the Madame X designation is that it can only apply to four-door closed vehicles. Cadillac record references to "coupe with Madame X windshield" confirm this understanding. Other people are willing to apply the Madame X sobriquet to coupes that share the Madame X styling features.

Mr. Kahlberg has saved some photographs he took of the Madame X coupe after its demolition derby performance. It's sitting up on blocks beneath a knot of trees in the middle of a field. The massive headlights are gone. The right front fender has been folded back vertically and the clamshell leading edge has been crimped up under the crown, with the hood taking some damage in the process. An old-fashioned truck marker light has been substituted for the original jewel-like parking light. The other front fender has been buckled by a severe front impact. The right rear fender is moderately bashed, as is the edge of the left-hand running board. The covers for the battery and tool compartments are missing, and otherwise, the car is surprisingly solid, considering the ordeal it has been through.

In the photos, this V-16 looks shorter than it is. The effect is partly due to the missing headlights and crumpled front clip. But the wheelbase is still 148 inches, one of the longest ever for a passenger car. It still wears the rustically hand-painted door numbers from the race and the driver's name on the hood—Moe? When Mr. Kahlberg ceased to have access to land on which to store the cars he had rescued, he was forced to sell them. The V-16 coupe was

Awaiting restoration. The coupe in the background is the same car Karl Kahlberg rescued from the crusher. Unlike some of its fellow contestants in that long-ago demolition derby, this car has been returned to its original magnificence (courtesy Rick Kellman).

sold to Grover C. Phillips in Chillicothe, Missouri, for $225. When Mr. Phillips died the car went to his relatives, and during the 1970s, it found its way to Kansas City, Kansas, and into the hands of "Cadillac Jim" Pearson. It was unrestored and partly disassembled at that time.

Most recently, this car has been fully restored by noted V-16 specialist Sonny Elliott at his shop in Kansas City. It now sports a pearl-gray and black color combination with tan leather interior and chromed wire wheels. Following completion of the restoration, the coupe was entered in the 2013 Pebble Beach Concours d'Elegance, where it took second place in its class. That's quite a comeback story, and it is a tribute both to Mr. Elliott's considerable abilities, and to the quality and substance of the V-16 motor cars. At last word, this 1930 Series 4376 rumble seat coupe was available for a fortunate new owner to purchase at KC Vintage Cars in Kansas City, Missouri.

44. A Latter-Day Hardtop Sedan

In fall 2008, my friend Theron Baganz (owner of Ferdinand, a 1930 V-16 five-passenger sedan saluted elsewhere in these pages) said that his daughter had seen a very unusual V-16 while traveling through Ogden, Utah. The car was exhibited with a group of classic motor cars in an old railroad station that had been converted into a museum. The cars had been given to the city of Ogden by the late Matt Browning, heir to a family fortune and one-time owner of a much larger collection of fine cars. The snapshots that Theron's daughter sent were quite tantalizing. The color scheme was unusual and quite vivid. But the styling diverged in a number of major features from anything seen among the body styles that Cadillac proposed to its prospective V-16 customers. It looked like an all-weather phaeton with a fixed, albeit cloth-covered, top, and with rear quarter windows. As on an all-weather phaeton, the posts between the front and rear door windows could fold down, leaving the same open vista that obtained with the phaeton (or, years later, with "hardtop" sedans). Although there was nothing like it in the standard "canon" of body styles, it is well known that Cadillac would have catered to a customer's desire for design changes, to the extent they could be accommodated. Clearly, some investigative work was called for.

In 1852, Mormon pioneer Jonathan Browning opened a gunsmith shop in Ogden, Utah. His son John Moses Browning was one of the most gifted firearms designers and inventors ever, and he designed or contributed to weapons produced by Winchester, Colt, Remington, Fabrique Nationale (of Belgium) and his family's company. His work was the basis of the Colt .45 caliber automatic handgun carried by GIs in two World Wars, Korea, and Vietnam. The Browning automatic rifle or "B.A.R." was a popular and effective light machine gun among U.S. forces from World War II through the early days of the Vietnam conflict. The Browning Arms Company was founded to market the non-military designs, including shotguns and sporting rifles. Organized in 1927, one year after John Moses Browning's death, it was acquired by Fabrique Nationale de Herstel in 1977.

John Moses Browning's great-nephew Matt Browning accumulated a collection of some sixty-five fine automobiles. He paid to have room prepared at Ogden's Union Station to serve as a museum, and he rotated various cars from his collection for exhibit at the museum. After he passed away in November 1996, the nine cars that were then on display in the

Driver's controls and instruments. The small round pedal on a stalk next to the accelerator (and partially obscured by the hand brake lever) engages the starter motor. Each side of the windshield is hinged at the top and can be tipped outward for ventilation (courtesy Steven Sherwood).

museum were donated to the city of Ogden, and they are kept and shown by the Browning-Kimball Classic Car Museum at Union Station. The rest of the collection was sold at auction in 2000. One of the cars now permanently with the museum is a very unusual 1930 Cadillac V-16 carrying engine number 700072.

According to Cadillac's records, engine number 700072 was originally installed in a Series 4330-S five-passenger sedan that was shipped new to Seattle, Washington. It is an early number in the production sequence and was probably shipped in the month of February 1930. That is all that is known of the first thirty years of this car's life, except for the fact that it was converted at some point into a tow truck, and the body was sawed off at the base of the windshield pillars and removed, leaving only the cowl, hood, radiator shell, front fenders and running boards.

Years ago, there was a unique establishment in Southern California that is now a legend among old car hobbyists. A gentleman named Mike McManus had a large piece of property in Gardena, California, and around 1955 he began driving big, old unwanted automotive relics of what is now known as the classic car era onto that yard and parking them in rows. Car nuts of varying sorts visited the lot to buy parts, chassis and whole cars. What many of us would give to go back in time and stroll through Mike's treasures! There were junkyards all over the land that gave sustenance to restorers, tinkerers and hot rodders in the years before civic beautification campaigns and environmental crusades made such businesses a rarity. But Mike McManus's place was heaven on earth for old car fans.

Classics rest in the California sun. This is how Mike McManus's salvage yard looked in the 1950s and early 1960s. In the foreground is a 1930 or '31 Cadillac V-16, missing its bodywork from the windshield back, and a late 1920s Packard. The row of cars facing includes a 1937 Packard sedan, a 1929 or 1930 Cadillac coupe, a 1938 Cadillac V-8, a 1941 Cadillac Series 61 sedan, a 1938 Cadillac Fleetwood Series 60 Special sedan, and a 1940 Fleetwood Series 60 Special. Savvy collectors and restorers made good use of establishments such as these before land values, countryside beautification projects and other forces conspired to eliminate them (courtesy Paul Schinnerer).

In 1961, V-16 enthusiast Paul Schinnerer (whom we meet elsewhere in these pages) paid Mike McManus $300 for the disembodied Cadillac V-16 chassis bearing engine number 700072. The fenders were pitted and banged up, and the radiator shell was well on the way to rusted. Paul didn't know just what he might do with this find, but he knew it had plenty of potential. About a year and a half later, he heard about three other Cadillac cars in Santa Barbara, behind a row of house trailers that had been there since 1947: a 1931 V-8 sedan that was too far gone for help; a '31 V-12 town sedan that a friend of his took a shine to; and a 1930 Fleetwood V-8 sedan with a fascinating body that he immediately wanted, in order to match it with the V-16 engine and chassis he had. The seller told him that this particular car had once belonged to the United States ambassador to the Republic of Ireland.

Fleetwood Series 3982 was a five-passenger sedan on the V-8 chassis of a type known as a "sedanette cabriolet." For advertising purposes, the 1930 Fleetwood body styles bore names that were variants of Fleetwood (for example, the roadster was "Fleetdowns" and a limousine was "Fleetdale"). The Series 3982 sedan was designated "Fleetwind" or "Fleetwing" (records are somewhat ambiguous). The same configuration was also used in the LaSalle line, designated Series 4082. The doors on the sedanette cabriolets were center-hinged like those on an all-weather phaeton. There was a two-piece, center-split and V'd windshield, and the pillars between the side windows were very slender. Those pillars could be folded down (again like the all-weather phaeton) to give a feeling of openness seldom found in a closed car. The roof was covered in Burbank cloth, emulating a convertible with the top raised. The advent of "hardtops" in the late 1940s would be hailed as a new development, but the Series 3982 is an example of a much earlier appearance of the same body type.

The Fleetwood bodies that were mounted on the 1930 V-8 chassis could be installed on the straight-sill V-16 chassis without any modification to either body or chassis. All mounting points lined up precisely, and hoods, fenders and body sills aligned normally. In fact, Cadillac records indicate that at least one 1930 V-8 body similar to this one (Series 3981) was installed by the factory on a V-16 chassis. Over the years, this interchangeability has allowed many metamorphoses from closed to open body styles. This particular car is an unusual example of a closed car becoming another closed style.

The body of the Fleetwood Series 3982 that Paul Schinnerer had to work with was quite solid in the metal parts, but it needed extensive replacement of the structural wood members. Remember that in the '20s and early 1930s, most cars (including Cadillacs) had "composite" bodies, constructed of metal panels stretched over a hardwood framework. The structural integrity and safe operation of such a vehicle is heavily dependent upon the soundness and security of the wood skeleton. If it has been rotted, dried out or damaged by insects,

Backyard progress check. Paul Schinnerer examines the new wood frame rails and cross members he has shaped, drilled and assembled for the sedanette cabriolet body. This framework for the floor of the body provides much of the structural stability. The cowl, door pillars and rear bodywork anchor to it (courtesy Paul Schinnerer).

the wood must be repaired or replaced before any other bodywork, interior restoration or painting can be undertaken. Mr. Schinnerer built all of the new wood parts himself, learning how to do it as he went. He didn't have a bandsaw of his own, but the marine electronics shop where he worked did. So at night, he would strap the lumber to the side of his work car and drive back to the shop to use the bandsaw.

After the chassis was cleaned and painted, and the repaired body was mounted on it, Mr. Schinnerer spent several years obtaining needed parts—better fenders and radiator shell, refinished emblems, hubcaps, engine parts and so forth. In an extensive article in the January 1965 issue of the Cadillac-LaSalle Club's newsletter *The Self-Starter,* Mr. Schinnerer tells the whole exciting story of acquiring and working on this project.

Eventually, Paul Schinnerer traded the V-16 sedanette cabriolet and a 1941 Fleetwood Sixty Special sedan to Mr. Wayne Bemis for a Series 4235 V-16 convertible coupe.[1] Mr. Schinnerer recalls that Mr. Bemis grew impatient with the restorer he was working with, and sold the Cadillac to Matt Browning.

According to Steve Sherwood, a volunteer at the Browning-Kimball museum, the museum's V-16 Cadillac has been dormant for some time. Mr. Browning is said to have driven it regularly, but there has recently been some difficulty getting the car running. The vacuum-driven fuel delivery system was bypassed at some point in the past, and electric fuel pumps were installed. In stock configuration, and under normal conditions, the fuel to the carburetors is pressurized only by gravity as it falls through the lines from the vacuum tanks. If an electric fuel pump is introduced into the system, the pump's output pressure must be regulated to keep it from overwhelming the needle valve in the carburetor and flooding the engine.

Exactly when Matt Browning acquired this particular Cadillac V-16 remains somewhat unclear, but one gentleman who used to work on his cars for him believes that the car joined Mr. Browning's collection in 1980. I encountered a number of secondhand tales about how that came to be. One story was that Mr. Browning's mother had the car constructed for him. Another explanation was that Mr. Browning himself contracted with a gentleman to put the Series 3982 body on the car. Another source told me that the body was installed by Cadillac according to the specific directions of the original owner. Mr. Schinnerer has the photographs and firsthand information to settle the question. Now if we only knew how the chassis and engine from that Series 4330-S five-passenger sedan that was originally purchased in Seattle ended up in Mike McManus's special wrecking yard ...

In the early 2000s, the Franklin Mint issued a limited-production ¼₄ scale die-cast model of a 1930 Cadillac V-16 sedan with the same color scheme as the Browning car. The model company did not replicate the unusual body style but used the molds for a previously-issued model of a 1930 Series 4375 seven-passenger imperial sedan. According to people at the museum, someone from the Franklin Mint did come and take measurements and photographs of the museum's V-16.

45. One-of-a-Kind Touring Car

Cadillac built one Series 4257-H phaeton. Just one. It was a large touring car with the "straight sill" treatment for the lower edge of the body above the running boards. The "H"

A dying breed. By 1930, the traditional touring car, a large, open car with the back seat all the way at the rear of the car and without windows, was falling out of favor and would soon be gone from the catalogs. Most Cadillac offerings in the four-door open configuration were either all-weather phaetons (convertible sedans with roll-up windows) or sport phaetons (with the rear seat brought up closer to the front seat) (courtesy Ronald Moore).

indicates additional headroom, meaning that the top bows and windshield frame were extended to raise the roof a bit. Many owners of fine motor cars of the time still insisted that they should be able to wear a hat without interference from the interior of the car.

This car was delivered new to the Inglis M. Uppercu dealership in New York City. It carries engine number 701849, and was shipped from the factory in June 1930. Something over 12 years ago, the owner of a carpet company in Chatsworth, Georgia, passed away at the age of 49. His estate included a four-acre building filled with antique automobiles. The extensive collection was largely unknown before the man's death. Mr. Ronald J. Moore of Birmingham, Alabama, was able to get into the building and see the cars. His wife got along well with the curator of the collection, and Mr. Moore was able to purchase some of the cars, including a Cadillac V-16 roadster and a 1935 Packard V-12 phaeton. At the time, Mr. Moore examined the Series 4257-H phaeton, but was put off by the "basket case" condition of the car, the large number of missing or incorrect parts, and the enormity of the work needed to bring it back to a presentable and operable condition.

Although he didn't purchase the one-off V-16, Mr. Moore told an attorney friend about it. His friend bought the car and brought it to the fellow in Birmingham whom Mr. Moore

Opposite: **Down to the bones. The body has been freed of doors, trim and other encumbrances and stripped of its paint. Primer is being applied and sanded. The wood framework that underlies and supports the metal panels of these "composite" bodies is visible in this shot (courtesy Ronald Moore).**

Somewhere on the road to restoration. From the two batteries sitting on the running board and the wires running into the engine and passenger compartments, it appears the engine is being encouraged to resume internal combustion after a significant hiatus. Sometimes that takes persistent persuasion (courtesy Ronald Moore).

Impressive proportions. The limousine-like dimensions of this rare body style are apparent in a side view. There is ample room for jump seat passengers between the fixed seats. Fixing side curtains in the event of a sudden storm could be a major adventure, though (courtesy Ronald Moore).

used for restoration work. Some time later, the restorer informed Mr. Moore that he had bought the phaeton from the attorney and had traded another car for a V-16 sedan in good unrestored condition that had all of the parts that were incorrect or missing on the Series 4257. With the availability of the needed parts as an inducement, Mr. Moore agreed to buy the phaeton and begin its rehabilitation.

Mr. Moore re-assembled the phaeton, adding in the parts that had been missing and getting it running before commencing a formal restoration process. The car was very solid, including the structural woodwork. It was a fine candidate for restoration quite apart from its impressive rarity.

The car went first to a restoration company in North Carolina, but after two years and a six-figure outlay, it became clear to Mr. Moore that the outcome was not going to meet his high standards for the project. So he cut his losses and moved the car to another restoration facility in Pennsylvania, where it resided for the better part of the next five years. The car is now a beautifully restored automobile that can be shown proudly in any venue. It achieved a perfect score at a Classic Car Club of America Grand Classic event in Baltimore, Maryland, and is a senior car with the Antique Automobile Club of America.

46. We Just Take Care of Them

It's a well-worn proverb of the old car hobby that we don't own these cars—we just take care of them until the next owner comes along. That summarizes the necessary sense of detachment that characterizes a grown-up and rational approach to material objects of all sorts. We are not the things we own, and our ultimate value is not determined by the quantity or quality of our possessions. Simply put, you can't take your cars with you. Either you'll transfer them to someone else or your estate will. Barring accidents, natural disasters or egregious neglect, the cars will outlast us and others will have the opportunity to appreciate and maintain them. Ideally, they will bear enduring witness through future generations to the genius, skill, care and hard work of those who built and handled them, and those whose lives they touched.

For approximately ten years, Mr. Herbert E. Mahn of Connecticut owned and cared for a very dark green 1930 Cadillac V-16 Series 4375 seven-passenger imperial sedan. That's the big limousine that was the second most frequently ordered style in the 1930–31 model run (only the 4375-S seven-passenger sedan was shipped in greater numbers). He acquired the car in 1955 or '56 from the widow of its most recent owner. The car had been sold new to a gentleman in Taunton, Massachusetts, and it was purchased from him by the famous operatic tenor and motion picture star James Melton. In addition to his pursuit of musical perfection, beginning in the mid–1930s Mr. Melton had sought out and acquired a collection of fine automobiles. He displayed his cars at a museum in Norwalk, Connecticut, and later at one in Hypoluxo, Florida (near West Palm Beach).

A gentleman named Hoyt purchased the 1930 Cadillac V-16 from Mr. Melton and still owned it when he passed away in the early 1950s. Mrs. Hoyt was left to manage their family alone, and her offspring were a handful. One of the grandsons presumed to tinker with the 1930 Cadillac, and he apparently connected two of the ignition wires to the wrong spark plugs, disrupting the firing order. That may have been what started a fire on the right-hand side of the engine that burned the spare tire right off of its wheel, and damaged the fender, the hood, the door and the right front window.

Mr. Mahn had opened an automobile repair shop in 1953, called the Model Garage. He named it after the shop featured in a recurring series of stories in *Popular Science* magazine, in which the wise, professional and conscientious mechanic Gus invariably solved one or more knotty automotive puzzles each episode, to the relief and gratitude of his customers. Subsequently, a writer for the series contracted with Mr. Mahn to provide him monthly with clever tricks Gus could use in upcoming installments of the fictional Model Garage's saga.

Mr. Mahn learned the trade of automobile mechanics in Boston at the Benjamin Franklin Institute of Technology, which opened its doors in 1908. The man who bored the cylinder blocks of the engines at the institute drove up every day in a 1930 Cadillac V-16 limousine, with all of his borers and related equipment in the roomy passenger compartment. The hand-built formal car was just his daily driver and tool wagon. That was the first Cadillac V-16 that Mr. Mahn ever saw.

In the early 1950s, Mr. Mahn joined the Horseless Carriage Club and attended many regional meetings. At one such meet in New Rochelle, New York (sponsored by James Melton), Mr. Mahn arrived in his 1940 LaSalle sedan that he drove on a daily basis. He made the acquaintance of another automotive technician, who had come with his 1934 Cadillac V-16 sedan. They encountered each other again at subsequent old car meets and Mr. Mahn found himself wanting a V-16 of his own.

One day a man walked into the Model Garage seeking help in locating a Lincoln Continental from the 1940s that he could purchase. Mr. Mahn was able to send him to a prospective seller, and the man subsequently purchased a Continental. In return, he provided Mr. Mahn with a lead for a 1930 Cadillac V-16 imperial sedan, which happened to be the fire-scarred car that Mrs. Hoyt had inherited from her late husband.

Mr. Mahn approached the widow at her home in East Norwalk, Connecticut, and it did not take long to settle on a price of $400 for the car "as is." Returning the next day, he brought the money for the purchase, an air tank to pump up the tires, some insect spray to get rid of the bees that made their home in the interior shortly after the fire, and his 1948 Ford one-ton tow truck for the nearly four-mile drive to his garage in Westport. The tires held air and the tow was successful, but the great weight of the car (something over 6,000 pounds) caused the front wheels of the truck to leave the ground with each bump in the road.

But for the fire damage, Mr. Mahn might not have been able to purchase the opulent and otherwise well-preserved limousine for such a low price. But for the bees, the youngsters might have wreaked havoc with the interior. As it was, he had a significant restoration project to deal with, and he set to his task with purpose.

It turned out that Mr. Mahn had bought the Cadillac right out from under a would-be purchaser who said he had expended considerable time and effort locating and arranging to buy it. That gentleman introduced himself to Mr. Mahn, who was able to turn aside his frustration and become acquainted. His name was Albro Case, and he was a member of the family that founded and ran the Case tractor company. He had a collection of Cadillac V-16 automobiles stored on his homestead in several barns and sheds, which he showed to Mr. Mahn and his friend Charles McCullough.

Mr. Case was invited to stop by the Model Garage any time he liked, and during the course of the restoration of the 1930 Cadillac, he did so frequently. After repeated requests, Mr. Mahn agreed to trade the elegant flying goddess radiator ornament for an authentic accessory trunk in fine condition with fitted luggage, together with a plain radiator cap to keep the cooling system in order. Although Mr. Mahn always thought that he'd gotten the worse end of that deal, today a trunk like that would easily bring a four-figure price.

Others who visited the shop made their own contributions to the project. One noticed the empty tube in the passenger compartment designed for storage of an umbrella, and on his next visit, he filled it. Another saw a place for a flower vase and supplied one. Mr. Mahn secured the wood pieces that he used for running board treads with dozens of screws. One friend spent a morning aligning the slots on each of the screw heads. A man to whom Mr. Mahn had sold a Chrysler roadster noticed that the dashboard clock was missing and gave him a clock that fit "like a glove." Another collector offered a complete hide of leather if Mr. Mahn would cover the damaged front seat cushion and back, and he was delighted to accept.

One of the distinguished automotive figures Mr. Mahn knew well was Briggs Cunningham, the noted race car driver and designer, whose 1950 Cadillacs took 10th and 11th places at LeMans, and who also captained the yacht *Columbia* to an America's Cup victory in 1958. Mr. Cunningham remarked about Mr. Mahn's V-16, "What a peasant crusher!" Mr. Cunningham owned a V-16 roadster that he asked Mr. Mahn to drive to a number of car shows (to the latter's delight!). That roadster is now owned by Robert and Brigitte Thayer of Atlanta, Georgia, and it is the subject of the chapter "California Dreamin'" elsewhere in this volume.

The restoration that Mr. Mahn undertook lasted ten years and made the car, in his words, "a wonderful display." The burned spare tire had to come off. The right upper hood panel had to be sent to a body man for careful straightening. A friend who ran a body shop inside the local Ford agency addressed that issue. He straightened and primed the hood panel, and did the same for the heavy gauge steel front fender. When he retrieved the fender, Mr. Mahn placed it in the back of his wrecker, but didn't tie it down securely. When the truck passed over a large bump in the road and the back end heaved upward, the fender was tossed into the air and tumbled to a stop at the curb. Stopping and running back to rescue his fender, he was relieved to find it undamaged.

Mr. Mahn opened the engine for inspection and any necessary repair. He removed the cylinder heads, pistons, connecting rods and oil pan. The internal parts were in excellent shape for a 29-year-old engine. New valves and piston rings were all that was required. He cleaned the right-hand carburetor, replaced the plug wires (correctly connected now), and installed and set new points and condensers. Once everything was in place, the engine fired up and sounded fine. Many parts were still available from the local Cadillac dealer, including a complete engine gasket set (very expensive today!).

A complete cleaning of the fuel system (which is actually two independent systems from the single gas tank forward, with separate lines, vacuum operated pumps, strainers and carburetors) was undertaken. Because the vacuum tanks that draw fuel from the main gas tank were not working well, an electric fuel pump was installed. Brakes, wheel bearings and tires were seen to. The tires were hard to find in the correct size, but the local Goodyear dealer came up with four blackwall tires. Even though they were not quite the correct size, because of an unusual bead shape they fit the rims and worked well.

Car clubs provided contacts and sources for some of the parts the car required. A missing

The 1930 Series 4375 when Herbert Mahn owned it. These cars are seldom seen today with blackwall tires, although that was more common when they were new. Whitewalls could be considered ostentatious, particularly during the opening years of the Great Depression. Note the wood strips that have replaced the original black rubber running board treads. Another unusual feature these days is the standard unadorned radiator cap (courtesy Herbert Mahn).

Another view of the Series 4375 limousine. The exterior door handles are the type found on Fisher-bodied Cadillacs (generally V-8s or V-12s) and would not likely have been original equipment on this Fleetwood-bodied car. The blackwall tires add to the impression of length. At eighteen and a half feet long, these cars fit comfortably in most standard garages. The 1934 V-16s would achieve a twenty-foot overall length (courtesy Herbert Mahn).

horn trumpet was obtained from a club member in Michigan, and a complete dual exhaust system was located through the recently-formed (1958) Cadillac-LaSalle Club.

Once the car was repaired and spiffed up, Mr. Mahn showed and enjoyed his elegant limousine. He relates that he "visited almost every corner of Fairfield County [Connecticut]" and "entered dozens of antique car shows." He recounts an impromptu drag race with Charlie McCullough's '34 Packard sedan after a car show in Orange, Connecticut. They both entered the Connecticut Thruway through separate tollbooths, paid the toll and hit the gas. The V-16 easily outran the Packard from the start. But at sixty m.p.h., the Packard began to slowly pull ahead. In fairness, at around 5,500 pounds, the Packard would have had a 500 to 1,000-pound weight advantage over the Cadillac, together with the aerodynamic benefit of the streamlining craze that was in full cry in the mid–'30.

In 1965, domestic fiscal and logistical needs caught up with the Mahn family. Herbert Mahn had two daughters in college, and after he sold the Model Garage, storing the big V-16 was more difficult. He made the decision to sell the 1930 Cadillac. The buyer was another collector on the order of Mr. Melton. He had about 100 cars, all of them prime examples from the period 1925 through 1935 when the great classics roamed the earth in substantial numbers. At his request, Mr. Mahn delivered the V-16 limousine to a restoration shop in New Jersey. Until recently, Herb Mahn had no idea what became of the car after he dropped it off.

The V-16 limousine is one of many automobiles Mr. Mahn has owned. His last antique car was a 1931 Ford Cabriolet that his daughter now owns. The Cadillac played a significant part in his life for a while, then left to be shared and enjoyed by someone else. Forty-four years after he parted with the car, his memories and his admiration for the exquisite workmanship remain fresh. Those of us who are privileged to be stewards of great works of art cannot help but be touched by them and find that our lives are changed. But like the man said, we never really own them.

In 2006, at the Concours d'Elegance of the Eastern United States, a black (or nearly so) 1930 Cadillac V-16 Series 4375 limousine with green wheels was shown, and photos of that car showed up on the Internet. Certain characteristics seemed to indicate that the car was the same one with which Herb Mahn had parted company in the mid–1960s. The rubber strips on the running boards had been replaced by wood strips held in place with countersunk screws the slots of which were aligned front to rear. The side-view mirror mounted to the hinge on the driver's door had the same long, curved mounting arm. With some amateur detective work, it was possible to determine that the owner of the car at the concours was Edward Crane of Brick, New Jersey.

Mr. Crane's father, Robert, of Toms River, New Jersey, had bought the car in 1972. A gentleman named Frank Thompson had advertised it in the Antique Automobile Club of America magazine, and by the time Bob Crane found out about it, the Cadillac had been

A remarkably well-conserved veteran. The limousine that James Melton once owned and that Herbert Mahn cared for is now under the careful guidance of Edward Crane. It retains a majestic presence in spite of all that it has been through (courtesy Robert and Edward Crane).

sold. But he asked if he could come down and see the car anyway, and Mr. Thompson agreed. Mr. Thompson had a half dozen other cars in various states of repair, and in the course of the visit, he asked Mr. Crane (a professional mechanic) if Mr. Crane could work on them. He agreed and over the course of some weeks got the cars running. During that time, the buyer of the Cadillac V-16 had not come to pick it up. Mr. Thompson had noticed how thoroughly taken with the big limousine Mr. Crane was, and said he'd tell the buyer that he had changed his mind about selling—just wait a month. Mr. Crane sweated out the month-long wait and returned with the requested price ($6,000 in cash). Mr. Thompson put the cash in his freezer and Mr. Crane drove the car home.

On his journey back, the two electric fuel pumps that had been installed on the car kept overwhelming the valves in the vacuum tanks and the carburetors, causing the engine to flood and die. In order to get home, Mr. Crane resorted to switching off the electric pumps long enough to let the engine's fuel consumption catch up with what the pumps were supplying. Once home, he removed the electric fuel pumps and the car has run on the original vacuum feed system ever since.

Herb Mahn's Cadillac V-16 limousine has found a new home. It has passed through several sets of hands and several generations, a source of fond memories and current pleasures, as it embodies another time, a rarefied world that we today can only imagine.

47. Dry Lakes Record Holder

The Southern California Timing Association was organized in 1938 by a group of clubs. The clubs, in turn were organized by men (mostly) who loved building and running fast cars. Then as now, the SCTA has relied upon the volunteer services of the club members to organize, staff and run racing events on dry lake beds. El Mirage Dry Lake is used today, but other venues were utilized in the past, including Muroc Dry Lake, which is now part of Edwards Air Force Base. In the 1930s, "hot rod" had a negative connotation in the public mind, signifying juvenile delinquents flouting traffic laws, endangering pedestrians and other drivers, and generally wreaking havoc with their homemade, hopped-up jalopies. Enthusiasts banded together to change that image and to legitimize and civilize what was a hobby for some and a lifestyle for others.

The club members who built and raced their roadsters, streamliners, sports cars and other creations at SCTA events were incredibly resourceful and creative. Frames, engines and chassis components were sourced from salvage yards or used car lots. Bodywork was adapted from discarded or secondhand cars, or it was hand fabricated. Some builders even used entire war surplus aircraft fuel tanks for their car's bodies, cheating the wind and saving money at the same time. Builders and drivers dreamed, designed, constructed, tested, ran and raced, learning as they went. It was a crucible in which knowledge and technology were refined by experience.

As the name implies, the SCTA was very much about timing cars and proving just how fast a particular car and driver could go. The best entrants came away with records and bragging rights. Everyone got the chance to participate in an exciting and fast-changing sport, and to be part of a lively community of like-minded folks.

One of the people who raced on the dry lakes was a young man named Clint Seccombe. In the late 1930s, he decided to see how fast he could run with a Cadillac V-16 engine. In 1940, he set a new SCTA record with a speed of 125.52 m.p.h., which wasn't broken until after the war. What follows is the story of the roadster that he built and what he did with it, as told by Mr. Seccombe (now in his nineties) to his son (also named Clint). Only minimal editing has been done to the text.

I was racing anything I could those days and I wanted to find and get my hands on the biggest engine I could, aside from a tractor or something, and put it in my 1929 Ford Model A Roadster. At that time racing classes were determined by body type, Roadster, Modified and Streamliner, but you could run whatever you wanted under the hood. Back then, the Southern California Timing Association sponsored speed contests out on the dry lakes in the Mojave Desert. We'd go out four times a year when the lakes were dry and hard, once in the spring, twice in summer and then again in the fall. Muroc was the preferred lake owing to the composition of its surface. That place later became Edwards Air Force Base.

So, in 1939 I found a complete and fully functioning 1930 model Cadillac limousine with a Series 452 V16 engine for $200 on a cheap assed used car lot on Santa Monica Blvd. in West Hollywood. Nice old Caddies like that weren't of much interest to people any longer. The Depression was getting to be over and if someone wanted a Caddie they wanted a new one. Two hundred dollars wasn't a small amount of money to me at the time, but I got it together and bought the car. I drove right away to the San Fernando Valley, to a lot beside the home of my buddy Ted Cannon, where I and some of my pals proceeded to dismantle it. The heavy wire wheels went onto my 1931 La Salle convertible. They fit nice and looked real good. The engine, manual transmission, radiator and gas tank were to go into my roadster. The rest of it was "junked out" and sold off as parts to wrecking yards. I don't remember getting any real money to speak of selling what parts I could salvage.

Now, this project of putting together a race car proceeded without the cognizance of my parents who, had they known, would have asked, "What the hell are you, a 21 year old father of two boys doing putting together a contraption to drag out to the dry lakes to race?" Well, when they finally did find out and did ask me, and then insist that I cease and desist, in characteristic fashion I continued to proceed with my plans.

Working out of Ted Cannon's shop, and he had a good one for doing all this kind of playing around, the first thing was separate off the Ford body from the frame because each one had its own problems to solve to get that monster engine in. On the body I started by removing the fuel tank. The tank in the Ford in those days was part of, actually integral to the cowl, there between the dashboard and the hood. It was one single tank which had to be sawn up and removed. That had to be done carefully, first so I wouldn't be blown to pieces in the process, but also so that it didn't compromise either the cowl structure or profile. Roadsters, "open knob jobs" as we facetiously referred to them, were the preferred vehicles around Los Angeles in those days among guys who liked to race in or outside of town. Many of them were chopped and altered but I wanted to remain compliant for Roadster class. That meant doing nothing which would alter the outside appearance of the Model A shell or alter the interior space where two persons had to be able to be seated side by side.

I next set about reinforcing the Ford's frame. That stock frame was a C channel and I took long, one-eighth inch thick by eight inch wide pieces of band steel, laid them up the length of both sides of the frame and arc welded the seams making it a rectangular tube. That made the frame heavy but it was going to be able to take the weight of that engine and whatever fast and rough conditions I'd be putting it through.

Back then there were "traffic buttons" placed in the ground at intersections to dissuade people from making dangerous turns into oncoming traffic. "No cuttin' the button," they'd say and it was a violation if you did. These things were like big red painted plugs which sat high enough and were strong enough to do damage to the underside of a car if any part of it were too low to the

Model A cowl makes a handy tool tray. Clint Seccombe (left) makes adjustments as interested bystanders watch. The rear half of the V-16 engine is visible between the cowl and instrument panel. Several spark plugs can be seen between the cylinder banks. Note the car's skeletal steering wheel (courtesy Leslie Long).

ground. So I had to be careful with my geometry when I was putting all this together. I had the radiator, the engine and the expectation of increased spring flex to think about.

I first carefully set the engine up on blocks at the height I'd wanted and then brought the frame down around it. With all that in place I made new engine mounting blocks. They were crude looking things made out of heavy iron water pipe which I welded to the band steel of the frame. Some heavy rubber between the engine and the mount completed it.

I needed the Caddie's radiator to cool that big engine. The Model A's just wasn't going to hack it. I removed the roadster's radiator from its shell and fitted the Caddie's behind the shell. The

Engine layout. The Ford radiator is retained for cosmetics, just in front of the actual heavy duty unit. The cloisonné V-16 emblem from the rear deck of the car that donated the engine has been mounted on the Ford radiator shell in place of the blue oval badge. Three of the four downdraft carburetors can be seen—the left rear unit had been removed when this photo was taken (courtesy Leslie Long).

height of the Caddie's radiator, being considerably greater than the roadster's made it necessary to place it so that it hung below the Model A's frame.

I put Ford V8 hubs and 16 or 18 inch wheels on the car. Those were strong wheels which I felt I needed to carry that engine and frame, and wheels that size would give me a little more speed. I put the Caddie's gas tank back in the rear of the roadster where it would be totally concealed where the rumble seat would have been. With the body in place I sat kind of stuffed into the thing. It was tight in all directions. The transmission stretched rearward further than my ass and to be able to shift gears I had to make a specially shaped gearshift lever. It came out of the transmission a few inches, turned 90 degrees and forward about a foot, then 90 degrees up so that the knob was about in line with my lowest rib. It took some leverage to shift that thing.

When I first took it out it went like a son-of-a-bitch, but there was no way of determining the car's actual speed. I was certainly running faster than the Model A's speedometer could gauge but it would have been no good to me anyways because of gearing differences. And the Caddie's speedometer would have been no good to me because it was never expected to go as fast as I was running either. George Temple, the brother of Shirley Temple, had a pretty fast car in those days but he couldn't keep up. Word got out in Los Angeles that I was taking unfair advantage by putting so big an engine in my car, even though others had tried it themselves.

After running well at high speed for a time the car began to show signs of irregularity in firing, rough running and reduced speed. It was a puzzle just what was amiss and we never resolved with absolute certainty what had gone wrong. Ted Cannon was the guy to go to if you wanted a good opinion on the best thing to do with the least money, and he was darn good at solving engineering problems. Ted's dad, Walt, was referred to as "The Oracle" by his kids and others owing to his general wisdom and technical intelligence. He'd taught himself German in order to be able to read books on German engineering. He'd built his own telescope, grinding and polishing the lenses himself, and through it I remember viewing the Galilean Moons of Jupiter. Well, Ted was a chip off the old block, I thought, and he'd become an excellent machinist, and we set about trying to solve this firing problem.

Ted had a pretty good working machine shop then, which is where I'd been doing all this work. During that time Ted had a chance to buy some used equipment, a vertical mill, a lathe and a shaper. With loans from his dad, from my folks and folks of another buddy he bought the stuff and with what he already had he'd made a real working shop for himself.

As I said, we never determined with certainty why the engine developed firing problems after initially running quite well. It may have been that the high rpms I was running had degraded the coil or something in the Caddie's system. The best we could make of it was that it was no longer getting the dwell time needed for optimal firing in the cylinders. After much pondering and scratching our heads it was decided to scrap the entire Caddie electrical system and run it all through a dual Ford system that we devised. I fabricated a two tiered distributor with each tier carrying eight points apiece. This increased the dwell time allowing the needed 50,000 volts to develop. That did the trick, and naturally more racing ensued.

First time I ran was out at Muroc on June 30th. I took first place and was clocked at 125.52 miles per hour.

I remember driving solo out to Muroc to the races one Saturday. I was feeling pretty good about my car. I was running slicks on it and I wanted to see if I could break traction just by jumping on the throttle. Well, it broke traction all right and the rear wheels started to slide hard. Before I knew the car had swapped ends and was rushing backwards somewhere between the sagebrush and the power poles. When it all settled down and I'd wiped the sweat off my head I found that there was no harm done. No one observed this and I had a pretty good time telling that story on myself out at the lake.

Of course, if you're racing competitively the goal is to keep working to go faster. So the next exercise was to do what could be done to the engine to squeeze more power out of it. I'd learned from Ted how to operate whatever machinery I was going to need. And I purchased an overhaul manual for the Caddie V-16 but it wasn't much good for what I intended to do.

The winner. Clint Seccombe finished well ahead of the other cars. SCTA certificate gave bragging rights (courtesy Leslie Long).

Naturally, I wanted to increase my compression ratio. At the rpm's I was running those heavy, cast iron Caddie pistons were putting a lot of extra strain on the crankshaft and connecting rods and I wanted to replace them. I found a used set of lighter, three inch bore aluminum racing pistons which I had to regrind slightly on account of a little flat that had worn in them. They came to about thirty thousandths over three inches. With a boring bar precisely set up I opened up the cylinder chambers to make room for those new pistons and increase my sweep volume. That was a Caddie Series 452 engine when I began and I believe the displacement by the time I was finished was about 492 cubic inches.

The factory V16 had separate exhaust and intake manifolds for each side or set of eight cylinders. But they only ran one carburetor on each side and I wanted to get more fuel in there than that. The intake and exhaust manifolds were cast iron. Their inside surfaces were rough and flow retarding. Model A hop-up guys would bore those passages smooth. I ignored the exhaust manifold altogether but I replaced the factory intake by fabricating a new one. I used two inch steel tube that I had a lot of work to do opening up and welding flanges to. The Caddie had updraft carburetors but Ford had very efficient downdrafts on its V8 which I decided to acquire and install. I optimally located two of those Fords on each of my intake manifolds.

I raced that car most all of 1940 and sold it in 1941 for two hundred dollars. I stopped racing it because to go further trying to get more power out of it was going to be too costly and involve too much time and effort. There'd be grinding the camshaft for more valve opening and improved timing, and having to go whole hog on the crankshaft by grinding the throws so as to increase the piston sweep. Ted had developed a super-charger that he put with good result on a Model A and I could have done a similar thing on the Caddie but again, at a lot of time and expense.

About that time I'd acquired a Marmon V16 which was an aluminum block engine that was larger and more advanced than the Series 452. I wasn't going to run a roadster this time but as a modified one seat affair. I'd been pretty cramped up beside that Caddie V16. Left and right, fore and aft I was squeezed in. It made that drive out to the dry lakes a challenge with all its opportunities for mishap. I spent some time trying to get that Marmon going but at the same time I was becoming increasingly interested in airplanes. And finally airplanes won and took practically all of my attention.

The last time the car was seen by me was at a show in the Armory building in downtown Los Angeles late in the '40s or early '50s. A young fellow owned it. I talked with him a while about it, curious to know just what kind of work he'd done on it. I finally introduced myself as the guy who put it all together in the first place. He was about floored and grateful for the meeting as I remember.

It's not known what became of Mr. Seccombe's car after that one sighting by him almost sixty years ago. Perhaps someone in Southern California has tucked away in a garage or shed an aging old-school hot rod with an engine so long that the driver sits next to the flywheel housing and the shifter knob is in front of the transmission. Of course, the car may have been junked or parted out, but there's still a chance that it will come to light someday.

Photos of the roadster appeared in *Rod & Custom* magazine and have shown up on the Internet.

Dean Bachelor in his book *Dry Lakes and Drag Strips* says:

Clint Seccombe set a new SCTA roadster record in 1940, at 125.52 mph, but because he set it with a Cadillac V-16-powered roadster, they made a new Unlimited Class for 1941 and moved Seccombe and his record into that new class. This record stood until 1945.[1]

48. Hot Rod Cadillac

Bob Blake of Phoenix, Arizona, died suddenly in October 2004 from heart disease. His passing was a hard blow for his son Dave, who had worked closely with him since Dave was five (in 1961). Among the other things they had been doing together was restoring Bob's hot rod that he had first acquired at about the time that Dave was born. Bob Blake was a history buff, in addition to being a master mechanic. His son marveled at how much he knew and remembered, because as long as Dave had been aware, his father had spent most of his waking life building, fixing or doing things with his hands. Their life together had been intense, productive and rewarding. As in all real collaborations, there had been tensions and difficult moments. But they meant the world to each other and when one was suddenly gone, the other was knocked for a loop.

Bob's hot rod was a 1923 Dodge Brothers roadster mounted on a 1932 Ford frame and powered by a 1930 Cadillac V-16 engine. For some time after his death, his son wasn't able to return to the restoration project. The pain of loss was too fresh and the car was too much a part of his father and the memories. Bit by bit, though, the edge has worn off the grief, and the car is now running and show-worthy. In June 2007, Dave brought it to a show in Carpinteria, California (along with a 1934 Ford with a Duesenberg J engine).

The V-16 hot rod was built in 1950 by 19-year-old Leon Moore, known as a talented metal fabricator, and his 16-year-old childhood friend George "Wayne" Perry, both of Phoenix. They had gotten the engine from a friend, who had bought it from Bell Auto Parts in California. They owned and drove the car for several years and even ran it a time or two at the Perryville drag races. Perryville was an abandoned military airstrip that the county

A hot rod so cool you have to use a stick to keep the girls away. That's how George "Wayne" Perry captioned this shot. He would later marry the pretty blonde (courtesy Blake Machine Collection).

had designated as a place where young car nuts could take their cars and race them, hopefully leaving residential and business streets to slower and less competitive drivers.

The car exemplifies the dominant philosophy behind the original hot rods—put a light-weight, bare-bones body on a light but strong chassis, bolt in a powerful engine, tweak things and see how fast you can get it to go. Used components were favored to save the time, expense and expertise required for fabricating parts to order. Most of the young men who participated in the hot rod craze were working with limited budgets, and they had to stretch their dollars. In 1950, salvage yards and even used car lots were rich sources of inexpensive raw materials for intrepid hot rod builders. And some of the most exotic engines ever built waited neglected and disregarded for someone with an idea and the motivation to execute it. This car was not the only time a Cadillac V-16 was installed in a hot rod. *The Street Rodder's Handbook* notes that of the 95 hot rods entered in the Southern California Timing Association's May 19, 1940, Lakes Meet, one was powered by a V-16 and another by a V-12. "They were strong runners," says the author, "but the engines were too expensive to entice a serious following."[1]

In the mid–1950s, Bob Blake, together with his high school friend Ken Dobbs, purchased the hand-built Cadillac hot rod from Leon Moore and Wayne Perry. The plan was to make a "rail job" out of it—a dragster consisting basically of an engine, a chassis and a seat. They never got around to making that transformation, and the car retained its roadster

The Cadillac V-16 engine as initially installed. Leon Moore and George Perry mounted the engine in a more or less stock configuration. Thick S-shaped pipe is the air intake horn for the Cadillac-Johnson updraft carburetor in the center of the picture. Fuel is supplied by an electric pump through the tube resting on the steering gear box (courtesy Blake Machine Collection).

configuration. Bob and Ken owned the car jointly until Ken moved to California. Bob Blake's long-time friend Urban "Humps" Porterie still recalls the excitement the hot rod caused when it pulled into Bob's Big Boy restaurant, a popular hangout for hot rodders along Phoenix's Central Avenue in the early and mid '50s. Ken Dobbs used the car for transportation while he was a student at Arizona State University, where it must have been a grand source of entertainment for his fellow students. People frequently asked, "Is that an Allison?," recalling the big V-12 aircraft engines built by General Motors and installed in many of the American warbirds during World War II. Interestingly, today the same question is still asked. The answer is the same today as it was back then: "Nope, it's a Cadillac V-16!"

Originally this hot rod had sported a smaller radiator with a proper painted shell, but that wasn't enough to dissipate the heat from the 452-cubic-inch 16-cylinder engine. So a truck radiator was installed that provided adequate cooling, but was too big for the radiator shell. The builders never got around to crafting a bigger radiator shell, so when Bob Blake acquired it, the radiator was still exposed. The Blakes took the car to a Los Angeles Roadster Show once, where they were refused entry because the club rule book required a grill shell— no exceptions. So they parked their roadster outside the show field and got more attention than any of the cars inside.

When Bob and Ken bought the hot rod, the doors and trunk lid had been welded shut. Bob freed them up, and they now open and close. Bob also replaced the original updraft

Bob Blake fields onlookers' questions from the driver's seat. Before he died, Bob and his son began restoring and upgrading the roadster. The fabricated intake manifold on each side now accommodates dual downdraft carburetors (courtesy Blake Machine Collection).

Opposite: "Three amigos" and a roadster. From left, Bob Blake, Urban Porterie and Bob Richards at a St. Patrick's Day party in 2004. The three high school friends participated in drag racing and circle track racing together. Bob Blake passed away later that year (courtesy Blake Machine Collection).

carburetors with a pair of Stromberg 48s, and he reported that this made a great difference in performance. Over the years of his life, with his eye for what later would become sought-after, and with his son's help, Bob assembled a quite respectable collection of unusual and desirable cars (fine classics, muscle cars and hot rods). This hot rod is not their only representative of Cadillac's V-16 supercar of the 1930s. There's a five-passenger coupe or victoria, two convertible coupes with the V'd "Pennsylvania" Fleetwood windshield, and a Series 4276 sport coupe with an aluminum body, Madame X–style windshield and roofline, and a golf bag compartment door on each side. There's also a V-16 sedan limousine parts car.

In the years before he died, Bob and his son had begun restoring the hot rod to its earlier glory. They had decided to "hop up" the engine with forged pistons, a billet camshaft and other performance enhancements. The engine was removed and disassembled as this process got under way. Unfortunately, Bob did not live long enough to see the engine work completed, and Dave has been hesitant to pick up that project and finish it. In the meantime, the Series 4276 coupe has lent its engine (number 702594) to the hot rod so that car can be driven and shown. Ultimately, the coupe will get its engine back, and Dave imagines driving it around with the hood off, showing off the engine like the early "mild" hot rod drivers (and some folks who owned V-16s in the forties and fifties) used to do.

Dave says that the V-16 hot rod is "very peppy." It's "more torquey" than high speed, and the power band is narrow. That isn't really surprising, since the designers had in mind the needs of wealthy buyers of heavy, luxurious, custom-bodied cars. These buyers were looking for smoothness and the ability to move out briskly and surely from low speed up to a swift cruising speed. The Blakes' hot rod may not have been the hottest racer around, even in its day. But it's a very unusual car, it's historically significant, it's a family heirloom, and it's guaranteed to draw a crowd at any show.

49. The Carash Custom Roadster

Craig Carash of Sandpoint, Idaho, has a very special remembrance of his late uncle Bill Carash. It is a beautifully designed and executed, hand-built roadster from the golden age, if you will, of West Coast hot rodding. And it's powered by a Cadillac V-16 engine.

In 1945, at the age of 17, Bill Carash did what a lot of California teenagers did at that time. He set out to build a hot rod. Only they weren't generally known as hot rods back then. They might be called customs, or roadsters. Or just cars. People just went to the local used car lots or salvage yards and looked for a strong but lightweight chassis, and maybe a light body, like a coupe or roadster. Some builders looked to military surplus sources and used things like aircraft belly tanks to make super-streamlined vehicles. And, of course, you needed an engine. Some worked with the four-cylinder Fords. Others started with flathead Ford V-8s. Some adventurous folks sought out the big powerplants that drove the great luxury cars of the previous generation—Marmons, Duesenbergs, Cadillacs.

Bill Carash started with the engine and built the rest of the car around it. He cruised wrecking yards until he located a junked Cadillac V-16, out of which he bought the engine and transmission. The serial number of the engine he acquired is 701866, and surviving

Cadillac records indicate that the donor car was a 1930 seven-passenger sedan that was shipped from the factory during June of 1930.

It took the young man a couple of years to accomplish a thorough overhaul and reassembly, and then he began building the rest of the car. The engine is only mildly modified—two Stromberg 97 downdraft carburetors replace the Detroit Lubricator updraft units it came with. And the fuel is fed by an electric pump.

Again looking to wrecking yards, Carash selected the frame, front axle and steering components from a 1936 Plymouth. Semi-elliptics spring the front of the car with a single transverse leaf spring in the rear. He substantially reinforced the chassis and prepared it to accept and support the big Cadillac engine.

The rear axle came from a Ford, and between that and the Cadillac transmission Carash inserted a Columbia overdrive unit. Taking into account the gear ratios and the rolling radius of the 7.00" × 16" tires, the theoretical top speed in overdrive was estimated at 138 m.p.h. A great deal of the work in constructing the car was done by Carash himself. He had a professional shop do some of the body panels, but he bent and welded his own tubular bumpers ("nerf bars" in the parlance of the day). A raked windshield offers some protection to the occupants, but this car is all about the open air. The result of all the work was a nicely proportioned, skillfully finished roadster, reminiscent of some of the open-wheeled Indianapolis 500 race cars of the late '40s and early '50s.

Side view of the V-16 engine. Stromberg 97 downdraft carburetors feed the engine in place of the original Cadillac updraft units. A generator originally sat under the forward end of the manifolds and next to the crankcase (replaced here by an alternator mounted on the other side of the engine) (courtesy Craig Carash).

Bill Carash and his car in November 1950. He first painted the car red with full moon hubcaps on the front wheels (courtesy Craig Carash).

At the Oakland Roadster Show, 1950. Bill Carash's back is to the camera. His father is on the left and his brother is in the middle (courtesy Craig Carash).

The annual car show in Oakland, California, was an established event by the late 1940s. Bill Carash and some of his friends petitioned the people in charge of the show for the chance to show their cars, and an area was set aside for them. That Oakland Roadster Show evolved into the National Roadster Show, and it's now known as the Grand National Roadster Show. The Carash Custom was shown there in 1950, and it took first place for originality in the Street Division, and third place in the Construction Street Division.

On March 14, 1950, Mr. Wilbur Shaw, president of the Indianapolis Motor Speedway Corporation, paid Bill Carash a tremendous compliment. He had written to Wilbur Shaw about having his roadster pace the Memorial Day 500-mile race. Mr. Shaw wrote as follows:

> Dear Mr. Carash:
>
> You certainly have built a very unusual and beautiful automobile and I would like nothing better than to be able to use it for a pace car. However, we are committed entirely to American manufacturers and there just wouldn't ever be a possibility of our getting it in as a pace car.
>
> Thank you very much for your interest and a lot of good luck with it.
>
> Sincerely yours,
> Indianapolis Motor Speedway Corp.
> WILBUR SHAW, President

If the Carash roadster had run as a pace car at the Indianapolis 500, it would have been the only time that a Cadillac V-16-powered automobile paced the race. The 1931 pace car was a Cadillac V-12 convertible coupe driven by none other than the legendary Cadillac test driver Willard "Big Bill" Rader. There would be a 1934 LaSalle pace car, but no other Cadillac product paced at the Brickyard until a 1973 Eldorado did the honors.

Bill Carash's roadster was profiled in the November 1949 issue of *Hot Rod* magazine. In January 1951, it graced the cover of *Mechanix Illustrated*, Tom McCahill's magazine that pioneered the road testing of new cars for readers. A detailed article including the car's history, its construction and descriptions of its performance on the road appeared in the April 1955 number of *Rod & Custom*. The author of the *Rod & Custom* article was treated to a ride in the car on a highway outside Oakland and found the experience to be "one of the great motoring thrills of a lifetime." He went on to say that "the car's center of gravity was so low and the bite of the chassis so good that it seemed that a *Grand Prix* Ferrari, detuned for street use, could have no more to offer."[1]

The last time the car was licensed to drive on the road was 1956. After that the car pretty much stayed home. Mr. Carash continued to tweak the roadster and work on it, off and on, for the rest of his life. During summer visits, his nephew Craig would ask to see the roadster and then head immediately to the barn where it was kept. Bill let Craig sit in the driver's seat and would tell him about the car, and say that he was fixing it up for him.

In 1999, Bill Carash passed away, leaving no children, only Craig and two nieces. Settling his estate turned out to be a difficult process that took time, but ultimately Craig got the roadster that had engendered so many happy experiences and fond memories. He quickly set about getting the car running, replacing all of the fluids and rebuilding the fuel system and the radiator. The first time he ever saw the car run was when he got it started. He recounts that he has driven the car only about four miles, but he and his wife enjoyed a short ride in it recently. "It is a hoot!" he says.

The Carash roadster is a remarkable piece of American automotive history. The hot rods of the forties and fifties were products of the individual creativity and personality of dedicated car guys. And unlike today, when custom cars and street rods are largely "big ticket" items, most of the post-war roadsters were built by folks on limited budgets who had to be creative and resourceful. As such, the cars they created display widely varying degrees of polish and finesse. Some are clearly homebuilt, even crude. Others, like this car, present an integrated design, neatly executed, where everything looks like it really belongs.

INDIANAPOLIS MOTOR SPEEDWAY CORPORATION

MAINTAINING THE GREATEST RACE COURSE IN THE WORLD

INDIANAPOLIS 4, INDIANA

March 14, 1950

Mr. Bill Carash
4030 Elston Avenue
Oakland 2, California

Dear Mr. Carash:

You certainly have built a very unusual and
beautiful automobile and I would like nothing
better than to be able to use it for a pace
car. However, we are committed entirely to
American manufacturers and there just wouldn't
ever be a possibility of our getting it in as
the pace car.

Thank you very much for your interest and a lot
of good luck with it.

Sincerely yours,

Indianapolis Motor Speedway Corp.

WILBUR SHAW, President

WS/mlh

A letter from Wilbur Shaw. Although the V-16 Roadster would not be an Indy 500 pace car, the president of the speedway praised it and its builder (courtesy Craig Carash).

In January 2009, the Carash roadster made a reprise appearance at the 60th Grand National Roadster Show. A special section of the show entitled "Twice in a Lifetime" featured cars that had been in the show at least once before. A few days earlier, Craig Carash had discovered the actual plaque given to his uncle as a participant in the 1950 show. Displayed with the car were photographs and reprints of some of the period articles about the car. The cream and orange color scheme was a change that Bill Carash decided to make in the late

Out for a spin with friends. Bill Carash is at the wheel. He would later marry Phyllis, and Dave Moore was his lifelong best friend (courtesy Craig Carash).

1950s from the original flame red paint job. Other than that, the car was very much the way it had been in 1950.

Craig Carash wants to continue the process of fixing up his uncle's pride and joy, reinstalling a correct generator and determining whether he needs to install a fan (Bill Carash apparently believed that the V-16's original fan was not needed). Craig intends to preserve and enjoy this legacy from his uncle for years to come.

50. A Chrysler Lion with the Heart of a Cadillac

Sometimes the story is about the car and its unusual attributes. Sometimes it's about the adventures the car had over the years and the crises it survived. Sometimes it's about the interesting or famous people who owned the car, and sometimes it's about the experiences of the people involved. Sometimes it's about all of that.

Lou Fageol was one of the most colorful and legendary figures in motorsport, on land and on the water. He associated with pioneers in high-performance automotive equipment such as Louis Meyer (Offenhauser racing engines) and Ed Winfield (camshafts and carburetors). During World War II, Packard Motor Company hired him to help develop the V-12 engines for the U.S. Navy's PT boats, and the Merlin aircraft engines that Packard built under Rolls-Royce license and that powered the Army Air Corps' P-51 Mustang fighter planes.

He built and piloted some of the fastest speedboats around, collecting many prestigious trophies, and he built race cars as well (including Indy 500 contenders). He was known as a hard-driving competitor and he won many important powerboat races. His boat racing career ended in 1955 when the craft he was piloting at a speed in excess of 160 m.p.h. became airborne and performed a perfect backwards aerial somersault, a "loop-the-loop," before returning to the water and coasting to a stop. This was all recorded on a video of the race. He survived the serious injuries he sustained in that accident, and retired from racing. Until his death in 1961 he was, in the words of American Boat Racing Association historian Fred Farley, a "respected elder statesman of the sport he loved."[1]

In 1933 Lou Fageol purchased a new Chrysler CL Imperial Custom Phaeton. That car would have come with a 384.8-cubic-inch straight-eight engine rated at 135 horsepower with 280 lb.-ft. of torque. By some estimates that would take the 4,900-pound car to 60 m.p.h. in just over 20 seconds with a top speed of 95. In 1934, dissatisfied with the car's performance and wanting to tow racing boats with it, Mr. Fageol replaced the Chrysler powerplant with a Cadillac V-16 (engine number 700132, which originally came with a 1930 Series 4375 seven-passenger sedan). Cadillac advertised at various times 165 or 175–185 horsepower for the 1930 452-cubic-inch V-16, and 320 lb.-ft. of torque at 1200 r.p.m.

Mr. Fageol personally engineered the engine transplant and associated chassis and

Lou Fageol sitting at the wheel of *Slo-Mo-Shun V*. He drove this boat to win the first unlimited hydroplane race held in Seattle, the 1951 Gold Cup. During qualification trials for the 1955 Gold Cup race, the boat flipped backwards in a complete 360-degree loop and landed upright in the water. Seriously injured, Mr. Fageol retired from active competition. *Slo-Mo-Shun V* has been restored (courtesy Ray Fageol).

suspension adjustments. At 146 inches, the Chrysler's wheelbase is only two inches short of the centerline distance between a 1930 Cadillac V-16's wheels. But the Cadillac V-16 sedan weighed over 6,000 pounds, while the Chrysler phaeton didn't reach 5,000. In a letter to a subsequent owner, Mr. Fageol said he could "definitely state that it made an excellent high performance highway automobile with the new power plant."

Because the Cadillac engine is essentially two straight-eights tethered to a common crankshaft and cam, the Chrysler's engine bay was adequate. The V-16 looks quite at home there. Carburetion was changed to two Stromberg 97 downdraft units, and an electric fuel pump was installed in place of the pair of big vacuum tanks that normally fed a 1930 V-16 engine. A right-hand exhaust manifold (and additional exhaust piping) had to be fitted to the driver's side of the engine to allow room for the Chrysler steering gear box. Otherwise, the exhaust outlet would try to occupy the same space as the steering box. So the waste gases leave the engine to the rear on the passenger side, and to the front on the driver's side.

The second owner of the Chrysler phaeton was the Austrian-born movie actor Turhan Bey. His family had moved to the U.S. after Hitler's 1938 Anschluss takeover of Austria, and Turhan Bey worked extensively as a leading man in films produced during the 1940s and 1950s, mostly in adventure pictures. Later he returned to the screen and was featured in several TV shows in the 1990s.

Next the car was owned by a now-anonymous student at Stanford University. One can imagine what fun he and his friends had running around in such a flashy (and quick) old-fashioned car, whenever they could feed the thirsty engine.

Cadillac V-16 engine number 700132. The stock updraft carburetors have been replaced by two down-draft units. Otherwise, the engine is quite comfortable in the Chrysler engine bay (courtesy Paul Schinnerer).

Legendary collector Jack Passey (subject of the book *For the Love of Old Cars: The Jack Passey Story* by Ken Albert) is the next character in the story. Our unnamed college student showed up on his doorstep in the early 1950s when Mr. Passey was in his mid–twenties. The student offered to sell the Chrysler for $200, which Mr. Passey didn't have. Intent on selling, the student proposed a $25 payment up front and subsequent payments for the balance. A deal was struck, the car changed owners, and the student was never heard from again.

Jack Passey replaced the late '30s Cadillac headlights that had found their way onto the Chrysler's front with correct units, before trading the car to Earl Hill and Dick Wells for a 1930 Cadillac V-16 coupe.

Laurence Dorcy, who always went by "Baron," was the great-grandson of James J. Hill, builder of the Great Northern Railway, which ran from St. Paul, Minnesota, to Seattle, Washington (now part of the Burlington, Northern and Santa Fe Railway). James Hill is said to have inspired the character of Nathaniel Taggart in Ayn Rand's novel *Atlas Shrugged,* and in F. Scott Fitzgerald's novel *The Great Gatsby*, Jay Gatsby says that his son would have equaled Hill if he had lived. In 1955 at the age of 19, Baron Dorcy had joined the air force, but was not yet on active duty. He found the Chrysler that Earl Hill and Dick Wells had acquired, and he thought it would be quick with a V-16 engine. He bought the car for $200, and he garaged it on the Mayfield Ranch, a property owned by his family. His girlfriend had warmed to the fancy phaeton when she saw what a hit it was everywhere they went, and young Mr. Dorcy decided to give it to her as a surprise Christmas present. But when he took her to make the presentation, they discovered that during the previous night's storms a large tree had fallen and crushed the garage and the Chrysler inside. He couldn't bear to look at the wreckage.

Baron Dorcy, three-time owner of the 1933 Chrysler V-16 Phaeton. Mr. Dorcy passed away in 2011 (courtesy Paul Schinnerer).v

Baron Dorcy went on active duty with the air force and his mother sold what was left of the 1933 Chrysler for $100 to Douglas O'Connell of Mountain View, California. Although Mr. O'Connell was not able to restore the car, he did a considerable amount of research and documentation, corresponding with Mr. Fageol, among others. After Mr. O'Connell passed away in 1975, Baron Dorcy bought the car back from his widow and took it to accomplished restorer Hal Orchard. Mr. Orchard told Paul Schinnerer that he'd been brought a chassis piled with wood and metal that would take a year of work to bring back to its proper state.

But another of Mr. Dorcy's adventures intervened in the form of a four-masted ocean-going sailing vessel he was building. Needing to devote his full attention to that endeavor, he forsook the restoration of the phaeton, which found a new owner in the person of Sid Colberg of San Francisco, California. Mr. Colberg continued working with Hal Orchard. The restoration began in April of 1985, and was completed in the first part of 1987. Although the car was very complete, most of the structural wood of the body had been wrecked and a complete new wooden framework had to be constructed and assembled. The metal panels were re-usable, but had to be refurbished and reattached to the new wood.

The body was painted a bright yellow hue, with black on the top panels of the hood, the tops of the doors and the fenders. The chromed wheels and new whitewall tires added to the spectacular presentation of this renewed beauty. Mr. Colberg had the late Gene Babow appraise the newly restored car and he estimated a fair market value on December 1, 1987, of $225,000.

Mr. Colberg applied to the Classic Car Club of America for "Full Classic" status for the V-16 Chrysler. The CCCA recognizes 1932–1933 LeBaron-bodied Chrysler Imperial cars as Full Classics, but the fact that this car had an engine from a different Full Classic of the same time period brought into question whether the Full Classic designation would apply. As part of his application, Mr. Colberg obtained a letter from famed race car driver Fred Agabashian, who knew Lou Fageol and had discussed the engine swap with him at the time it was done. There was also an affidavit from the restorer attesting to the authenticity of the LeBaron coachwork for the car. Sadly for Mr. Colberg, the application was denied, with the chairman of the Classification and Technical Service Committee only holding out the hope that the club was considering establishing a class for classics that had been tastefully altered in a way that improved their touring capability.

At some point subsequent to the 1987 appraisal, V-16 engine number 700132 was replaced with engine number 701289 (which powers the car today, and which came from another Series 4375-S seven-passenger sedan). Possibly engine number 700132 was damaged when the tree crushed the car in the mid–1950s.

Sid Colberg owned the phaeton until 2001, when he sold it to Ken Daniel of Los Altos Hills, California. A classic Chrysler enthusiast who owns two early '30s Imperial open cars, Mr. Daniel had known of the existence of this unusual automotive specimen for about 25 years. As it happened, Baron Dorcy lived in the same community as Mr. Daniel, and when he saw the Chrysler V-16 again, youthful memories came flooding back. He approached Mr. Daniel and worked for some time at persuading him to part with the car. Ultimately, a deal was struck, and Mr. Dorcy acquired the car for the third time. He located a replacement for the aging aluminum original hood. And he repainted the car the same red color it had worn when he had owned it before. Then he situated it comfortably at his mountain retreat on the Hawaiian island of Maui. Baron Dorcy passed away in 2011.

This Chrysler has survived a great deal—hauling boats, falling trees, college students and car collectors. Two Cadillac V-16s contributed to the making of this story, and unfor-

The Chrysler V-16 as it is today. Lou Fageol's creation, thrice owned by Baron Dorcy, awaits a new caretaker (courtesy Jeff Peterson).

tunately, we know almost nothing about their particular tales. A 1933 Chrysler CL Imperial Custom Phaeton is a rare and unique car in its own right. But having been equipped by the original owner with a Cadillac V-16 engine (and appropriately re-engineered chassis) makes it one of a kind, and something of a supercar in performance terms. With the more powerful engine sporting downdraft carburetors, the suspension modifications, and a body lighter than what the engine was built for, one wonders just how fast this Chrysler could run. Let's hope the next owner treasures it as greatly as it deserves.

51. A Visit with Cadillac Jim

In late August 1931, a Series 4302 V-16 roadster left the Cadillac factory and was taken to Mabbett Motors, Inc., in Rochester, New York. At least part of the journey was by boat, and the build sheet contains the notations "SOLD RUSH" and "PHONE G W." The car carried engine number 703165 and body number 94. With the exception of the usual chrome trim items, the Burbank cloth top, the stainless steel wheel spokes and the ivory pinstripe, the car was finished entirely in black. Even the tires were specified as "BLACK SIDE WALL SURE."

Who ordered and took delivery of this shiny black roadster is not known today. But sometime in or before 1961, a man named Lou Moore of the town of State College, Pennsylvania, sold it to Jim Pearson of Kansas City, Kansas. Mr. Pearson shows up several times in these pages, and he proudly carried the nickname "Cadillac Jim," reflecting his extensive

Lou Moore's 1931 V-16 Roadster. This photograph was probably taken in the 1950s and it shows a nearly new car. The black paint rings near the circumference of the hubcaps appear to have been rubbed off, and the door handle looks upside down, but otherwise the car looks quite correct and sharp. Note the stainless steel wheel spokes (as specified in the build sheet). Later the car would receive full chrome wire wheels (courtesy William Locke).

knowledge of, and experience with, early Cadillac motor cars. He would enjoy this roadster for several years before passing it along to another owner.

On June 23 and 24, 1961, the Veteran Motor Car Club of America held a national meet in Kansas City, Missouri. The VMCCA had invited the Cadillac-LaSalle Club to join them for a joint national event, and the CLC had accepted the invitation. One of the members in attendance was Jack Wade, Jr., of New Orleans, Louisiana. Jack and his wife Sue were friends of Jim Pearson and his wife Louise, and they took the occasion to stop in and see the Pearsons at their home in Kansas City, Kansas, hoping to see an enormous inventory of Cadillacs and Cadillac parts. An idea of the wonderful phenomenon that was Jim Pearson can be formed from the description that another visitor penned in the August 1961 issue of *The Self-Starter*:

> After a warm welcome from Jim and his wife Louise the travelers were led through a wonderland the likes of which old Cadillac and LaSalle lovers dream of but dare not believe exists outside the imagination. Need a Pilot-Ray?—here's a few over here! Cadillac heaters?—Yup—They're upstairs! Radio?—Sure thing—V-8, V-12, or V-16 please? Spotlights?—only a few less than were manufactured, to begin with. Here are new headlamps in original boxes, here's a drawer full of Cadillac Jaeger clocks, here's a flock of stone guards, there's a mountain of crank hole covers. Over here are the carefully wrapped tail light lenses, over there the complete tail light units, Cadillac and LaSalle, what type, what year—you name it!

The author of that description, Mr. Al Rodway (then executive vice president of the Cadillac-LaSalle Club), and his friend Paul Marut had come to the Pearsons' home a few days before Jack and Sue Wade arrived, in order to buy a V-8 roadster from Jim. (At the time, Jim Pearson was a national director of the CLC.) After a day of conviviality that passed well into the

First, we see Jim and Louise Pearson standing behind the Cadillac roadster. The rear panel of the folding top (that includes the glass rear window) has been unsnapped and lowered to aid warm-weather ventilation, and to allow the rumble seat passengers to converse with the couple in the front seat. By comparison with rumble seats on lesser cars, this Cadillac's back seat was high luxury. There were three chrome-plated steps up to the crest of the rear fender to aid the passengers' entry. There were cushioned, leather-covered armrests, and a full-width footrest. And the leather upholstered back and seat cushion were very comfortable. But any rumble seat is open to the elements and quite bouncy, owing to its position directly over the rear wheels (courtesy Jack Wade).

evening, Jim sent Mr. Rodway and Mr. Marut back to their hotel with the keys to his own V-16 roadster.

As Jack Wade relates the story, he could tell they were getting close to Jim Pearson's place because he began to see old Cadillacs in various states of repair lined up one after the other. Jim and his family lived with, in and around these fine cars and their various components. Some might have called it a junkyard, but any self-respecting old Cadillac enthusiast would think they were peeking through the pearly gates.

The Wades and the Pearsons had a long visit that day, as they waited for the return of Jim's V-16 roadster. It wasn't until evening that the car showed up, and the two couples piled in and went driving around Kansas City, each taking turns at the wheel. At that time the Cadillac had 50,000 miles on it and it was a fine-running example of the V-16 model line. The wheels had been painted red at some point, but the factory-specified black paint on the rest of the car and its ivory pinstripe were still sharp.

A young Jack Wade poses next to the roadster with his hand on the top. The sporting effect of the stainless steel spokes is easy to appreciate from this vantage. The red wheels and whitewall tires contrast with the way the car was delivered new (black wheels and black sidewall tires). Once upon a time, whitewall tires were white on both sides because the inner side could be seen, especially on the front wheels, and this picture is a good illustration of that (courtesy Jack Wade).

When the party returned to the Pearsons' home, photos were taken (flash, of course) and through the courtesy of the Wade family archives, we can look back across 48 years and share the moment.

In the years that followed, Jim Pearson sold the roadster to Dick Gold of Minneapolis, Minnesota. Mr. Gold was a devoted collector, and he had the car thoroughly restored. The black paint was replaced with a two-tone scheme—a silver-beige body with brown fenders, deck lid and body moldings, and a scarlet accent stripe. Pilot Ray lights were mounted on the front frame crossbar. Mr. Wade got to see it again after the restoration, but he was only able to peek inside the car's trailer.

Mr. Gold showed the car and received top honors in CCCA and AACA competitions. In 1989, he sold the roadster to noted restorer Fred Weber of St. Louis, Missouri. Shortly thereafter, Mr. Weber sold the car to the Hans Luscher Collection in Europe, from which it was transferred to Belgian collector Bob Lallemont. Mr. Lallemont passed away in November 2007. Subsequently, this distinguished Cadillac crossed the block at RM Auctions' Automobiles of London event on October 28, 2009, for £247,500. The new owner was reported to be a collector in the United States.

52. Presidential Provenance

The target "demographic" (a word not generally used back then) for the Cadillac V-16 was a stellar group populated by heads of state, captains of industry, successful professionals, stars of screen, stage and sport and others with substantial independent wealth. The 31st president of the United States rode in a V-16 in his official capacity, and later purchased one for his personal use.

Herbert C. Hoover was elected in 1928. During his single term as president, the White House garage acquired a 1930 Cadillac V-16 Series 4375 seven-passenger imperial sedan. It is not clear what became of that automobile, but it is known that President Hoover enjoyed it. The closest I have come to tracing its fate is the information that the engine from a Series 4375 limousine that was delivered to the White House garage (engine number 702631) survives, but the car's body was likely junked.

It had been William Howard Taft who converted the White House stables into a motor car garage, stocking it initially with a pair of Pierce-Arrows. Warren Harding actually learned to drive an automobile, and Calvin Coolidge was the first presidential Cadillac fan. President

Cadillac V-16 limousine in White House service. This photograph, taken in November 1930, shows a policeman and a chauffeur standing next to a Series 4375 seven-passenger imperial sedan. The presidential and United States flags snap smartly in the breeze as the gentlemen pose with the car. The front license plate is District of Columbia plate number 101. The same plate number graced the Pierce-Arrow touring car in which President Hoover rode (with outgoing President Coolidge) to the Capitol for his inauguration in 1929. Immediately behind the Cadillac in this photo is a Pierce-Arrow sedan (Library of Congress, Prints and Photographs Division, LC-USZ62–99513).

Increased use of curves for 1932 is readily apparent from this angle. The inexorable advance of stream-lining had begun, and has continued to the present day (courtesy Worldwide Auctioneers).

Hoover, according to one account of an interview with presidential chauffeur George Tolan, noticed the 1930 V-16 in his entourage pulling easily ahead of the car he normally rode in on steep grades, and he directed that thenceforth the V-16 would be his personal car. President Hoover had the nasty misfortune of serving as chief executive at the moment when the supposedly unstoppable economic expansion of the Roaring Twenties exploded into vaporized fortunes, massive unemployment and a decade of hardship. According to Jim Motavalli writing in *The New York Times*, Hoover was ridiculed for riding in the White House V-16 limousine while the Great Depression was tightening its grip on the country.

White House records are incomplete at this date, so it's not easy to verify another account that holds that President Hoover purchased the 1930 V-16 upon leaving office. What is more likely is that he bought a new model and left the 1930 behind. There are records available to confirm that he purchased and owned a 1932 Cadillac V-16 and that he kept that car well into the 1940s. It was a 1932 Series 5175 seven-passenger imperial sedan, an updated model of the White House car he'd gotten to know. In 1932, the vacuum fuel delivery system was replaced with a mechanical fuel pump. If the car ran out of fuel, there was no need to refill the vacuum tanks in addition to filling the gas tank in order to get running again. The body lines were gently rounded and the irresistible trend toward streamlining had begun. Some, including General Motors' then–styling chief Harley Earl, consider the 1932 models to be the epitome of Cadillac styling in the classic era. The 1932 V-16 line was given the designation 452-B, with the number representing the engine's displacement in cubic inches and the letter indicating that this was the first real model year changeover. 1930 and 1931 V-16 Cadillacs were virtually identical, and are generally designated 452 (or in later records and manuals, 452-A). Due to the effects of the Depression, only 300 V-16s were sold in 1932, as against 3,251 for the 1930 and '31 model years.

Returning to private life, Mr. Hoover and his wife took their 1932 V-16 first to New York City. Not long afterwards, they returned to California. In the 1940s they sold the car to their friend Gordon Garland, who was a California legislator and state official. The Garlands kept the Cadillac for several years and it next shows up in the hands of Frederick Ronstadt, a student at the California Maritime Academy in Vallejo. In 1951, a fellow named Russell S. Dempster (now deceased) acquired the car. It had been abandoned at a service station in Vallejo, and Mr. Dempster's brother Jean (who attended the Maritime Academy at about this time) spotted the car. A cashier's receipt from the California Department of Motor Vehicles records that on July 18, 1951, Frederick Ronstadt (who gave the California Maritime Academy in Vallejo as his address) filed to transfer the ownership of a V-16 Cadillac, engine number 1400200.

The Dempsters got the car running and drove it to San Luis Obispo (where Russ was attending California State Polytechnic College). Russ told a friend that it had just run out of fuel and needed a prime (unlike the Dempster brothers, Fred Ronstadt was not very mechanically inclined). Russ Dempster had planned to use the car to make some money as a chauffeur, and had obtained a chauffeur's license in 1951 while visiting relatives in San Diego. But the big Cadillac was expensive to operate and maintain, and the venture did not work out. Russ sold the car in San Diego and it went into storage in a barn. The last time the license plates were changed was for the year 1956.

Instrument panel. For 1932, Cadillac moved the instruments from the center of the dash to the area directly in front of the driver. Convex cover glass cuts glare. Beautiful interplay between burled walnut and other inlays is clearly seen in this view. Choke knob is a replacement (courtesy Worldwide Auctioneers).

Receipt for title transfer fee. The California Department of Motor Vehicles issued this receipt, dated July 18, 1951, for title transfer fee paid by Frederick Ronstadt in connection with President Hoover's 1932 Cadillac (courtesy Russell Taylor).

A California chauffeur's license issued to Russell Dempster, then owner of President Hoover's 1932 Cadillac (courtesy Russell Taylor).

In August 2007, President Hoover's 1932 Cadillac (engine number 1400200) was consigned for auction at Quail Lodge Resort and Golf Club in Carmel, California. It was unrestored and very well preserved. The interior was intact, and the dark blue paint was presentable. The trim showed some rusting and pitting in the cast parts, but the overall condition was such that the car could easily be shown at any major event. It would be certain to win kudos for originality, rarity and historical significance. A suitable ornament, consisting of an eagle with spread wings, holding the national shield, still graced the radiator cap.

The pictures accompanying the auction write-up afforded the viewer a peek inside the engine compartment. What could be seen gives a hint of how hard it was, before the big classic cars were "rediscovered," to keep these cars running. Dealers no longer stocked parts for the very unique engines, and the limited production numbers meant that finding parts cars in junkyards wasn't always easy either. Qualified service also became hard to find, and the owner was generally left to his own resources.

Someone struggled a great deal to keep this car running, and at some point the owner must have simply thrown up his hands. The stock Detroit Lubricator carburetors have been replaced by units from a different manufacturer. That required a homemade choke linkage cable, jerry-rigged to work off the firewall-mounted lever, with a mounting bracket bolted to the exhaust manifold. The cable appeared to have broken, though.

The replacement carburetors also meant that the stock air cleaner/intake muffler units

Radiator mascot on President Hoover's 1932 Cadillac. The rampant eagle with the American shield on his chest is an obvious reference to the presidential seal. Unfortunately, the pot metal radiator cap has begun to deteriorate. Winged cloisonné Cadillac crest and sunburst is a 1932-only feature (courtesy Worldwide Auctioneers).

were removed from the firewall, along with their flexible hoses that would connect them to the carburetor air intakes. The stock ignition coils no longer occupied their holes in the top tank of the radiator. Instead, two mismatched aftermarket coils had been fastened to the firewall with a homemade bracket. One can imagine the blank stares of the clerk at the local auto parts store, or the parts man at the local Cadillac dealership in the mid–1950s, when asked for two coils for a 1932 V-16. The indications are that the Dempsters had to do a lot of making do with what was available.

The car sold at the Quail Lodge auction for $87,750, including buyer's premium. Three years later, in early September 2010, the car was again offered at auction, this time at Worldwide Auctioneers' third annual Auburn Auction. The sale price was $137,500, although the estimate that had been given was $160,000–$180,000.

53. Old Money

It is very rare that an automobile is diligently cared for and preserved in "as-new" condition for the better part of eight decades. Normal life changes and ordinary exigencies in the lives of regular people tend to thwart even the best intentions, and cars generally pass from one owner to another. The miles add up and natural forces take their toll. Occasionally, the means of the owner and the stability of his or her circumstances provide a haven in which a fine car can rest unaffected by the things that age and degrade most automobiles. This is the story of a 1933 Cadillac V-16 that remains in nearly perfect original condition, ensconced in the household to which it was first driven as a new purchase.

Even in the current history-averse climate, the idea of family fortunes and generational wealth brings to mind certain names, and one of those is Vanderbilt. Cornelius Vanderbilt, known as the Commodore, was a larger-than-life figure in the development of railroad and water transportation in 19th-century America. He quit school at 11, and by 16 he had his own ferrying business in New York Harbor. By the middle of the century his steamships plied the Hudson River and the transatlantic lanes, and carried gold rush traffic to California. By the time he died in 1877, he had built the New York Central Railroad, whose Grand Central Terminal in midtown Manhattan is still a metaphor for people going places in a hurry. He left the bulk of his fortune to his son William Henry Vanderbilt and disowned William's brothers.

William Vanderbilt survived his father by only eight years, but he expanded the family railroad empire and nearly doubled the fortune he had inherited. His philanthropy included funding to establish the Metropolitan Opera, endowing Columbia University's College of Physicians and Surgeons, and supporting the eponymous university that his father had established. He was considered the richest man in the world when he died. William Vanderbilt's fortune was divided among his widow and eight children, with the bulk going to William K. and Cornelius II.

The third son of William Henry Vanderbilt was Frederick William Vanderbilt. He married Louise Holmes Anthony Torrance (known to friends as "Lulu"), but their union was childless. Their doting was done on their nephews and nieces. The Vanderbilts kept residences in Manhattan, Hyde Park (New York), Newport (Rhode Island), Bar Harbor

(Maine), and Upper St. Regis Lake in New York's Adirondacks, and they kept a stable of fine motorcars, including Rolls-Royce, Crane-Simplex and Minerva.

In 1920, Mr. Douglas Crapser became a driver for Frederick and Louise Vanderbilt. Mrs. Vanderbilt's preference was for Packards, and she preferred maroon for the color. Mr. Vanderbilt sought out unique and exclusive cars, and generally chose conservative shades of gray. Mrs. Vanderbilt passed away in Paris in 1926, and her husband carried on without her until his death in 1938. In 1933, Frederick Vanderbilt determined to replace a 1928 Minerva with a new limousine. He discussed the idea with his driver, who suggested that he consider a Cadillac V-16. After all, the president of the United States had one. Mr. Vanderbilt liked the idea.

The Cadillac that was selected was a Series 5530-FL, a five-passenger imperial sedan with filled-in rear quarter windows and a leather roof covering—"F" for "formal" or no quarter windows, and "L" for leather. The V-16 engine was number 5000088, the body number was 14, and the price was $12,500. The car was a special order designated "#5270LX." The body bore a coat of maroon lacquer, perhaps in honor of the late Mrs. Vanderbilt. An accessory trunk was ordered with fitted luggage, including a hatbox. The seats were individually fitted to the driver (a taller man) and his passenger (not as tall). Each traveled separately to New York City to be measured so that the cushions could be sized and proportioned.

Mr. Crapser took his employer to the landing so he could board his yacht, and Mr. Vanderbilt told him to expect delivery of the new Cadillac. He wanted the car broken in so that they could take long trips in it as soon as he returned. When he did return, Mr. Vanderbilt

Engine of Frederick Vanderbilt's car. Louvered cylindrical object on firewall is intake noise muffler for carburetor. Actual air filters would come later. Vacuum tanks have been replaced by mechanical fuel pump on left side of engine. Note chromed air scoop for cooling generator. Distributor cap with eighteen terminals on top (two coil wires and sixteen plug wires) contrasts with the flat-top model used for 1930 and '31 (courtesy Bud Juneau).

asked how the car was. Mr. Crapser told him it was ready for the road, and handed Mr. Vanderbilt a $100 check that the Cadillac dealer in New York had made payable to Mr. Crapser. Mr. Crapser didn't feel right about accepting the payment, which was a common practice in those days, slipping a little treat to the chauffeur to encourage him to put in a good word for the brand when trade-in time came around. Mr. Vanderbilt said he knew about it, insisted that the money belonged to his driver, and expressed surprise that the amount wasn't greater. The next morning, he came to the garage and gave Mr. Crapser another hundred dollars.

A concession to decoration. Optional gold-plated radiator ornament graces the otherwise subdued front ensemble. Over the years, the carefree wind-buffeted goddess offered on the 1930 Cadillacs evolved into a very stylized figure before disappearing in the late 1950s (courtesy Bud Juneau).

The Cadillac was generally used for long trips. Mr. Crapser described the usefulness of the ride control lever, damping the up-and-down motion when the car encountered a bump in the 1930s roads. The Rolls-Royce was used only for New York City. And there was a Buick that the housekeeper normally used and which Mr. Crapser would take to meet Mr. Van-

Seen from the side, the effects of the streamlining craze are readily apparent—fenders are skirted, lights are teardrop shaped, windshield header is softened. This is the first year for vent windows in the front doors ("No-Draft Ventilation"). Slight water damage to paint on hood louvers is only visual clue that this isn't a brand new car (courtesy Bud Juneau).

derbilt at the train station if he would be arriving alone and the weather was nasty. That way the extensive clean-up and de-mudding of the big car could be avoided.

In 1938, the Cadillac received its second set of tires. A few months later, Mr. Vanderbilt died, leaving the Hyde Park, New York, estate, including the 1933 Cadillac, to his niece, Mrs. James Van Alen. Mr. Crapser continued to live in the area. Two years later, Mrs. Van Alen donated the estate to the United States government as a historic site, and took the Cadillac V-16 to Newport, Rhode Island. She continued to use the car until 1954, and then gave it to the government to be returned to the Hyde Park estate. The car had 19,700 miles on the odometer, and still had the second set of tires. Mr. Crapser helped the National Park Service to preserve the car after its return from Rhode Island. He passed away in the early 1980s.

Today, Frederick Vanderbilt's Cadillac V-16 imperial sedan is kept at the mansion in Hyde Park National Historical Site, under the auspices of the National Park Service. Unfortunately, the trunk with its fitted luggage seems to have disappeared. The Park Service sells a booklet about the car and its distinguished owner, but the general public is not able to view the Cadillac. Douglas Crapser was interviewed by the Park Service in 1973 to preserve his recollections about the Vanderbilts, which necessarily included information about the Cadillac V-16.

54. A DuPont Convertible

For 1934, Cadillac significantly restyled its line of automobiles. The fenders were now pontoon-shaped (or "airfoil-shaped" as the designers would say). The front fenders faired

Attracting attention. Olde Salem Days in 2007 was the occasion for this outing. "Biplane" bumpers, exclusive to the 1934 model year, were stylish and flashy and had spring-loaded brackets. But they proved to be fragile and were replaced with a more conventional design (courtesy Louis Barnhart).

right into the radiator shell, and on the V-8 and V-12 models, the effect, when viewed from the front, was like the prow of a ship splitting the water and pushing aside the waves. The "face" of the V-16 line was more staid, but no less changed from what had gone before. The new (and short-lived) biplane bumpers were a stylish, if fiendishly impractical, addition to the look.

Convertible sedans ceased to be called "all-weather phaetons." There were no longer any ordinary phaetons or touring cars in the lineup from which to distinguish a four-door convertible with roll-up windows. The Series 5880 convertible sedan provided the freedom and openness of a touring car and, with the top raised, the comfort and privacy of a limousine.

Edith DuPont was twenty-one in 1934, the year she married Richard Eveland Riegel. She was the great-great-great-great-granddaughter of E.I. DuPont, the founder of the DuPont Company who amassed a family fortune. Her marriage to Mr. Riegel would last thirty years until his death in 1964. A 1934 Cadillac V-16 convertible sedan was sold to her new, bearing engine number 5100038. Mrs. Riegel's car was equipped with a roll-up divider window between the driver's seat and the rear compartment. The paint color was "blue hour blue" (a hue frequently selected by DuPont family members) and chrome wheel covers and painted metal spare tire covers were included. A radio was installed, as well as the optional flexible "banjo" steering wheel. And a silver goddess perched atop the radiator shell. The build sheets for Cadillac automobiles shipped during the 1930s do not often identify the actual purchaser, showing only the dealership to which the car was sent. This one, however, is unambiguous regarding the buyer's identity. It contains the instruction "TAG—MRS. EDITH DU PONT RIEGEL."

Roy Licari, of Alexandria, Virginia, acquired this car in 1952. In 1963, a young man named Louis Barnhart purchased it from Mr. Licari for $1,000. Mr. Licari was living in Fairfax, but the car was in Philadelphia with a fellow named Bill Walters. The car had been sitting for a long time. All four tires were flat, and the general condition of the car had begun to suffer from prolonged outdoor exposure. Mr. Barnhart and a friend drove to Philadelphia in a truck, put air in the tires and got the car running. Then, without really thinking about what they were doing, Mr. Barnhart climbed into the Cadillac, his friend started the truck, and they proceeded to drive directly back to Salem, Virginia, over 350 miles. They made the trip without incident, but Mr. Barnhart wouldn't think of repeating it today.

Mr. Barnhart owned, enjoyed and cared for the car for the next 44 years. He was not in a position to undertake a full-blown restoration, but he maintained its very serviceable original condition. He showed the car locally on a regular basis, and at the Antique Automobile Club of America's 2005 Eastern Spring Meet in Roanoke, Virginia, it was certified as an "HPOF" vehicle (historic preservation of original features).

Recently, an article about Mr. Barnhart and his car in the publication of the local region of the AACA was picked up and published in the July/August issue of *Antique Automobile*, the national club's magazine. Mr. David Kane of Bernardsville, New Jersey, saw the article and sought out Mr. Barnhart to buy the car from him.

Mr. Barnhart said that he didn't want to sell. Mr. Kane offered to trade several different cars, including a mid–1930s V-12, but Mr. Barnhart didn't want to be without a V-16. He knew he'd never be able to replace the one he had if he sold it. Mr. Kane found out about a 1935 Cadillac V-16 sedan that Tom Crook was selling in California. He bought that car and offered it to Mr. Barnhart in trade for the 1934 convertible sedan. Mr. Barnhart accepted, and in November 2007, the cars were exchanged.

CADILLAC MOTOR CAR CO.
DETROIT, MICHIGAN

DUPLICATE GN

DISTRIBUTORS ORDER 3/20/34 TYPED 3/30 SALES ORDER NO. _____

MONTH	SERIAL	ORDER
5	A	3181

SHIP TO ORDER OF CADILLAC MOTOR CAR CO.   AT ___ WILMINGTON DELA.

NOTIFY ___ DELAWARE MOTOR SALES COMPANY ___ AT ___ "

CHARGE TO ___ " ___ AT ___ "

DRAW THRU ___ WILMINGTON TRUST COMPANY ___ Will hold
75.

CAR NO. 66 TAG- MRS. EDITH DU PONT RIEGEL

G.R.A. NO.	GEAR RATIO	JOB NO.	BODY NO.	DATE SHIPPED	INVOICE NO.
	4.64	5880	25	6-19-34	

CAR ___ CADILLAC "60" FLTD. CONV.   ENGINE NO. ___ 5100038

SEDAN WITH DIVISION.   UNIT ENGINE NO.

UPHOLSTERY ___ E.O. K-31 BLACK LEATHER   51-35

ROOF OR TOP ___ HAARTZ JONARTS 5000   FREIGHT CAR NO.

REVEALS   ROUTE

MOULDING ___ CHROME

BODY PANELS ___ BLUE HOUR BLUE 2441634   BILL OF LADING NO.

FENDERS AND CHASSIS ___ BLUE HOUR BLUE   IGNITION KEY ___ 6378

WHEEL COLOR ___ BLUE HOUR BLUE   COMPARTMENT KEY ___ 6616

WHEEL DISCS ___ 6 BLUE HOUR BLUE

TYPE WHEELS ___ 6 WIRE   CARRIER ___ FENDERWELLS   51-38

TIRE SIZE ___ 7.50-17   MAKE ___ ROYAL   EXTRAS ___ 2

ORNAMENT ___ - (WHITE SIDE WALL)

GODDESS - SILVER A1042

HUB CAPS- CHROME.

1 PR PAINTED METAL COVERS A878-30

INSTALL RADIO (MASTER)

INSTALL FLEXIBLE STEERING WHEEL 1096288.

LICENSE FRAMES A-1090.R.4

SEE SPECIAL FLTD. BODY ORDER NO. 223 FOR DETAILED SPECIFICATIONS.

TOOL KIT

CHECK

DOUBLE CHECK

"Birth certificate." This is the "build sheet" for the 1934 Cadillac V-16 convertible sedan. It is quite rare to see the initial owner's actual name on the build sheet. Optional equipment selected is listed in lower left corner, and includes a silver-plated hood ornament (courtesy David Kane).

When Mr. Kane got the '34 convertible, he says, it was a good car in good shape. That was said by way of contrast with a 1933 V-16 he had owned that had been missing parts, and that had required a very extensive restoration ("That one almost ended my career!"). The 1934 convertible sedan was taken to Stone Barn Automobile Restoration in Vienna, New Jersey. In a matter of months, the car emerged in showroom-new condition. Mr. Kane took

Freshly restored. This shot finds the 1934 V-16 convertible sedan at Stone Barn, Inc., restoration facility in Vienna, New Jersey. In less than a year the car has received an extensive restoration, and it would go on to take high honors at the 2008 Pebble Beach Concours d'Elegance (courtesy David Kane).

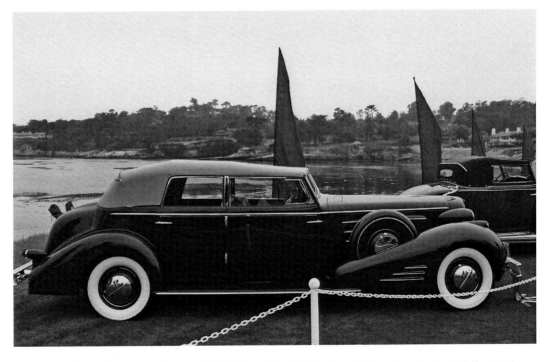

Best in Class. The car was shown at Pebble Beach in 2008 and took first place in the Cadillac V-16 class. Subsequently it has won other awards as well (courtesy Joseph Scott).

it to the 2008 Pebble Beach Concours, where it won Class C-4 (Cadillac V-16). Cadillac V-16s were featured that year, and Mr. Kane's car faced some formidable competition.

In January 2013, the auction catalog for RM Auctions' Scottsdale event included this glorious 1934 V-16, and it sold for $825,000.

55. Grace

Sometimes people give their cars names. Sometimes it's out of a personal attachment to the vehicle or involvement with it, like "Ferdinand," a 1930 V-16 sedan described elsewhere in these pages. Sometimes it's a reflection of the personality of someone who owned or used the car, like Franklin Roosevelt's "Sunshine Special," denoting his fondness for open cars. Sometimes it's a droll statement about the nature of the car itself, like the "Queen Mary" and "Queen Elizabeth" monikers the Secret Service bestowed on the twin massive 1938 Cadillac V-16 parade cars that served U.S. presidents well into the 1950s. Sometimes a subsequent owner names the car in honor of an interesting or distinguished prior owner. That's how a certain 1934 Cadillac V-16 coupe became known as "Grace."

1934 stationary coupe. This was the year when Cadillac really took the plunge into streamlining. Pontoon fenders, wheel shields (their name for fender skirts), teardrop lights and fully concealed undercarriage mark a break with the past. "Biplane" bumpers and leaping hood goddess evoke flight. The bumpers were spring-loaded to absorb impacts, but proved too delicate to be practical (courtesy Monty Holmes).

Series 5776 was known as a "stationary" coupe, as opposed to a convertible. On the 1934–37 Cadillac V-16 chassis, it cut a figure at once dashing and imposing. An elegant forerunner of what would later be called "personal luxury cars," the V-16 stationary coupe makes full use of the '34 V-16's twenty-foot length without looking bulky or ungainly.

The stationary coupe that was built around engine number 5100050 was sold new on July 19, 1934, for $8,000 cash in mid–depression dollars. The purchaser was Mr. Daniel B. McDaniel, oil drilling contractor, owner of a distributing business and owner of the Houston, Texas, Cadillac and LaSalle dealership. His wife Grace McDaniel was vice president of the dealership. A subsequent owner of the car would name the car after Mrs. McDaniel.

Mr. Stan Squires was employed by the Pontiac Division of General Motors when he bought this V-16 coupe in 1962. He purchased it from Bob Mellin of Detroit, a fellow GM employee who used to buy old cars and hang on to them. Mr. Mellin had bought the V-16 coupe in 1958 from a fellow in Blue Island, Illinois, named George Willy. Mr. Mellin says that he had intended to restore this Cadillac, and he had acquired a V-16 limousine (that was actually in better shape) to use as a parts car for it. He recalls that he had "too many cars" at the time, and decided to sell. Mr. Squires bought the coupe from Mr. Mellin, and began a 45-year-long relationship with it.

A good deal of the car's early history remains obscure. When D.B. McDaniel sold it, and to whom, are not known. What is known is that in the middle 1950s, the Cadillac was subjected to the indignity of being run in stock car races (at Blue Island, Illinois, according to Stan Squires's recollection). A number of modifications were wreaked on it—the sidemount spare tire brackets were welded to the frame, and the engine manifolds had been

Ready for Bob Mellin to pick up. This photograph was taken in early 1958 in Blue Island, Illinois, on the day that Bob Mellin retrieved his purchase. The car had survived its experience in stock car racing and would now begin a long restoration journey. The running boards are missing and the fenders are somewhat battered, but overall the car appears pretty solid (courtesy Stan Squires).

This photo was taken on the day that Stan Squires bought the car. The scale of the restoration project he undertook is clearly evident. In 1962, big classic cars were only beginning to be appreciated as more than ungainly, obsolete used cars. It was not unusual in the '50s and early '60s for such noble vehicles to wind up in demolition derbies and salvage yards (courtesy Stan Squires).

altered for the installation of downdraft carburetors. There was a switch in the trunk to provide 12-volt current for starting and six volts for normal operation. Mr. Mellin remembers that Mr. Willy bought the Cadillac from the people who had been racing it, and Mr. Squires has a photograph taken after the car was retired from the races.

Mr. Mellin was able to provide Mr. Squires with replacement manifolds and correct Detroit Lubricator carburetors as a result of an unfortunate incident. David Holls, former director of corporate design at GM, had lost a 1935 V-16 convertible sedan to a house fire, and Mr. Mellin acquired what was left when the insurance company sold it for salvage. Mr. Squires was able to get the engine parts as well as a frame that had not been altered for racing.

In carrying out the car's restoration, Mr. Squires traveled all over the country tracking down necessary parts, and he benefited greatly from his experiences and contacts at GM. Working at GM, he was able to speak with people who had firsthand knowledge of how the V-16 cars were built, and to consult the original Cadillac mechanical and electrical drawings. As he had been in charge of wiring the prototype cars built for the Pontiac Division, making a new wiring harness for his V-16 coupe was not a difficult task at all. Over the years, the car would be transformed into an award-winning show participant.

In recent years, Mr. Squires retired and moved to North Carolina. Prior to that move, he had worked on the V-16 coupe for many hours. But between managing 53 acres, building a home and other responsibilities, he was no longer able to devote time to the '34 Cadillac, and it languished in the garage. Meanwhile, he became acquainted with a gentleman who'd been purchasing V-16 parts from him, and they struck up a solid friendship over their mutual interest in these enormous classics. When Monty Holmes of Seattle, Washington, arrived at Mr. Squires's place in North Carolina to pick up a truckload of parts and met Mr. Squires and the V-16 coupe in person, he asked if he could be its next caretaker, should Mr. Squires decide to sell it. About a year later, satisfied that Mr. Holmes would take good care of the car and "not make a hot rod out of it," Mr. Squires called and invited him to become the next owner. It was Mr. Holmes who named the car Grace, and he treated her to new upholstery, new paint, some chrome work and new tires, among other enhancements.

Grace has been shown at the 2007 "Coming Out Party" of the Classic Car Club of America's Pacific Northwest Region, followed by Pebble Beach later the same year, and the Kirkland Concours d'Elegance (where she received the Chamber of Commerce Award). She won Best in Show and People's Choice awards at the Cadillac-LaSalle Club Pacific Northwest Region picnic.

I first saw a picture of Grace in the summer of 1968 when I joined the Cadillac-LaSalle Club and received the club's newsletter *The Self-Starter*. One of the features was a photographic account of a meet in Michigan called the "Carnival of Cars." One of the cars in particular caught and held my imagination. The caption identified the owner as Stan Squires from Pontiac, Michigan, and said that he had driven the partially restored 1934 Cadillac V-16 coupe in the picture to the meet. It also said that he had received the "Most Improved" award. The fenders and running boards were missing, as were the grille, the hood and hubcaps.

Restoration under way. According to Stan Squires, this photograph was taken in about 1966 at a Cadillac-LaSalle Club meet at the Ford Engineering grounds in Dearborn, Michigan. The rehabilitation had progressed to the point where the car could be driven. It looks like a very large home-built "old school" hot rod (courtesy Charles Beesley).

But there the big car sat, proudly lined up with the rest on the show field. My 16-year-old mind was thrilled at the idea that one could participate in a car show without completing every last detail point of the restoration of one's car. I was still dreaming of finding my own unrestored V-16 to drive as I worked on it, and this little photo was enormously encouraging. Recently I made Mr. Squires's acquaintance, and I learned the rest of the story of this magnificent motor car.

At the 2012 Pebble Beach sale conducted by RM Auctions, the beautiful black 1934 V 16 coupe that Stan Squires brought back to life brought $396,000, and found a new owner.

56. Helen

Thomas Humphrey Wittgenstein Stonborough was born in Berlin in 1906. He came to the U.S. in 1908 and lived in New York City and Washington, D.C. After studying in Cambridge, UK, he returned to Vienna to work towards a Ph.D. in psychology under Charlotte Bühler. An American citizen, he traveled often between Europe and the U.S. He was a silent partner in Shields & Company, a New York stockbroker, and for a period of time an assistant at Columbia University. Sometime in the 1930s he joined the Office of Price Administration or OPA, one of the group of agencies established as part of Franklin Roosevelt's New Deal. During World War II he would enlist in the Office of Strategic Services, the forerunner to the CIA. In the late 1920s, he met Helen Engelhardt at Columbia University. They were married in 1932 and had a son, Pierre.

Thomas's father was a well-to-do chemist named Jerome Herman Steinberger, who changed his name to Stonborough before he married Margarete Wittgenstein (also known as Gretl) and before Thomas was born. Margarete's father, Karl Wittgenstein, commissioned the Austrian artist Gustav Klimt for a now-famous portrait of her in her wedding gown, which painting her son Thomas sold to the Munich Pinakothek. Margarete's was a very interesting family. Karl Wittgenstein was a wealthy industrialist. Her brother Ludwig is considered by some to have been the greatest philosopher of the 20th century. Brother Paul was a concert pianist who lost his right arm in World War I. Maurice Ravel wrote his *Piano Concerto for the Left Hand* for him to perform. Johannes Brahms, Gustav Mahler and Richard Strauss frequently visited the household in Vienna.[1] Sisters Hermine and Helene were determined not to leave their beloved homeland, Austria, even after its annexation by Nazi Germany, and in spite of the Nazis' unmistakable intentions toward the Jews. As now–German citizens they had to convert a great deal of their foreign currency holdings—an enormous amount of gold—into Reichsmarks, which ensured their safety, as in consequence their grandfather Hermann Christian Wittgenstein was changed (on order by Hitler) from a Jew into an Aryan. Margarete, as a U.S. citizen, helped to arrange pioneering psychoanalyst Sigmund Freud's escape to England in 1938.[2]

Thomas Stonborough purchased a new 1934 Cadillac V-16 Series 5780 convertible sedan with engine number 5100040, ordering it through the New York Cadillac showroom. The car was black, with a unique black Victoria leather top. The goddess perched atop the radiator shell was ordered in silver. Chauffeur-driven, the Cadillac was not equipped with a heater, as this was Mr. Stonborough's summer car (we don't know what car he used for the colder part of the year). We have an idea of the kind of people he kept company with, and it's not unlikely that Leonard Bernstein or one of the Gershwin brothers rode in this automobile.

Thomas's father committed suicide in 1938 after the loss of his and a great deal of his wife's fortune in the stock exchange crash.[3] The next year Thomas (having divorced Helen) married Elizabeth Churchill. That second marriage did not last and there were no more children. He left the U.S. after the war and probably sold the Cadillac at about that time.

In 1949, a 45-year-old railroad man and race car driver named Archie Marcotte bought the 1934 Cadillac and drove it back to his home in Dickinson, North Dakota. There he set about doing what a number of adventurous, mechanically inclined fellows did with these cars during the 1940s. He took the sixteen-cylinder powerplant out of the car and, with the help of his friend Richard Wehner, he built a race car around it. The stock camshaft was replaced with a ¾-race cam from the Los Angeles performance equipment company Harmon and Collins, Inc., and instead of the twin updraft carburetors Cadillac provided, Mr. Marcotte installed eight Stromberg 97 downdraft carburetors. He used the frame and chassis from a 1937 Ford, fabricated a streamlined sheet-metal exterior and called his creation "Sweet Sixteen." According to a 1951 newspaper account, the car used three fuel pumps and burned a mixture of gasoline, water, alcohol and castor oil.

The race car was intended for dirt track contests, but it was heavy

Portrait of Margarethe Stonborough-Wittgenstein. Austrian artist Gustav Klimt painted Mrs. Stonborough in her wedding gown in 1905. Countless posters and reproductions have been made of this memorable image (Neue Pinakothek, Bayerische Staatsgemaeldesammlungen, Munich, Germany/Austrian Archive/Scala/Art Resource, NY).

and the chassis unsophisticated. It proved to be impressively fast in a straight line, but turns and maneuverability were a different matter. So Mr. Marcotte set about lightening and sim-

"Sweet Sixteen" as raced by Archie Marcotte. Minimalist exhaust headers (simple straight tubes for each cylinder, like a World War II fighter plane) extend from the side of the engine. Homemade bodywork provides some streamlining. Seated at the wheel is a cousin of Archie Marcotte's friend Richard Wehner (courtesy Monty Holmes).

Getting ready to run. To the right, Archie Marcotte makes adjustments to the racer. Body sheet metal has been removed, revealing the bomber pilot's seat, simple I-beam and transverse leaf front suspension. To the left, the Series 5780 Cadillac convertible sedan that donated the racer's engine (courtesy Monty Holmes).

plifying the design. He replaced the '37 Ford chassis with a tubular space frame constructed for the purpose. The transmission and clutch were removed and the engine was mated up directly with a Mercury rear axle. The driver sat in the pilot's seat from a World War II B-29 Stratofortress bomber.

The rest of the Cadillac had not been discarded. Mr. Marcotte had inserted a Mercury flathead V-8 engine with a Ford transmission in place of the V-16 engine, and the resulting half-breed was used to tow the race car. Quite a pair. But for whatever reason, Mr. Marcotte lost interest in both cars. Archie Marcotte moved to Glendive, Montana, and somewhere along the line the cars were titled in someone else's name. Both vehicles sat around and weathered, although all of the parts remained in generally the same place.

In 1974, Monty Holmes of Washington State bought the racer and its convertible sedan engine donor. In 1975, he gave both cars to his son (also named Monty) with the exhortation, "Keep the dream alive." The younger man had helped his father restore cars for years. His dad's 1911 Stevens-Duryea Model Y was a three-time national champion. At the time, Monty the son couldn't afford to restore the elegant but weathered '34 Cadillac, but he did collect all of the parts, including the silver hood goddess, in anticipation of the day when he would be ready. In the late 1990s, he took the plunge and embarked on a no-holds-barred restoration.

The chassis was placed on a rotisserie to provide complete ease of access. The engine was brought back to the factory configuration, and it and the transmission were reunited with the rest of the chassis. At about this time, Mr. Holmes received an invitation to display

What was left. Here is what was left of the once-proud V-16 convertible sedan. The 154-inch wheelbase means the chassis barely fits onto the trailer. The enormity of the restoration job that Mr. Holmes undertook is startlingly clear from this image (courtesy Terry Wenger).

Twenty feet long. Exactly twenty feet from bumper to bumper, the 1934 Cadillac V-16s rode on a 154-inch wheelbase, longest of any production American car (and ½ inch longer than the Duesenberg). The car was awarded second place in its class at the 2009 Pebble Beach Concours d'Elegance (courtesy Monty Holmes).

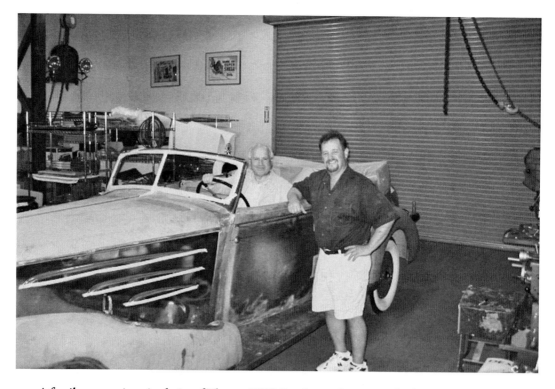

A family connection. A relative of Thomas H.W. Stonborough poses in the driver's seat of the 1934 Cadillac V-16 convertible sedan that his uncle bought new. Monty Holmes, restorer of the car, is standing next to the door. Lime-green painter's tape protects the chrome trim during preparation for painting the car's body (courtesy Monty Holmes).

the restored chassis at the Pebble Beach Concours d'Elegance. That provided additional motivation to really get the drivetrain and chassis right. In a full restoration, the upper surface of the frame on a 1934 Cadillac will never be seen. In a chassis-only display, it had better be beautiful. And so it was. Mr. Holmes showed the chassis at Pebble Beach in 2001 and had a splendid time.

The attention to detail was intense—new springs were installed for the brakes. New-old-stock bearings and seals were found and installed. Sonny Elliott in Kansas City, a renowned expert on these cars, replaced the compromised wood in the body. But other projects began to intrude. There was a Packard, the elder Mr. Holmes's Marmon had to be prepared for the Kirkland Concours, and Stan Squires called and informed Monty that he'd been chosen to be the next owner of Stan's 1934 V-16 stationary coupe (see the chapter in these pages about "Grace"). The coupe made it to Pebble Beach in the late oughts, and then the focus returned to completing work on the '34 convertible sedan (now known as "Helen" after Thomas Stonborough's first wife). As before, the watchword was to use the same techniques in restoring the car as Fleetwood had used in building it.

To assist in ferreting out the history of this beautiful car, Mr. Holmes enlisted a genealogist. In due course he made the acquaintance of a living member of Mr. Thomas Stonborough's family. During a trip to the U.S., that gentleman arranged to visit Mr. Holmes. At that point the car had been stripped to the bare metal in preparation for painting. Nevertheless, the visitor posed for photographs sitting in the car that his forebear bought new.

The leather upholstery and convertible top were done by the same specialist in Michigan, and with the long process complete, the car was ready for Pebble Beach in 2009, where it took a second place award, followed by a first place at Kirkland—an impressive finish for a long road back.

Three years later, the splendidly restored convertible sedan was offered for sale at the auction accompanying the Pebble Beach Concours and it brought a very respectable $550,000 price.

57. A Very Long Sedan

By 1934, the Great Depression was in full swing. Franklin Roosevelt had been elected president two years previously and was working to implement the first New Deal. The market for fine motor cars had contracted severely, and the prospects for a turnaround were not rosy. Peerless was gone. Marmon, Duesenberg and Pierce-Arrow were not long for this world, and Packard was struggling. Lincoln and especially Cadillac had the benefit of substantial parent companies to help them survive.

The multi-cylinder program at Cadillac continued for a number of reasons. It gave the Cadillac and LaSalle lines an incalculable dose of "prestige by association." It offered a glimmer of inspirational optimism in a tough economic phase. It gave an edge over the remaining competitors in the luxury field. And there were still people with the means and the desire to own the best car money could buy.

Four years of development and improvement had brought a mechanical fuel pump, cooled and muffled intake air, higher compression ratio, independent front suspension, and no-draft ventilation. Styling across the automotive industry had taken up the streamlining theme and art deco accents. Horns, radiator cap, chassis parts and most spare tires were concealed by the body sheet metal. Cadillac V-16s reached an astonishing twenty feet in overall length with the longest production car wheelbase ever (154 inches). Cadillac advertising warned that production of the V-16 for the 1934 model year would be limited to 400 cars. As it turned out, no more than 60 of these magnificent conveyances were built that year.

One of the 1934 V-16s was originally shipped from the factory to the New York City branch on July 17. On July 25, it was diverted to Philadelphia. Then in late November it was diverted to Wilmington, Delaware, and a handwritten note on the shipping document seems to indicate that the ultimate destination may have been Atlantic City. It was a seven-passenger sedan, style number 5775, according to the body tag. The car had engine number 5100016 (which makes it the sixteenth built that year), and body number 9. The body number is somewhat deceptive because only five 1934 V-16 cars with this body style were built. The explanation is that the same Fleetwood bodies were used for V-8, V-12 and V-16 cars, and this was the ninth such body (although not the ninth V-16 with that style).

There are some unique features that may indicate that this car was an experimental model, or that it was used to try out some structural variations. Unlike other first-generation V-16s, the front of the engine is secured with a single center mount, and not with two corner mounts. The steel plate bolted to the front of the crankcase on most of these engines extends to the sides to form two feet that sit on and bolt to diagonal frame members that attach to

Twenty feet long. All right, an inch or two shy without the 1934-only biplane bumpers. But many owners replaced the ornate but fragile two-blade bumpers with the more conventional design used on the 1935 Cadillacs. The 1934 V-16s were the longest production cars with the longest wheelbase Cadillac ever manufactured. Combined effects of the streamlining theme and Art Deco esthetic considerations make these some of the most fascinating motor cars of the Classic Era (author's photograph).

the frame side rails and the cross member under the radiator. This engine is supported in the front at one location in the center of the engine.

The second unusual feature has to do with the "knee action" independent front suspension, a new and revolutionary change to Cadillacs for 1934. The lower A-arms of the front suspension of this car pivot at the frame on rubber bushings. Most 1934 Cadillacs had lubricated metal-to-metal bushings with fittings so that they can be periodically greased. This car's build sheet mentions this variation and the corresponding part numbers. Since independent suspension had just been developed and introduced, it's conceivable that this car was built as a test vehicle of some sort to see how the rubber bushings would fare as against the greased bushings.

The bumpers for 1934 Cadillacs were a one-year-only design consisting of two flat horizontal blades connected by bullet-shaped mounting struts protruding from the frame ends. This "biplane" bumper design was very attractive but easily damaged, and many owners replaced them with the sturdier, more conventional bumpers Cadillac installed on the 1935 cars. Such is the case with this car.

In 1963, *The Self-Starter* shows the car as owned by Mr. Robert E. Harrison of Philadelphia, Pennsylvania. Later it is believed to have been owned by Cadillac dealer and noted collector Dave Towell of Akron, Ohio. For a good twenty years, the big Cadillac was owned by

Goddess mascot appears to hold the hood wings aloft. 1934 saw the radiator fully enclosed, the headlights removed from the fenders, and the front wheels and suspension entirely enclosed. Paradoxically, one of the breakthrough features for this model year—independent front suspension—is hidden from view (author's photograph).

Gene Zimmerman, displayed in his Automobilorama at Harrisburg, Pennsylvania. In 1973, Mr. Zimmerman had to sell his Holiday Inn and put the cars in his museum up for auction. A gentleman bought the 1934 V-16, but soon found it was more than he was prepared to deal with. A large number of parts were missing—the carburetors and intake silencers and tubes, the fender-mounted parking lights, the clock behind the front seat, and others. Cliff Woodbury, Jr., of Media, Pennsylvania, made the owner an offer, and he accepted it. Mr. Woodbury earnestly set about replacing the missing parts. He went to Hershey every year to sift through the various vendors' parts bins until he spotted items that his car required. Mr. Woodbury had been around these cars all his life. His father had bought a 1934 Cadillac town sedan that had the 1935 bumpers when it was sold new. Mr. Woodbury had a music studio in Manhattan in the 1930s, and he'd seen all the big classics when they were new driving through the Big Apple traffic.

Mr. Woodbury's son (Cliff Woodbury III) used the '34 V-16 for his wedding limousine. It was a hot day, and the old girl didn't want to start for the trip to the reception. So the wedding couple had to wait around a bit while the engine cooled off before they could continue with the celebration.

The elder Cliff Woodbury died in 2007, and the car is now owned by his son. The son has continued to care for the sedan and to share its stately beauty with others. He has decided to remove the pale gray paint and return the finish to the original black, and has undertaken an engine overhaul. He has biplane bumpers and is considering installing a set for that correct 1934 look. He would also like to pin down the early history of the car and answer the open questions regarding the unusual front engine mount and suspension bushings.

58. Opposition Research

For most of the twentieth century, Rolls-Royce benefited from an aura of almost divine hand-crafted perfection. The very name was synonymous in most people's minds with ultimate precision, flawless engineering and the most opulent luxury. It was assumed that a Rolls was so well designed and built that it would last a lifetime. Hardly ever has a manufactured product achieved such a hyperbolic axiomatic reputation.

Today, of course, things are somewhat more matter-of-fact. The Rolls-Royce automobile is now manufactured by a unit of the German BMW Group, an irony of immense profundity to anyone who lived through (or who has studied) the Second World War. And while the motor cars are still eminently luxurious, solid and exclusive, the mystique that enveloped the brand in ages past is much reduced, if indeed it remains.

From the vantage point of the present day, and with the help of careful historians (such as the distinguished New Zealander Maurice Hendry) it is possible to discern periods of time during the days when Rolls-Royce was a magical phrase that the vaunted reputation of the company was more myth than actual fact. During the late 1920s and into the 1930s, at least from an engineering perspective, the company found itself lagging behind many of its competitors. At a time of rapid transformation of the very nature of the automobile, Rolls-Royce were somewhat slow to realize that even hand-crafted works of art could become outmoded or even obsolete if proper efforts were not made to keep abreast of (if not to form the vanguard of) innovations in propulsion, chassis design and construction techniques.

Driver's controls. From 1932 on the instruments are placed before the driver. Art deco influence is apparent in the instrument faces and the background panel. Moving the hand brake lever to the cowl wall increases front seat legroom. Steering wheel hub is designed to be engraved with the owner's name (courtesy RM Auctions).

By the time the multi-cylinder craze hit the United States, Rolls-Royce were still relying on big six-cylinder engines to power their cars. The heyday of the big six was already well in the past. Packard and Duesenberg used straight eights. Lincoln and Cadillac had been running V-8s since the teens. By 1930, Peerless had gone to all eight-cylinder engines. The problem was that with the technology available at the time, a six-cylinder engine powerful enough to carry the big, luxuriously appointed bodies that buyers of fine motor cars preferred tended to be rough running. To achieve adequate power and refined smoothness, the solution was to add cylinders. The greater the number of power impulses in each revolution of the crankshaft, the less they were felt individually by the passengers. And so the cylinder wars commenced. Rolls-Royce came late to the contest.

As the reader knows by now, Cadillac introduced its V-16 in 1930. Marmon followed with its own V-16 the following year, and Peerless had brought a V-16 car to the working prototype stage before that venerable company was overtaken by financial difficulties in 1931 and transformed into a brewery. In 1932, Auburn, Franklin, Lincoln, Packard and Pierce-Arrow brought out V-12s. Cadillac's own V-12 had appeared the previous year. Duesenberg stayed with its mighty straight eight, but began offering supercharging in 1932.

Maurice Hendry has identified a number of instances in the 1920s and 1930s when Rolls-Royce obtained, examined and emulated in one degree or another contemporary American motor cars. One of the vehicles so utilized was a 1934 Cadillac Series 5875 V-16 imperial

A bit more businesslike. By 1934 the fashionably styled V-16 engine has evolved a bit. The thick black tube that parallels the valve cover brings cool air from in front of the radiator through an intake noise muffler and down to the carburetor. The ignition wires are a bit unruly, compared to the tidy arrangement of the 1930–31 engine and its "flat-top" distributor cap. And the knobs that secure the metal cover between the cylinder banks no longer have enameled and gilded Cadillac crests (courtesy RM Auctions).

sedan, engine number 5100024. The build sheet for this car indicates that it was shipped directly to Rolls-Royce in Derby, England, with the typed notation "SHIP NOT LATER THAN APRIL 25." The specifications include Thessalon Green exterior color, a silver goddess radiator ornament, a Master radio in the rear compartment, fender-mounted spare tires, and a rack for an accessory trunk. Someone has handwritten on the build sheet copy "THIS DELIVERED TO AMERICAN EMBASSY IN ENGLAND FOR JOSEPH KENNEDY," but during the period 1934 through 1937, Joseph P. Kennedy, Sr., was serving in Washington, D.C., as the inaugural chairman of the newly-established Securities and Exchange Commission, and then as the first head of the United States Maritime Commission. He was not appointed ambassador to the United Kingdom until February 1938. It seems likely that the notation on the 1934 Cadillac's build sheet is not authentic.

In his book *The Cars in My Life*, Walter O. Bentley had this to say about the 1934 Cadillac V-16:

Many years later, when I was with Rolls-Royce, I often drove another Cadillac owned by the company and used for experimental purposes. This was a V16 of such mammoth dimensions that it would have dwarfed even that earlier American car. My chief memories of this automobile (although that term is inadequate) were its astonishing refinement with perhaps the most completely successful elimination of evidence that explosions were occurring under the bonnet ever obtained in a motor car. The word "torque" also took on a new meaning with this V16, which could reach 90 m.p.h. with a sort of endless limousine body of goodness knows what weight. Finally—and one could never get away from this—there was the impression of sheer size this car has left; and of attempting, like the captain of the *Queen Mary* docking during a tugboat strike, to manœuvre this Cadillac through the gates of Hyde Park and into the dock basin of Marble Arch.

Mr. Bentley was understandably impressed by the remarkable dimensions of the 1934 V-16 cars. With an overall length of exactly twenty feet, these cars had the longest wheelbase (154 inches) of any production car ever built, exceeding even the mighty Duesenberg by ½ inch.

British automobile enthusiast and author Mr. Robert Maidment has in his possession a copy of an internal communication from Rolls-Royce archives that reads as follows:

Ev.

There is a 16-Cylinder Cadillac now at W. in the Experimental Department's possession, the body of which you would no doubt like to look over to see some of its more important features such as method of construction, method of mounting, etc.

Sg arranged for Hoopers to have a look over this car before it went to the Works, and Mr. Sclater Booth rang me up and said that, whereas he understood it was all-steel construction, this apparently is not the case and there is some wood in it. He even found that the door hinges were fixed with wood screws.

When you next go to W. would you take an opportunity of looking at this body and let me have a report on its most interesting points.

We should particularly like to know what the weight of the body is, and if W. remove the body for the purpose of getting at the chassis, would you ask them to have it weighed and let us know what the weight is and of course what the weight includes.

Cx.

Twenty feet of opulence. 1934 Cadillac V-16s were exactly 20 feet long, with a 154-inch wheelbase that exceeded even that of the Duesenberg long wheelbase chassis. Increased horsepower, independent front suspension and other chassis improvements make these very drivable cars (courtesy RM Auctions).

Mr. Maidment informed me that not only did Rolls-Royce purchase and examine the car, they took it for a 10,000-mile extended run around Europe, after which they dismantled it extensively, only to reassemble and sell it.

It's not clear, at this distance from the events, who purchased the '34 Cadillac V-16 once Rolls-Royce were finished with it. What is known is that a subsequent owner had an interesting time at a car meet with it. Mr. Maidment has provided the following account as told to him by Mr. Peter Baines, the late long-serving secretary of the Rolls-Royce Enthusiasts' Club (the only Rolls-Royce club in the United Kingdom, with some 6,000 members):

> In the late 1960s at an early Rolls-Royce Enthusiasts' Club one-make meet, a gentleman (name never recorded) showed up driving a large 1934 V-16 Cadillac. He was politely told the meet was only for Rolls-Royce motor cars and that he could not come onto the field. Whereupon he pulled out definitive documentation in the form of the car's "log book" proving that the Cadillac was originally owned by Rolls-Royce Limited. At the time, neither Peter Baines nor [the club's co-founder and original chairman] knew anything of such a car being owned or purchased by R-R. However, in the face of the overwhelming evidence, the gentleman and his V-16 were welcomed onto the show and afforded the hospitality warranted by such an unexpected discovery.

The identity of the owner who brought the Cadillac to the RREC meet is lost to us now. But eventually the car that had so awed Mr. Bentley made its way to an Oklahoma collector who had the engine rebuilt and the electrical system converted to 12-volt. On August

Center "imperial" division. Folding auxiliary seats ("jump seats") are covered by zippered upholstered flaps. Lidded storage compartments behind the polished wood strip flank the crank to raise and lower the divider window (courtesy RM Auctions).

6, 2005, it was sold at auction at the Vintage Motor Cars at Meadow Brook Hall sale conducted by RM Auctions. The price was $83,600. The lucky purchaser was a businessman and collector from California, Mr. Charles Swimmer. He admired the car's originality and integrity, but in due course he traded it to the Blackhawk Collection in Danbury, California. They, in turn, offered the car at the 2005 Hershey Auction conducted by the Kruse organization. Today the car is in a private collection.

59. Let's Make a Deal

The Cadillac V-16s built during the years 1934 through 1937 are extremely similar and the model years are hard to tell apart without reference to the engine number and the body number plate. Although the 1934 cars were equipped with the one-year-only "biplane" bumpers, those decorative appurtenances were quite fragile, and some owners replaced them with the single-bar bumpers used for '35–'37. All of these cars rode on the longest wheelbase ever used on a production passenger car, 154 inches. The elegant bumpers on the 1934s brought the overall length to exactly twenty feet (the later cars were two inches shy of that mark). That said, Cadillac remained eager to accommodate a purchaser's individual preferences and desires wherever possible.

In 1934 and '35, V-16s could be ordered either with flat windshields or with V'd windshields. The factory used separate body style numbering sequences for the cars equipped with one or the other. V-windshield jobs were of the 5800 sequence, while flat-windshield cars bore a style number in the 6200 sequence. There were far fewer flat-windshield styles offered and far fewer were built (fourteen each in 1934 and 1935). They were all either variations on the 6275 style (6275 limousines, 6275-B formal limousines, 6275-S seven-passenger sedans and even a Series 6275-H3 with three inches of added headroom), or five-passenger Series 6233 town sedans.

In 1935, one of the seven Series 6275 limousines shipped from the factory was sold new by the Don Lee organization in California. Painted a deep green color that Cadillac called "Champlain Green," it had engine number 5100123. According to veteran V-16 enthusiast Joe Mikula, Champlain Green was similar to the hue that mailboxes were once painted, back when mailboxes stood on many municipal street corners, and before they were painted red and blue in the 1960s.

As was often done with the 1934–1937 V-16 cars, the original purchaser's name (T. T. Prepoutse in this instance) was engraved by the factory on the steering wheel hub. Mr. Prepoutse had the car tailored to his particular preferences. The divider between the front and rear compartments was deleted (making this, in effect, a Series 6275-S car). It's hard to say from this vantage point why he didn't just order a dividerless sedan in the first instance. That way, the car would have had an adjustable driver's seat, as well.

Mr. Prepoutse also requested that the vent windows on the front doors and rear quarter window openings be deleted. Pivoting vent windows were introduced in 1933 as part of General Motors's "No-Draft Ventilation" system, but for some reason, this buyer preferred not to have them. Also deleted at the owner's request was the armrest in the rear compartment that would normally split the rear seat when pulled into place. Otherwise, tucked up into the seat back, it would have been flush with the back cushion. Again, for some reason, he preferred not to have it, and Cadillac obliged.

Optional equipment selected for the car included a radio and a heater. By this point, Cadillac-installed radios were reliable and could hold a station consistently. The technology had improved vastly since radio sets were first offered in 1930, and by 1935, those who ordered them could confidently expect enjoyable listening as they drove. The antenna for the car is suspended beneath the driver's-side running board, an odd location to modern minds, but an efficient and unobtrusive choice at the time.

Personalized touch. A special feature available on 1934 Cadillac V-16s was a horn button engraved with the owner's name and the car number. The owners who chose this option have greatly assisted those who try to uncover the histories of these cars (courtesy Louis Barnhart).

During the Second World War, an aftermarket overdrive unit was installed on the car in order to improve its gas mileage. Ordinarily, when a car's transmission is in high gear, the driveshaft is turning at the same speed as the engine's crankshaft. With an overdrive, the driveshaft can be made to turn *faster* than the engine. If two examples of the same make and model car are running at 60 m.p.h., one with overdrive and the other without, the engine of the car with an overdrive is running slower, wearing its moving parts less and using less fuel than the other engine. According to two former owners, this overdrive-equipped Cadillac runs extremely well, and the overdrive unit is a great help for touring.

In 1963, Jim Weston of San Francisco heard that Mr. Ross Prepoutse (the original owner's son) wanted to sell the car. Mr. Weston told Craig Watrous and Gunnar Henrioulle, who followed up on the lead and went for a ride in the car. The seller spoke about his history with the big Cadillac, beginning near the end of his high school years. It was he who engineered the installation of the Chrysler overdrive just to the rear of the transmission (he still had the car's original propeller shaft and brought it out to show the men). During World War II, Ross Prepoutse had been in army intelligence working as a courier. For some time during 1943 and 1944, he was making weekly round-trip runs in the V-16 Cadillac between San Francisco and a military facility near Salt Lake City carrying documents and information. He would travel by way of U.S. Highway 50 over the Sierra mountains, and on one or more occasions, a special snowplow service was arranged to facilitate his run. Civilian vehicles were frequently pressed into service in the war effort, but one rarely hears of this happening to a Cadillac V-16.

Mr. Henrioulle and Mr. Watrous agreed to buy the Cadillac. Mr. Henrioulle drove the V-16 back home from San Francisco, accompanied by his wife. Mr. Watrous and a friend rode separately in a 1935 Pierce-Arrow that Craig had bought from Jim Weston. Both cars traveled at a brisk pace, and on one long incline, the Pierce-Arrow slightly outperformed the Cadillac (even with overdrive engaged).

The two men kept the V-16 for a while, then agreed to let Mr. Watrous find it a new owner. An ad was placed in the *Sacramento Bee,* and it came to the attention of Mr. Ronald Renaldi, who traded a 1962 Chrysler 300H for the Cadillac sedan. Five years later, Mr. Renaldi sold the V-16 to Joe Mikula. During the fifteen or eighteen years that Mr. Mikula owned the Cadillac, he re-covered the interior door panels and the front seat. In the 1980s, Mr. Renaldi re-purchased the car from Mr. Mikula, and he retained ownership until very recently, selling it to Mr. Tom Crook of Washington State.

In 2007, this grand Cadillac was offered for sale by Mr. Crook, a respected dealer who advertises in various old car enthusiast publications. Meanwhile, Mr. David Kane of Bernardsville, New Jersey, had read that Louis Barnhart of Salem, Virginia, had a 1934 Cadillac V-16 convertible sedan in good unrestored condition. Mr. Kane wanted to acquire that car, but Mr. Barnhart declined to sell it for cash, and Mr. Kane was trying to find a car that he would accept in trade. Mr. Barnhart had lived with a V-16 for forty-some years, and he was not eager to be without one. When Mr. Kane offered to buy the black 1935 V-16 sedan, Mr. Barnhart agreed to do a swap. So, in November an enclosed trailer arrived at the Barnhart home and out rolled the 1935 sedan.

For the occasion of the exchange of the 1934 convertible sedan for the 1935 limousine, Mr. Barnhart's wife Trish donned a lovely period dress with matching gloves and hat. Of

Before the 1934 convertible left for its new home in New Jersey, the Barnharts took a picture with both cars. Trish Barnhart wore fine period clothes for the occasion (courtesy Louis Barnhart).

Imposing front end of Mr. Barnhart's 1935 V-16 limousine. Upholstered trim panels for the doors had been redone (portion around sides and tops of windows is original material). In person the difference between the old and new work is imperceptible to the eye (courtesy Louis Barnhart).

course a photo was taken of the two cars together. One Cadillac V-16 by itself is a remarkable sight—two together is magnificent.

In the ensuing months, Louis got to know the sedan and its unique personality. He enjoys driving it, and he's discovered some minor mechanical issues to which he can apply his skills. Remarkably, it is only in photographs that the difference between the older upholstery material and the newer is readily apparent.

Mr. Barnhart has a California ownership certificate in the name of Joseph Mikula that shows Mr. Mikula as the registered owner for the period February 23, 1980, through August 24, 1980. The certificate has been signed by Mr. Mikula and the Wells Fargo Bank by way of transferring ownership and it has been stamped "VOID."

Mr. Barnhart also has a sheepskin rug that was an original accessory for these cars (and fits the passenger compartment floor exactly), and a correct accessory trunk.

60. Shiny, Streamlined and Sleek

One of the most interesting body styles of the Cadillac V-16 cars was the closed or "stationary" coupe on the 1934 through 1937 chassis. During those years, the cars were a full twenty feet in length, automobiles of monumental proportions. The relatively small passenger compartment of a coupe served to emphasize the long tapered hood and the gentle downward curve of the deck. Not as flashy as the convertibles, and not as opulent as the sedans and limousines, these were still unmistakably extraordinary conveyances. They were just as carefully built, just as well engineered and just as capable of being custom fitted to the purchaser's individual taste.

In the first half of the last century, tobacco companies were considered to be respectable enterprises, and their executives were admired businessmen. The P. Lorillard Company (now known as the Lorillard Tobacco Company) was founded in 1760 in New York City by Pierre Lorillard. It calls itself "the oldest continuously operating tobacco company in the United States." In 1886, Griswold Lorillard, a descendant of Pierre Lorillard, introduced a men's evening wear outfit at his father's estate, Tuxedo Park, in upstate New York, that would thereafter be known as "the tuxedo." In 1937, an executive of the company named George Hummel ordered a new Cadillac V-16 stationary coupe.

Engine number 5130315 with body number 43 is a Series 5776 coupe. The list price, including destination charge, was $7,400, and four cars like it were built in 1937. A story is told about this one to the effect that Mr. Hummel bought it as a wedding present for Mrs. Edward Hummel, but that has not been verified. Another uncorroborated legend is that it was left to Mr. Hummel's butler. In any event, it stayed "in the family" into the 1970s.

During the 1970s, the car was sold at auction, and Richard Gold bought the black V-16 coupe. He later sold it to Tom Barrett, cofounder of the Barrett Jackson Collector Car

1937 Cadillac V-16 Stationary Coupe. Photographed at the Amelia Island Concours d'Elegance in 2010. The triumph of the teardrop shape, characteristic of the styling trend of the 1930s, is clear in this view of a very sleek motor car (courtesy Randy Denchfield).

Posing at Pebble. The lean and elegant profile of this car easily makes the case that "personal luxury cars" were not an invention of the 1960s and '70s. It's just short of twenty feet long, but pleasingly proportioned; there is nothing ungainly about it (courtesy Joseph Scott).

Auction. Mr. Barrett may have repainted the car while he owned it. He sold it to a Pennsylvania collector and dealer in payment of a debt.

New Jersey car collector David Kane's grandfather had owned a 1937 V-16 coupe that he had bought slightly used. Mr. Kane had hoped that he would eventually own the car, but somehow it slipped away. Over the years, Mr. Kane let it be known that he was interested in finding his grandfather's Cadillac again (or one just like it), and in due course, the Pennsylvania dealer contacted him. But events intervened, and Mr. Kane was unable to effect a purchase at that time. Subsequently, the dealer sold the car to another collector, Mr. Ronald Benach of Lake Forest, Illinois. Mr. Benach recalls the car as having been in superb original condition when he owned it, with only 17,000 actual miles. But he sold the car back to the dealer and to this day he regrets having done so.

Mr. Kane recounts that about this time some thought was being given to removing the coupe's roof and transforming it into a convertible. He again let it be known that he really wanted the car. The dealer in Pennsylvania had reacquired it from Mr. Benach, and around the turn of the century, Mr. Kane was able to become the owner of the V-16 coupe. It still had about 17,000 miles on the clock, and in 2002, the car took Best of Show and Best American Closed Car 1935–1939 honors at the Greenwich Concours.

In the intervening years, Mr. Kane sold the car to another collector in New Jersey, and not long ago, he bought it back. In 2008, he displayed the car at the Pebble Beach Concours, and took it to the Kirkland Concours in Seattle, Washington. With a friend helping out as copilot, he drove the car on a 150-mile tour, and reports that each day it drove better than the day before, proving the old saw that these cars were meant to be driven. Today, the mileage is 20,600. Mr. Kane has been actively enjoying this prime example of a real personal luxury car.

61. 1938 Town Sedan

In 1938, Cadillac introduced to the world a startling new series of V-16 motor cars. The Great Depression was still ravaging American businesses and families, and annual sales of the original overhead-valve V-16 never exceeded 60 in the period 1934–37. Venerated names in the fine car business—Marmon, Pierce-Arrow, Peerless, Duesenberg—had been consumed by the creditors and receivers. Yet Cadillac had poured resources into developing and manufacturing a new, and in many ways improved, supercar. From our perspective, it seems like an imprudent move, at best.

The timing of the new Cadillac V-16 was not as foolhardy as we "retrospectators" might think. By the middle of the 1930s, there was an economic turnaround, with employment and the gross national product steadily increasing. It was not until the summer of 1937 and a plunge back into a deep recession that people understood that the hard times were not yet over. The introduction of the new sixteens shortly after the economy again turned southward echoed, in a way, the debut of the original Cadillac V-16s shortly after the great stock market crash in the fall of 1929.

Aside from the economic turmoil, or perhaps because of it, Cadillac had been losing competitors in its struggle to dominate the luxury automobile market. Packard was still a force to be reckoned with, though it introduced a lower-priced eight and even a six-cylinder car to compensate for lower luxury sales. Lincoln had Ford behind it, but it, too, was compelled to bring out the less expensive Zephyr. Cadillac had had its smaller sibling the LaSalle since 1927 (which borrowed an Oldsmobile straight eight engine for 1934 through 1936), but Cadillac also had the financial strength of General Motors behind it. By the mid–1930s, the Cadillac V-16 was the most spectacular automotive engine still offered, and even with minimal sales figures, its halo continued to grace the rest of the product line. Cadillac was in a position to score a final triumph that would assure its leadership for the foreseeable future.

The 1930s were a period of rapid development in automotive engineering, petroleum chemistry and aerodynamic design. Better fuels, better engine technology and the "longer, lower, wider" design imperative meant that the priorities and limiting factors car builders worked with in the late '30s were quite different from those of the late '20s, when the first generation V-16s were brought into being. If the V-16 was going to continue, it made sense to update the (now eight-year-old) engine.

So, for a variety of reasons, Cadillac brought out a new sixteen-cylinder engine in a dramatically restyled car. The original 45-degree cylinder angle was opened out to 135 degrees, making a much lower profile and permitting the use of downdraft carburetors. The crankcase and cylinder blocks were a single casting. The total number of parts was slashed dramatically, and even though the engine was smaller in displacement and lighter in weight, it produced the same power as its predecessor. Importantly, the new design allowed more modern chassis and body design—lower hood, a passenger compartment moved forward on the frame.

The second series V-16, designated the 90, would be produced for three years—1938, 1939 and 1940. The first year Cadillac sold over 300 cars, benefiting, in part, from the partial economic recovery that was dissolving back into recession. In 1939, less than half as many cars were shipped, and the final year saw only about 50 produced.[1]

Dramatically low profile of late-series V-16 engine. With a wide 135-degree angle between cylinder banks, the "flathead" V-16 engine is almost flat. In contrast to the V-16 cars from the early 1930s, where the engine was a strikingly designed conversation piece, the later engine is buried deep within engine compartment and hard to see at all, when all of the bodywork is in place. Cadillac engineers got the same power with less weight and fewer moving parts (courtesy Brad Ipsen).

Twenty of the cars built in 1938 were style number 9039 town sedans. In the design parlance of the 1930s, a town sedan was a four-door model with front and rear seats, but without the extra legroom in back required for jump seats or even the smaller "opera" auxiliary seats. Generally, the upper rear quarter was blanked out or windowless. It was an owner-driven, relatively private conveyance for four or five people. The rear wall of the passenger compartment was somewhat farther forward than on a regular five- or seven-passenger sedan, and in earlier examples, there might be a permanently-mounted trunk, in addition to a folding rack for an additional trunk. Once the body sheet metal engulfed the formerly separate trunk, a town sedan would simply have a larger trunk (or boot, as the English say) than an ordinary sedan.

Mr. Brad Ipsen of Marysville, Washington, owns one of the surviving examples of the 1938 Series 9039 town sedans. He believes that the car was most likely built on speculation, without a purchase order in hand. The factory build sheet indicates no special equipment, but shows that the car went through two Cadillac distributors before it found a home. Apparently it had to be repainted a different blue color to please the original purchaser.

In the course of restoring his car, Mr. Ipsen has learned a great deal about how the body was constructed. By 1938, Cadillac bodies, including the V-16 full sedan and limousine bodies, were generally all steel. The town sedan body was a partial exception to this rule. As he

Left rear quarter of Brad Ipsen's 1938 V-16 town sedan. This area of the car was largely handmade. The rear window area of a regular sedan body was moved forward about a foot, requiring removal of material from the roof and lengthening the top of the trunk lid. The rear quarter windows of the sedan body were filled in for an elegant privacy feature for the rear seat passengers (courtesy Brad Ipsen).

disassembled and worked on his car, it became clear to Mr. Ipsen that when Cadillac built a town sedan body, a great deal more work was required than to construct than the regular five- and seven-passenger sedans and limousines. The town sedan rode on the same wheelbase as the others, but the passenger compartment was noticeably shortened. That was done by taking the standard body shell, cutting a section out of the roof, moving the rear window and aft portion of the roof about a half-foot forward, lengthening the trunk lid and its opening, and filling in the rear quarter window. In the process, the trunk lid and the rear portions of the back door openings were hand made in the old "composite" technique—wood framework with sheet metal covering. The solid upper rear quarter was achieved by filling in the window opening with a steel plate, and a great deal of lead was used to smooth and fair the portion of the body above the rear fender to make the surface flow correctly. The result was a graceful symphony of curves that is somewhat more relaxed to the eye than the formal shape of the regular sedans.

Brad Ipsen's car had been for sale in Illinois at one point (V-16 enthusiast and owner Terry Wenger has an advertisement for it). Subsequently it came into the possession of a gentleman in Canada known for creative restorations of older cars.

During the 1990s, a friend told Mr. Ipsen about an ad in *Hemmings Motor News* for a

1938 V-16 town sedan for sale in Canada. As it happened, Mr. Ipsen had a business trip to make that took him close enough to stop and look at the car. The owner who placed the *Hemmings* ad seems to have used the town sedan as a parts car, and it was priced accordingly. Mr. Ipsen bought what was left. As such, the car was in need of some critical (or at least hard to find) parts. The body parts forward of the firewall (comprising what's called the "front clip") except for the top hood panel, were all missing, incorrect or in poor shape. Plain fenders had been substituted for the originals (which had wells for spare tires). The hood side panels and the radiator shell were gone. A number of the horizontal bars in the grille were broken, but the frame was usable. The engine (and not the one that was originally installed) was in terrible shape, with extensive cracking of the block casting and firmly frozen pistons. The whereabouts of the original engine, number 5270137, are presently unknown. Most likely it was installed by the Canadian owner in another car, but that is not certain.

Since he became the owner, Mr. Ipsen has been steadily working on returning this Cadillac to the glorious presence it had when first delivered. The engine in the car was cracked, and Mr. Ipsen had to drill out the pistons in order to determine whether the block could be used at all. A man in California had a second engine and some parts, and although the engine required rebuilding, there were no cracks in the block to deal with. Front fenders with spare-

Widened rear door of town sedan body. The swivel vent window in the rear door allows the main window to be lowered completely into the door, even with a cutout for the front of the rear fender (courtesy Brad Ipsen).

tire wells were procured, but Mr. Ipsen elected to use the original (plain) fenders to keep the cleaner look. He also obtained a radiator shell and a good grille. The hood side panels have remained elusive, but V-8 panels can be modified to serve, if all else fails. A great deal of painting and finishing have been done, but there is still some interior work and reassembly required before the car's restoration is complete.

62. 1939 Limousine

In late 1978, Brad Ipsen of Marysville, Washington, acquired a 1939 Cadillac V-16 Series 9033 imperial sedan owned most recently by a gentleman named Archie Marcotte in Livingston, Montana. Series 9033 describes an elegant limousine with glass division between driver and passengers, and full-width jump seats. Mr. Ipsen completed a thorough restoration in 1985 and has owned and enjoyed the car ever since. It has covered 20,000 miles since the restoration (including several CARavan tours with the Classic Car Club of America) and it remains very presentable. Recently Mr. Ipsen has been able to undertake some reconstruction of the car's history, with the help of his friend Mr. Terry Wenger of Ferguson, Missouri.

In 2006, Mr. Wenger was looking through old copies of *Hemmings Motor News* and in a 1972 issue he found an ad for a 1939 Cadillac V-16 limousine. The ad indicated that the

Brad Ipsen's 1939 Cadillac V-16 limousine. The third series V-16 cars are less "showy," perhaps, than their predecessors, but they are fully as elegant and refined. Grille, hubcap emblems, "V16" badge on spare-tire cover, louvers on fenders and hood, and distinctive hood ornament are among the features that contrast the "Series 90" V-16s from the V-8-powered Series 75s (courtesy Brad Ipsen).

car for sale was the 73rd V-16 out of the 134 sold in 1939, and it provided an address in Forsyth, Montana, for a man named Purkett. Mr. Wenger shared what he'd found with Brad Ipsen, who hoped it was part of the history of his 1939 V-16 Cadillac. Taking the information in the ad as a starting point, Mr. Ipsen performed an Internet search with the seller's last name and the Montana town. Then he sent e-mail inquiries to the candidates he identified. A young lady with the Purkett family name responded and directed Brad to the man himself, who was then 84 years old. The car he had offered in the ad had engine number 5290073, which would indeed have been the 73rd 1939 V-16, but Mr. Ipsen's car has engine number 5290072 (making it the 72nd). This raised the intriguing possibility of two 1939 Cadillac V-16s with consecutive serial numbers in a state where none were sold new (records survive for 1938 and 1939, but not for 1940.)

The car in the ad had been sold to the casino owner and legendary car collector Bill Harrah, but Mr. Purkett did have an old picture, which he shared with Mr. Ipsen.

Mr. Purkett had known Archie Marcotte, who had earlier lived in Glendive, Montana. Both of them had been railroad men, and that's probably how they came to be acquainted. At one point, Mr. Purkett disclosed, he had tried to buy the car Mr. Ipsen now owns (number 72) from Mr. Marcotte, but when he saw it, it was in poor condition with extensive dog damage in the rear seat. That description was consistent with what Mr. Ipsen had encountered when he bought the car and began restoring it.

By the time Mr. Ipsen had begun researching his car, Mr. Marcotte had passed away. Mr. Wenger and Mr. Ipsen found his son and daughter, and discovered that Mr. Marcotte had been a bit of an eccentric. He'd bred wolf-dog hybrids, for one thing, and he had built a hot rod out of a Cadillac V-16 from the early '30s. He had purchased the '39 V-16 seven-passenger limousine that Mr. Ipsen now cares for in the 1950s.

The build sheet discloses that Mr. Ipsen's '39 limousine was delivered new in Wilkes-Barre, Pennsylvania. Could a coal mine owner or mining company executive have been the initial purchaser? In 1939, Wilkes-Barre was still a center of the coal industry, having once been known as the "Diamond City" when the discovery nearby of rich anthracite coal deposits brought thousands of job seekers. According to the Luzerne County Historical Society, in the late 1930s there was also a great deal of manufacturing in the Wilkes-Barre area, including textile mills and cigar factories. The Vulcan Iron Works was supplying locomotives for the railroads and the mines. There were certainly potential V-16 owners in the area, but without more information, one can only speculate as to which one of them bought this particular car.

The only further clue to the car's first owner was a set of three initials that, according to the build sheet, were ordered for a monogram on the car's doors. One of the options available for these cars was to have the factory paint up to three initials on the doors, just below the side window. It's a bit difficult to make out, but the letters on the build sheet appear to be "WWY," or perhaps "MMY."

Continuing his sleuthing, Mr. Wenger wondered how a Montana resident in the 1950s would have found this car, which was located at the time in Pennsylvania. He reasoned that the only publication with a national circulation in those years that would have featured old car ads would have been *Motor Trend*. That was fortunate, because Terry Wenger had a collection of *Motor Trend* back issues extending back well into the '50s. So he began flipping through the pages, and eventually he came upon an ad for a 1939 V-16 limousine under the name Williams with a Wilkes-Barre address. That answered one question and posed several more: Could Mr. Williams be traced and could his identity be ascertained? Could he be

Photograph that Mr. Purkett provided to Brad Ipsen. Damage toward the rear of the running board edge molding helped identify the car in the picture as the one owned by Mr. Ipsen. The name of the Hotel Redington is partially visible toward the top center of the photo (courtesy Brad Ipsen).

pinned down as the original owner? And could that be a lead to more information about the early years of the '39 limousine?

Remember the photograph that Mr. Purkett sent to Mr. Ipsen, telling him it was a shot of the car he had sold to Bill Harrah? Mr. Ipsen had sent a copy of it to Terry Wenger for curiosity's sake, and had put it aside. But Terry noticed that the beltline chrome strip on the car in the picture was painted over, and he recalled that the build sheet for Brad Ipsen's car had specified that same modification. And Brad confirmed that his car had the same dent in the running board edge molding that the car in the picture had (he still has the dented molding). It suddenly became clear that this was a period picture of Mr. Ipsen's car! Mr. Purkett must have acquired the photograph from Mr. Marcotte while trying to buy the car from him. And Mr. Marcotte must have obtained the photograph when he bought what is now Mr. Ipsen's car back in 1952. Did you follow all that?

In the background of the photograph is a hotel, with its name painted across the top. Our two researchers took what they could make out of the hotel's name and tried to find Montana towns with lodging places similarly named. But when they input what they thought was the name, the city of Wilkes-Barre was the first hit. The Hotel Redington, at 77 East Market Street, was for years a landmark in Wilkes-Barre. The National Federation for the Blind was founded there in 1940. Today the Best Western Genetti Hotel and Conference Center encompasses the site of the former hotel.

So far Mr. Ipsen has been able to determine that the address given in the *Motor Trend* ad for what is now his car was a cash register repair business from 1948 through 1952. He hasn't taken the search to the level of tracking down all of the listings for the name "Williams" in the Wilkes-Barre phone book. Someday that may yet lead him or a subsequent owner to the man who first took delivery of this big, elegant car.

63. And Power Everything

In 1938, Cadillac defied conventional logic and instead of retiring its V-16 model line, introduced a completely new V-16 engine. The first series engine, installed in 1930 through 1937 cars, was a visual spectacle in polished aluminum, black porcelain, enamel and chrome. It was an overhead valve powerplant with a narrow 45-degree angle between the cylinder banks. The level of technology was cutting-edge for the time, with hydraulically silenced valve mechanism, among other features. The new engine was a side-valve or flathead configuration with a 135 degree V angle that let it sit lower in the engine bay (allowing a lower center of gravity and a lower overall body profile). It used two downdraft carburetors, two distributors and two water pumps. It achieved the same horsepower with less weight and with far fewer moving parts. But for all its advantages, it wasn't much to look at. When you opened the hood, you saw the two air cleaners and not much else. You had to peer over the side panels of the engine compartment and down into the dark chamber to see the engine itself.

The second generation V-16s are rare—just under 500 cars over the years 1938 through 1940, as opposed to 3,889 during 1930 through 1937. By 1938, engine technology and fuel chemistry had brought power, torque and smoothness to V-8 engines that rivaled what a 16 could produce. And the national economy was stumbling again, just in time for the new engine's arrival.

In the fall of 1937, Mr. Johnston A. Bowman of Evanston, Illinois, who owned Bowman Dairy in Chicago, purchased a new second-generation V-16 Cadillac. It was a convertible coupe, engine number 5270108 and body number 4. Mr. Bowman was still driving the car in 1951, when he suffered a stroke. No longer able to operate his big Cadillac, but wishing to keep enjoying it, he sought to have his car modified to accommodate his difficulties. The dealer told him that it would be cheaper to buy a new car, with modern power accessories, than to retrofit his 1938 coupe. But Mr. Bowman insisted that if the dealer wanted to keep his business, he would have to convince Cadillac to make the necessary alterations. Mr. Bowman also happened to be one of the largest private shareholders of General Motors Corporation, and a request from him would certainly be considered by the GM tech center. The car was sent back to the factory, and the foreman of Cadillac's experimental garage, a Mr. Burrell, adapted and installed one of the new dual-range Hydramatic transmissions and a new rear axle gear set with a 3.07:1 ratio. The car was also fitted with power steering and power brakes. The price tag was about $2,400. Mr. Bowman was able to keep driving his elegant Cadillac until 1968, racking up 49,000 miles. When he was approaching 90 years of age, his doctor pressed him to stop driving, and he sold his car.

Joseph Bortz of Highland Park, Illinois, has become renowned in car collector circles for searching out, locating, acquiring and lovingly restoring some of the rarest old cars around—the hand-built show cars and concept vehicles that GM and other manufacturers presented at automobile shows to test public interest in new styling and engineering features, and to whet customer appetites for future products. Typically these cars would be shuttled around the country for a year or two and then destroyed. Often they were non-running mockups, or if they ran, they might not be fully tested or finished to the point of being reliable transportation. From a product liability standpoint, the logic behind destroying these prototypes was sound. Nevertheless, some of these dream cars from the past have survived, either because salvage yard personnel hadn't the heart to execute their orders, because the vehicle was lost in corporate paperwork, or because someone at the factory "lost" it.

From time to time some of the show cars that had been condemned to demolition have turned up in unlikely places. Mr. Bortz has found some of these cars as literal basket cases, requiring monumental restoration work. Over a period of years, he has assembled a mind-

Never seen on another V-16. No other V-16 Cadillac had a factory-installed automatic transmission. Visible here is the shifter quadrant on the steering wheel hub, showing which gear has been selected (courtesy Robert Smits).

boggling collection, and car buffs are in awe of his accomplishment. But in 1967, he was a young man in his mid–20s, collecting old cars and recently involved in boating in the Chicago area. One of his fellow enthusiasts at Montrose Harbor told Joe Bortz about a 1938 Cadillac V-16 convertible coupe, whose owner was no longer able to drive it and had decided to sell it. He recognized the seller's name, as Bowman's Dairy was well known in the Chicago area, and he phoned right away and was invited to come see the car.

Mr. Bortz was astonished to see no clutch pedal, and to find a shift lever with a pointer and a row of letters such as one saw in cars equipped with an automatic transmission. He knew that Cadillac had first offered an automatic transmission in 1941, and that the car he was looking at predated that debut year by three years. Mr. Bowman explained that the car had a factory-installed Hydramatic transmission and power steering as well, and he told him how that came to be. When he took the car for a drive, Mr. Bortz was delighted by the unusual sensation, with the automatic and the power steering. He bought the big convertible and drove it regularly for two years. Caught between the earnest begging of his boating friend Herbert Levin, who wanted the Cadillac, and his own desire to purchase a 1935 V-12 Packard dual cowl phaeton, Mr. Bortz parted with the V-16. But each time he saw the new owner driving it he regretted selling it.

Some few years later, Mr. Levin would sell the car to Harold Mistele, a gentleman in Grosse Pointe Park, Michigan, who owned a company that supplied coal for heating homes. Mr. Mistele was something of an eccentric, and he collected various sorts of older cars, as well as classic speedboats. In the early 1970s, he placed an ad to sell a 1940 Cadillac Series 75 V-8 town car. Mr. Ron Van Gelderen answered the ad and came to his home to see the town car. Driving the prospective purchase, Mr. Van Gelderen found it less to his liking than he had hoped, and he asked if the seller had any other cars he might be willing to sell. He said he had some Thunderbirds and some other cars, and he led the way to the back side of his property where there stood a small airplane hangar. Inside, packed closely together, was a large number of automobiles. Scanning the selection, Mr. Van Gelderen's Cadillac-attuned

Braving an Illinois winter. This photo was taken when Mr. Joe Bortz owned the 1938 Cadillac, probably around 1970. Mr. Bortz enjoyed driving the car and regretted parting with it (courtesy Bortz Auto Collection).

eye focused quickly on a car near the very back of the building. He asked if he could go over and take a look, and the owner agreed. After climbing and snaking his way across the crowd of cars, he reached Mr. Bowman's 1938 Cadillac convertible coupe. The door could only be opened part way, so the specially fitted Hydramatic transmission was not immediately apparent. It just looked like a well-preserved original car.

Mr. Van Gelderen looked at some of the other cars, and on the way out, he noticed that there was a slip from Lake St. Clair right up to the gentleman's house. He asked Mr. Mistele what that was for, and the fellow walked over and opened the door. Inside were a pair of Chris-Craft speedboats in their own sheltered mooring. One of the boats, a 38-footer, was powered by two Packard V-12 engines. Amazed, Mr. Van Gelderen asked him if it ran, and he started the boat. The sound of the two massive engines, exhaust burbling in the water, was music to Mr. Van Gelderen's ears.

The conversation returned to the 1938 Cadillac, and the fellow asked if Mr. Van Gelderen wanted to buy it. He asked to take another look, and when they returned, a closer inspection disclosed the unique transmission. The seller disclaimed any knowledge of how the car came to be so equipped, and asked again if he wanted to buy. He gave a price and wouldn't budge from it. At length, Mr. Van Gelderen said he didn't think he was interested. The seller then came down $1,000, and Mr. Van Gelderen decided to buy the car. That was when he found out about the rest of the car's unusual features.

Mr. Van Gelderen drove the car from Detroit to the Washington, D.C., area where he lived. Just in case there might be an overheating issue, he drove at night. But he needn't have worried. Because of the Hydramatic installation, the cooling fan ran at a higher r.p.m. than would normally have been the case. And between that and the special rear axle ratio, the car would always run quite cool for him.

The automatic transmission was very smooth and responsive, and the kick-down shift was instantaneous with powerful acceleration. At one point he noticed the speedometer needle indicating 80 or 85 m.p.h., and was startled to realize he had been going so fast. Fortunately, the speeding Cadillac had not been noticed by law enforcement, and no tickets were incurred.

Mr. Van Gelderen was able to meet and speak with Mr. Bowman, who was pleased that the car had found an appreciative owner. Although Mr. Van Gelderen enjoyed the convertible's smoothness and modern conveniences, he would later remove the power steering and brakes, but keep the Hydramatic.

When it came time to have the car repainted, things did not go well. While it was in the shop a large number of parts suddenly disappeared, whether because there was a break-in at the paint shop, or due to some other reason. Coincidentally, Mr. Van Gelderen found himself in need of cash. So he sold the car to Robert G. Smits, a plastic surgeon in Des Moines, Iowa, who collected replacements for the missing parts and gave the car a thorough restoration.

When he bought the car, Dr. Smits had no idea that the automatic transmission had a "right" to be in the car. For all he knew, it had been installed by a creative owner somewhere in the car's history, and if he showed the car with that feature, any judge would deduct a hefty point penalty for an incorrect transmission. A couple of days after he decided to keep the Hydramatic, he received documentation proving that it was a factory change. Dr. Smits has since retired, and moved first to Florida and later to Texas. The Hydramatic installation remains intact and continues to attract great attention—a unique driving experience.

Poise and presence. A recent photograph taken by the current owner shows the big convertible coupe to be in fine condition. Careful attention to proportion and line allow the car to impress without overwhelming (courtesy Robert Smits).

64. Dr. Brinkley's Coupe

Dr. John Brinkley, the famous radio-based virility specialist of the 1930s, owned various Cadillacs, including several V-16s. One of these was a 1939 V-16 coupe that he turned into a rolling advertisement for his professional activities. It was officially a Series 9057-B coupe for five passengers, with body number 1 (of five built that year) and engine number 5290048. The car was painted bright red and had white leather upholstery. The owner's name was painted on the car itself and on the special hubcaps that adorned the wheels. Dr. Brinkley's life and lifestyle were colorful in several senses of the word.

In addition to the car's built-in trunk, Dr. Brinkley wanted an old-fashioned separate trunk, such as would have been set on a rack on the rear of an older-style car. Because such an appendix would have been completely at odds with the styling and lines of the 1939 Cadillac coupe, the manufacturer politely refused to add an external trunk. In order to satisfy a well-to-do customer and keep his business in tough economic times, however, the local Cadillac dealer undertook to attach brackets to the frame and to mount a trunk from a 1933 Cadillac. As a result, this V-16 coupe has a truly unique presence.

After Dr. Brinkley's death in 1944, his widow, Minnie (who stood barely 4 feet, 10 inches), wished to keep driving the car, but she did not want the attention that it drew because of its late owner's decorations. So she had the body repainted Caroline Green, a turquoise color that Cadillac ordinarily made available only for cars sold on the West Coast, and she had the leather interior dyed a green color, as well (including the headliner). She had the wheel covers replaced with plain hubcaps, and kept as a remembrance of her husband at least one of the personalized hubcaps. The car remained in the Brinkley family until 1962.

In about 1971, Ron Van Gelderen purchased the Brinkley coupe from the gentleman who had bought it from Mrs. Brinkley. It was Mr. Van Gelderen's first V-16 (he was to own several others over the years) and he drove the car from the Brinkley residence in Del Rio, Texas, to his home in Michigan. Along the way he heard a grinding noise from the engine compartment, but was neither experienced nor nervous enough to worry about it. Once he was home, he discovered that only one of the engine's two water pumps was working, a situation that could have led to serious damage. Fortunately, the water pump was the only part that required servicing.

In a 1972 article in the Cadillac-LaSalle Club's magazine *The Self-Starter*, Mr. Van Gelderen described some of the other features specially ordered by Dr. Brinkley. These included a gold-plated hood ornament, a sumptuous rear bench seat with an armrest, a clock in the back of the right front seat for the benefit of rear-seat passengers, 11-leaf rear springs, and of course, that extra trunk. A photograph taken by Mr. Van Gelderen shows the hood ornament, the trunk and the unusual bumper guard arrangement with which Dr. Brinkley accessorized the car. In the photo, the big coupe still wears the paint color that Mrs. Brinkley selected.

When Mr. Van Gelderen acquired the car, the original rack for the trunk was missing, and a makeshift support was made. When he visited the Brinkley estate and made the acquaintance of Mrs. Brinkley, she took him to the garage (a large affair, with three bays and apartments overhead) and helped him locate and take possession of the rack, which he later reinstalled on the car.

During the 1970s. When Ron Van Gelderen acquired Dr. Brinkley's 1939 Cadillac V-16 coupe, Minnie Brinkley had repainted it in a turquoise hue instead of the bright red color the doctor had chosen. Standard Cadillac hubcaps replaced the caps that had "BRINKLEY" in block letters around the center emblem. Mrs. Brinkley kept the lettered hubcaps as a remembrance. The script-lettered monograms on the spare tire covers ("Dr. JRB") had disappeared (courtesy Ron Van Gelderen).

Red leather now covers the interior. Leather was unusual for an owner-driven car in the Classic Era, but not unheard of. When new, Dr. Brinkley's car was fitted with a white leather interior, later redyed green. The pattern is correct for the car (courtesy Sonny Abagnale).

At the time of his visit, Mrs. Brinkley showed to Mr. Van Gelderen one of the hubcaps that had been specially decorated for the car at Dr. Brinkley's behest. They were similar to regular 1939 Cadillac wheel covers, except that in the wide chrome band around the center Cadillac emblem, large block letters spelled out the doctor's last name twice. Mrs. Brinkley said that she was too emotionally attached to the hubcaps to part with them. Period photographs of the car (such as one that is now in the Kansas Historical Society) show the car with "Dr. Brinkley" in script across the left-hand spare-tire cover atop the front fender.

Mr. Van Gelderen drove the car a good deal and enjoyed its size, quality and smooth performance. In a 1966 issue of *The Self-Starter*, Ron Van Gelderen related his participation at the Classic Car Club of America's Upper Midwest Grand Classic event held on July 6, 1966, in Minneapolis, Minnesota. He drove Dr. Brinkley's '39 Cadillac coupe from his home in Elgin, Illinois, to Minneapolis and back, and the car scored 87.50 points (of a possible 100) for a third-place finish in the Primary Custom Late category. In Mr. Van Gelderen's words:

> A total of 871 miles round trip was driven without overheating (the water gauge refused to go past the half way mark), adding water, nor adding oil during 96–101[deg] weather at a constant 60 mph with an average of 9.1 miles per gallon (that's like 18.2 mpg on a normal 8 cylinder piece of iron) in luxurious comfort (except for the heat and humidity) ... end of boast!

At length Mr. Van Gelderen sold the car. A later owner wanted to remove Dr. Brinkley's anachronistic trunk, but he found that this idiosyncratic addition was the feature that most captivated people at car shows. So the fellow settled on selling the car.

Today this unique 1939 Cadillac V-16 is owned by Sonny and Joan Abagnale of Cedar Grove, New Jersey. Mr. Abagnale has given the car a new color scheme. But he, too, has retained the distinctive trunk, grille guard and gold hood ornament.

The V-16 coupe today. Sonny Abagnale selected a maroon color for the car. Several of Dr. Brinkley's personal design choices remain. The unusual external trunk has been retained, as has the gold-plated hood ornament. Recently, a similar "beyond-the-bumper" luggage rack configuration has been arranged for SUVs, with the rack attached to the trailer hitch bracket (courtesy Sonny Abagnale).

65. An Air Conditioned V-16 Limousine

Air conditioning in private motor cars did not begin to appear until just before the Second World War. In 1941 Cadillac introduced a unit that occupied most of the ample trunk space of the car. The on-off control was a serviceman opening the hood and attaching or removing the drive belt for the compressor. The same company with which General Motors contracted to build the system also provided units to Packard. Only 300 Cadillac cars were so equipped that year, and it was really an experimental enterprise. Cadillac did not re-introduce factory-installed air conditioning until the 1953 model year. Because the last Cadillac V-16 rolled out of the factory in 1940, an air conditioned V-16 is an anachronism.

William Fisk Harrah, generally known as Bill Harrah, was a Nevada casino owner whose Harrah's Automobile Collection became the archetype for private and public car museums and collections worldwide. There was a fully-stocked reference library as well as a complete restoration and maintenance facility supporting the enormous number of thoroughbred, rare, unusual and downright quirky vehicles that made up the collection. One of the fine motor cars was a 1939 Cadillac V-16 Series 9033 imperial sedan with engine number 5290065.

Mr. Harrah liked the Cadillac enough to make it one of his personal vehicles. He had his people install power steering and an air conditioning unit. The latter was one of those systems that consumed a lot of trunk space, but it left no outward indication that the car

Stately presence of the 1939 Series 90 limousine owned by Mr. Richard Maidman. Ten years of rapid evolution in automotive styling have generated a different sort of formal elegance from that seen in the first V-16 cars. The wind-cheating effects of streamlining combine with myriad engineering improvements to produce a very modern car (courtesy Richard Maidman).

had been modified. With its sumptuous Fleetwood interior appointments, the car would then have been very comfortable year-round, even in sunny Reno, and easier to drive than it had been with the stock manual steering configuration. Mr. Harrah is said to have used the big Cadillac to transport friends and VIPs.

Bill Harrah died in 1978 and his resort properties and automobile collection were purchased by a corporation in 1980. Public outcry at the proposed sale of the collection led to the donation of the research library and 175 of the automobiles to a tax-exempt entity formed for the purpose with the governor's help. Eventually, the National Automobile Museum was established and carries on as an enduring legacy of Bill Harrah. The 1939 Cadillac V-16 with its air conditioning and power steering is one of the cars that were sold.

Subsequent owner Jeffrey Gast had the car for about two years and put 1800 miles on it. He recalls that it was a delight to drive. Shortly after he sold it, it came into the possession of Mr. Richard Maidman of Port Washington, New York, who owns it today. Under his ownership, a more modern and efficient air conditioning installation has been made, taking up less trunk room. Mr. Maidman has shown the car successfully at Cadillac-LaSalle Club Grand National meets and enjoys driving it.

---

66. The Last V-16

In 1940 Cadillac had been building and selling V-16 motor cars for a decade. From the time of the surprise announcement in late 1929 that such a supercar would be offered to the public, the world had changed in so many ways. The Great Depression had weighed down nations, businesses and individuals. The Rome-Berlin Axis had begun wrenching Europe into a horrible war, into which the United States would soon be drawn. The Imperial Japanese Army and Navy were on the move in the Pacific. Movies now had lifelike color. Swing was the thing in popular music and dance. Commercial air travel was becoming more available (in 1939 Pan American Airways flew the first transatlantic passenger service). Cars were becoming sleeker, more powerful and more civilized.

The technological reasons for a sixteen-cylinder engine had faded over the decade. The new flathead V-8 that Cadillac introduced in 1937 was much smoother than its predecessor, and it rivaled even the silken power delivery of the V-16. Improved fuel chemistry and advances in metallurgy allowed higher compression ratios and greater power without adding cylinders. Streamlined styling, all-metal bodies and advanced construction techniques made for lighter weight that smaller and more agile power plants could easily manage.

Not incidentally, the perception of the automobile and its reasons for existence (and purchase) had evolved. Where once the fortunate and accomplished would travel in elaborate chariots built and appointed by the finest craftsmen, years of hard times had greatly restrained the ostentation of luxury automobiles, and most of the fine coachbuilding houses had died off or turned to other work. It had become much more difficult for an automobile manufacturer to concentrate on the carriage trade (pun intended). Packard survived the Great Depression by offering a lower-priced line. Cadillac survived with substantial assistance from its corporate parent. Many others disappeared.

The decision was made that the 1940 model year would be the final one for the Cadillac

V-16. The last major styling change had been for 1938, when the 135-degree side-valve ("flat-head") V-16 engine was introduced. The '38 V-16 cars used the same new bodies and chassis as the Series 75 V-8 models, with distinctive grilles and trim pieces to set them apart from their lesser siblings. For 1939, the V-8 cars got a new prow-style grille ensemble, but the V-16 line continued through 1940 with the 1938 bodies freshened by minor decorative changes. Calling the correct model year for a late series V-16 is a specialized talent among old Cadillac fans. Cadillac had sold just over three hundred of the new flathead V-16 cars in 1938, but less than half as many were delivered in 1939. The year 1940 would see just fifty new V-16 Cadillacs produced.

The last Cadillac V-16 had engine number 5320061. Research carried out by longtime owner Bill Tite (now deceased) disclosed that it was delivered to Green Bay, Wisconsin, and from there it was shipped to Honolulu, Hawaii. It was a Series 9019 five-passenger sedan (no divider window and no jump seats) and it wore a color exotically named Luzon Green, a shade somewhere between teal and sea green with a slight metallic quality to it. It's not known at this time who bought the car new—a pineapple company executive? the territorial governor? a general or admiral? In any event, the car eventually made its way back to the mainland. In 1961 Dean Brown, a used car dealer in Los Angeles, California, sold it and it was transported to St. Clair Shores, Michigan, in a van, together with a 1939 V-16 coupe. The purchaser of the Series 9019 was Bill Tite, and a fellow enthusiast was the new owner of the '39 coupe.

Bill Tite was one of the early members of the Cadillac-LaSalle Club and he owned many 1938–1940 Cadillacs and became quite knowledgeable about the V-16s. When this

Sleek and simple instrument panel. The dash and controls are shared with the other 1940 Cadillac models. The push-button AM radio in the center is an option (courtesy Douglas Tite).

Unassuming but historically significant. Longtime prior owner Bill Tite had stripped and primed the fenders, rechromed the bumpers and performed other work on the car, but did not live to complete the project. His family found an eager new owner to finish reviving this solid and very complete car (courtesy Douglas Tite).

particular V-16 sedan arrived in the Detroit area, it wasn't running. Mr. Tite rebuilt the engine, new pistons and all. But there were problems with the wiring and he was not able to really enjoy the car. A friend recalls that he might have driven it around the block a couple of times, but his wife said that he never started it. Mr. Tite had other projects, and the discouragement occasioned by the wiring difficulty meant that this car was put aside for later.

As things worked out, later never came, and when Mr. Tite passed away the last V-16 was still a project waiting to be tackled. In 2011, Mr. Tite's son put the car up for auction on eBay for his mother. The photographs showed a very complete car with the original paint on the body, re-chromed bumpers, and the fenders in primer. Some rust was visible on the lower

End of the Line. Majestic but weathered, the trunk emblem on the final car in the V-16 program bears mute witness to the dreams and aspirations of a car company and its employees, customers and admirers (courtesy Douglas Tite).

edge of the trunk lid, but the listing indicated that a new trunk lid and a new passenger door would go with the car. The upholstery and interior trim appeared to be complete and in good condition. The new owner would not have to conduct an extensive hunt for parts.

On October 8, 2011, Australian collector and Cadillac enthusiast Ross Morgan won the auction and purchased the big Cadillac for $30,301.89. Mrs. Tite was glad to see it go to someone who would appreciate it. It will be interesting to watch for pictures of this historically significant motor car, refreshed, reinvigorated and driven.

Epilogue

An imaginary twenty-one-year-old who bought a new Cadillac V-16 in the last year they were produced (1940) would now be more than ninety years old. From that arithmetic, it is easy to see that few, if any, of the original V-16 purchasers are alive today. Some people now living who were children at the time still remember a new V-16 becoming part of the family. A judge I know remembers the 1930 V-16 sedan his father bought and owned for just a short time (until the effects of the Great Depression compelled him to sell it). His most vivid recollection is getting his fingers caught when one of those massive doors closed. (Ouch!) As time passes, fewer and fewer folks will be around who knew these cars when they were new or nearly so. More and more, they are artifacts of the remote past, outside the memory of man.

In a similar way, time has taken an inexorable toll on the men who designed, built and trained to maintain these man-made thoroughbreds. Is there anyone alive today who sat through a viewing of the instructional filmstrips that Cadillac sent around to all of the dealers and distributors in March of 1930 to introduce servicemen to the new features and technical idiosyncrasies of the new V-16 models? Some of the knowledge, skills and talents that were an integral part of the gestation and birth of these cars have been passed on to succeeding generations, but inevitably, some have been lost, though perhaps not irretrievably. How many people today know how to service a distributor? Restore a Babbitt bearing? Rebuild a vacuum tank fuel system? And how many trim shops can replicate the elegant interior appointments of a classic Fleetwood body?

The multi-cylinder era came and went. Accurately or not, multi-cylinder was the term used to describe engines with more than eight pistons. And for a time, adding cylinders was a reasonable way to increase power while maintaining smoothness. But by 1940, the same smoothness could be had with a V-8 that was once specific to a twelve or a sixteen. Since the Second World War and for decades afterwards, the V-8 engine has been the gold standard for muscle cars, bone fide luxury vehicles and full-sized American automobiles of every stripe. But first in the 1970s (following the oil "crises") and more seriously now, the V-8 itself has been threatened. Between advancing technology (direct fuel injection, turbocharging, variable valve timing) and pressure for ever-lower emissions and ever higher fuel economy, the V-6 is finding increasingly broader acceptance on the V-8's home turf, at the bigger engine's expense.

For its time, the Cadillac V-16 was a technological and esthetic tour de force, a "super car" that helped establish the Cadillac brand as a premier luxury marque. Even today, it amazes and delights. It is wonderful that so many have survived. It is to be hoped that they will continue to be valued, conserved and used, even as their roles as primary transportation fade into history. They should be used, both because the cars benefit from being driven (having been built supremely well for that purpose), and because future generations should be able to experience travel in such a grand conveyance.

The stories of the cars and the people who purchased, drove and cared for them make an eloquent case for historical significance and cultural value. They were dream cars when they were new, and they still fire the imagination and inspire, even today. God willing, they will continue to bear splendid, elegant witness to a different time, a different age and a different world.

Chapter Notes

Chapter 5

1. Many car collectors and sellers use a number scale to describe a car's condition, with "Number 1" generally indicating a "trailer queen" car that has been perfectly restored (or even "over-restored" beyond like-new condition). Successive numbers indicate increasing levels of wear, damage or deterioration, with "Number 6" denoting a car that is usable only for parts and not worth restoring. Naturally, the grades in between are susceptible to a good deal of subjective impression, and reasonable people can disagree firmly, for example, on whether a car is closer to a "Number 2" or a "Number 3." Moreover, the same level of deterioration that might render a Ford unrestorable might not doom a Duesenberg.

Chapter 10

1. The dividing line between 1930 and 1931 V-16 Cadillacs is somewhat vague, because there was no model changeover from one year to the next. Although some minor running changes were made during 1930 and 1931 (such as carburetor air intake horns) the first restyling was saved for the 1932 model year. Thus, collectors and historians debate whether to distinguish 1930 V-16s from '31s on the basis of production date, shipment date, sale date or an arbitrary engine number cutoff.

Chapter 16

1. A detailed account of Mr. Struck's modifications and how they worked was presented in the December 1983 issue of *Special Interest Autos* (predecessor of *Hemmings Classic Car* magazine) in an article entitled "Mr. Struck's Clever Classic Cadillac" by William Locke.

Chapter 17

1. See Maurice A. Hendry, *Cadillac: Standard of the World—The Complete Seventy-Year History*. Automobile Quarterly, 1973.

Chapter 24

1. Shortly before 1920, Herbert Mason, the founder of a duck decoy manufacturing company, teamed up with a friend to start the Rinshed-Mason Company, which became the largest paint supplier to the rapidly growing automobile industry. Today it is a division of BASF Coatings.

Chapter 26

1. Another car described in this book was delivered new in Huntington, West Virginia, in 1931. It has been restored as a cane-bodied brougham.

Chapter 44

1. Subsequently, the convertible coupe was stolen. The person responsible for the theft was later found, drowned in an execution-style fashion, but the car was never recovered.

Chapter 47

1. Dean Bachelor, *Dry Lakes and Drag Strips*. MBI Publishing, 2002, page 115.

Chapter 48

1. Frank Oddo, HP Books, 2003, page 6. The year 1940 was the last year that Cadillac built V-16 cars. Ten years later, after the war and its gas rationing, a thirsty V-16 engine would have been significantly less expensive.

Chapter 49

1. Ken Kincaid, "Hottest Contender for Title of Biggest Cubic Incher Is Bill Carash's ... Classic Rod. *Rod & Custom*, April 1955, pp. 34–37.

Chapter 50

1. Fred Farley, "The Lou Fageol Story," on the website of the Hydroplane and Raceboat Museum, www.thunderboats.org/history/history0526.html.

Chapter 56

1. *Empty Sleeve: Der Musiker und Mäzen Paul Wittgenstein* by Irene Suchy, Allan Janik and Georg Predota presents, in a set of essays in English and German, fascinating information on the life, music and professional accomplishments of Paul Wittgenstein.

2. For those who read German, her life and world (including her assistance of Dr. Freud) can be thoroughly appreciated in *Margaret Stonborough-Wittgenstein: Bauherrin, Intellektuelle, Mäzenin* by Ursula Prokop. The Wittgenstein and Stonborough family lines are also clearly diagrammed in that work.

3. Although financial difficulties may have been an influence, it would be an oversimplification to fix that as the cause of Jerome Stonborough's suicide.

Chapter 61

1. The numbers differ if one is speaking strictly of completed cars, or including bare chassis with engines, and engine-only sales. Straight car sales for the three years were 308, 134 and 50, respectively. Otherwise, the figures are 315, 138 and 61. This information is from the careful compilation of production figures undertaken by Carl Steig in the 1960s.

Bibliography

Ackerson, Robert C. "Cadillac V-16: Worth Its Weight in Prestige." Reprinted in James T. Lenzke, ed., *Standard Catalog of Cadillac 1903–2000,* 2d ed. Iola, WI: Kraus, 2000: 217–221.

Adler, Dennis. "1930 Cadillac V-16 Madame X Imperial Landau Sedan—Best Foot Forward." *Car Collector and Car Classics* Vol. IX, No. 8 (Aug. 1986): 34–40.

Albert, Ken. *For the Love of Old Cars: The Jack Passey Story.* Evansville, IN: M.T., 2008.

Artzberger, Bill. "The 16 Cylinder Cadillac: Smoothness, Silence, Acceleration and Hill-Climbing Ability" in James T. Lenzke, ed., *Standard Catalog of Cadillac 1903–2000,* 2d ed. Iola, WI: Kraus, 2000: 222–223.

Bachelor, Dean. *Dry Lakes and Drag Strips: The American Hot Rod.* St. Paul: MBI, 1995, 2002.

Bentley, Walter Owen. *The Cars in My Life.* New York: Macmillan, 1963.

Bowman, Hank Wieand. *Famous Old Cars.* New York: ARCO, 1957, 1978.

Collins, Herbert Ridgeway. *Presidents on Wheels.* Washington, DC: Acropolis, 1971.

Donnelly, Jim. "Automotive Pioneers—Sam McLauchlin." *Hemmings Classic Car* #82 (July 2011): 74.

Farley, Fred. "The Lou Fageol Story." Posted on the website of the Hydroplane and Raceboat Museum, http://www.thunderboats.org/history/history 0526.html.

Ferguson, Clark. "1930 Cadillac V-16, Series 452A Roadster by Fleetwood, Style 4302." *Torque: Michigan Region Classic Car Club of America* (September-October 2002): 5–9.

Hendry, Maurice A. *Cadillac: Standard of the World—The Complete Seventy-Five Year History.* Princeton: Automobile Quarterly, 1973.

Hendry, Maurice A. *Cadillac at 100: Legacy of Leadership.* New Albany, IN: Automobile Quarterly, 2008.

Juneau, Bud. *The Vanderbilt Cadillac V-16.* Reprinted by permission from the Cadillac-LaSalle Club by Hyde Park Historical Association, Hyde Park, NY, 1987.

Kincaid, Ken. "Hottest Contender for Title of Biggest Cubic Incher is Bill Carash's ... Classic Rod." *Rod & Custom* (Apr. 1955): 34–37.

Locke, William S. "Mr. Struck's Clever Classic Cadillac." *Special Interest Autos* #78 (Dec. 1983): 28–33.

Locke, William S. "The Remarkable Rolling Laboratory of Henry W. Struck." *The Classic Car* Vol. XXXI, No. 2 (June 1983): 10–19.

Loe, Raymond. "1934 Cadillac V-16 Two-Passenger Stationary Coupe." *Bumper Guardian*, Pacific Northwest Region, Classic Car Club of America (Winter 2008): 4–7.

Melton, James, with Ken Purdy. *Bright Wheels Rolling.* Philadelphia: Macrae Smith, 1954.

Merkel, Alan. "Where Did All the 16s Go? A Documentary Study of the 1930–31 Cadillac V-16s." In James T. Lenzke, ed., *Standard Catalog of Cadillac 1903–2000,* 2d ed. Iola, WI: Kraus, 2000: 225–229.

Nordberg, Nils. *Karossmakarens berättelser: Glimtar från bilismens födelse och tillväxt i Sverige och om de stora bilälskarna.* Uddevalla, Sweden: Rabén & Sjögren, 1969.

Oddo, Frank. *The Street Rodder's Handbook.* Tucson: HP Books, 2003.

"Picture Restoration of a Madame X." *The Self-Starter* Vol. VI, No. 9 (July 1964): 10–11.

"The Poindexter Lives." *Automobile Quarterly* Vol. 11, No. 8 (Fall 1973): 258–263.

Prokop, Ursula. *Magaret Stonborough-Wittgenstein: Bauherrin, Intellektuelle, Mäzenin.* Vienna: Böhlau Verlag GmbH und Co. KG, 2003.

Saunders, Yann. *The (New) Cadillac Database.* http://www.car-nection.com/yann/Dbas_txt/ indx2001.htm.

Schild, James. *Fleetwood: The Company & the Coachcraft.* Columbia, IL: The Auto Review, 2001. Rev. 2d ed. published June 2011.

Schinnerer, Paul. "Cadillac Safari." *The Self-Starter* Vol. VII, No. 3 (Jan. 1965): 10–11.

Schneider, Roy A. *Sixteen Cylinder Motorcars: An Illustrated History.* Arcadia, CA: Heritage House, 1974.

Siuru, William D., and Andrea Stewart. *Presidential Cars & Transportation.* Iola, WI: Krause, 1995.

Smith, LeRoi, and Tony Hossain. *Classic Cars: Cadillac.* New York: Crescent, 1983.

Suchy, Irene, Alan Janik, and Georg Predota. *Empty Sleeve: Der Musiker und Mäzen Paul Wittgenstein.* Innsbruck: Studeinverlag, 2006.

Throttle: January—December 1941 The Complete Collection. South San Francisco: The Rodder's Journal, 2009.

Thurber, James. "Mr. Pendley and the Poindexter." Reprinted by permission of *Automobile Quarterly* Vol. 11, No. 8 (Fall 1973): 256, 257.

Tomaine, Bob. "Back in a Cadillac: V-16 Fan Tracks Down a Coupe Like his Grandfather Had." *Old Cars Weekly News and Marketplace* Vol. 40, No. 39 (October 13, 2011): 76–78.

Van Gelderen, R.E., and J. Juhring. "Upper Midwest Grand Classic—Minneapolis, MN." *The Self-Starter* Vol. VIII, No. 8 (Aug. 1966): 18–19.

Wenger, Terry, and Robert C. Mellin. "The 1934-'37 Cadillac V-16s." *The Self-Starter* Vol. 49, No. 11 (Nov.-Dec. 2006): 17–22 and Vol. 50, No. 1 (Jan. 2007): 17–20.

Whyte, Andrew. *Great Marques: Cadillac.* Secaucus, NJ: Chartwell, 1986.

Wood, Jonathan. *Great Marques of America.* London: Octopus, 1986.

Index